The Flamingos

The Flamingos

A Complete History of the Doo-Wop Legends

TODD R. BAPTISTA

Foreword by Terry Johnson

McFarland & Company, Inc., Publishers
Jefferson, North Carolina

LIBRARY OF CONGRESS CATALOGUING-IN-PUBLICATION DATA

Names: Baptista, Todd R., author.
Title: The Flamingos : a complete history of the doo-wop legends /
Todd R. Baptista ; foreword by Terry Johnson.
Description: Jefferson : McFarland & Company, Inc., Publishers, 2019. |
Includes bibliographical references and index.
Identifiers: LCCN 2019045507 | ISBN 9781476679822 (paperback : acid
free paper) ∞ |
ISBN 9781476637891 (ebook)
Subjects: LCSH: Flamingos (Musical group) | Singers—United States—
Biography. | Doo-wop (Music)—History and criticism.
Classification: LCC ML421.F5574 B36 2019 | DDC 782.42164092/2
[B]—dc23
LC record available at https://lccn.loc.gov/2019045507

BRITISH LIBRARY CATALOGUING DATA ARE AVAILABLE

ISBN (print) 978-1-4766-7982-2
ISBN (ebook) 978-1-4766-3789-1

On the cover: Chicago studio portrait, 1953—clockwise from top right,
Ezekiel Carey, Johnny Carter, Jacob Carey, Paul Wilson, and Sollie
McElroy (Maurice Seymour photo from the author's collection); *inset* for
their first End album George Goldner commissioned a color portrait of
the group—left to right, Zeke, Paul, Jake, Tommy, Terry, and (front)
Nate, 1959 (courtesy Terry Johnson)

Printed in the United States of America

McFarland & Company, Inc., Publishers
 Box 611, Jefferson, North Carolina 28640
 www.mcfarlandpub.com

This book is lovingly dedicated to my mom, Carol, with grateful appreciation for a lifetime of love, encouragement, and support.

Table of Contents

Foreword
by Terry Johnson

I first want to say that it is an extreme honor that Todd Baptista wanted to spend years of his life researching and compiling a comprehensive history of the Flamingos. There have been many excerpts and articles written about the group, along with interviews with various members, but nothing to this extent, and nothing as close to the truth. Todd had not yet been born at the time when the Flamingos started their dream of being one of the top vocal groups of their era.

Just reading the first chapters of this book will open readers' window of view as to what it takes in this business of show to be successful, revealing the struggles that the group suffered. It meant working house parties, performing at venues that didn't pay, and spending sleepless nights driving to reach the next gig. On many occasions, it meant having to stay in the worst motels. It meant not being able to stop and eat when you were hungry because you weren't the right color. It meant often having to go through the back door, experiencing curfews in certain parts of a town, or even fearing for your life as you drove through certain towns. It meant recording record after record on many different record labels with no real recognition or monetary reward, yet still believing that if you just keep going, it will pay off.

What got the Flamingos through those dark days was a positive mindset. It meant knowing that the only way to reach the top was to rehearse, rehearse, and rehearse! We danced like the Nicholas Brothers. We had four lead singers—Nate Nelson, Paul Wilson, Tommy Hunt, and me—who sang the love songs that made the girls go crazy. We had such intricate background harmonies that to this very day, other vocal groups are still trying to figure out how we heard our harmonies and how they were structured. There were good times and bad times, but the magic never failed once we hit that stage. We finally got our break when we signed with End Records and recorded our first crossover hit song, "Lovers Never Say Goodbye," which I wrote. Then, for the very first time, our record was being played on the pop or white radio stations. In those days, that was a true sign of success for black artists. It was a thrill. The Flamingos had their own unique sound and I'm very proud to have been a part of that sound.

What I like about this book is that Todd conducted interviews and preserved vintage interviews that allowed all the members to share their memories and their own versions of stories. With eight members and eight different personalities, we all had varying points of view of the events that took place during our climb to fame. This book allows the public to read and decide for themselves what the truth is. The Rock and Roll Hall of Fame was right to honor Johnny Carter, Jake Carey, Paul Wilson, Zeke Carey, Sollie McElroy, Nate Nelson, Tommy Hunt and myself, Terry Johnson. We all helped bake the cake!

I want to say more than thank you to all our fans, who fell in love with our music and still come to see us. It is you who have allowed me to make a living at what I love, music and performing. Without you, there would be no show. I especially thank those of you who have appreciated some of the different music that I have put into our show. Those are the songs that as musical director and arranger I would have loved to have recorded with the original Flamingos. Some were not even written at the time, but I felt they would entertain you and they are definitely in true Flamingos style. I've always been about the power of the show to move the audience emotionally, not just rest on the laurels of the past. I wish you all of the love and blessings that God has given me through you, and I truly thank you in advance for your continued support.

Introduction

When music historians, researchers, and aficionados of future generations reflect on the vocal group harmony sounds of the mid–20th century, the Flamingos will undoubtedly rank among the most prolific and influential. From their beginnings, at the Judaic Church of God and Saints of Christ at 39th and State streets in Chicago, the group rose to international heights, capturing the imagination of record buyers and aspiring artists with their unique blend of tight, minor-chord harmonies, floating falsetto tenors, velvety lead voices, eye-popping choreography, and original compositions and arrangements. From rhythm and blues and doo-wop, to rock 'n' roll, pop, soul, and even funk, the Flamingos, simply put, could do it all. That they have been able to find and maintain an audience for more than 65 years serves as a testament to the talents and perseverance of their original members.

As a second-generation fan of the Flamingos, I can vividly recall hearing "Lovers Never Say Goodbye," "I Only Have Eyes for You," and "Golden Teardrops" playing on the car radio and my dad's stereo at home even before the film *American Graffiti* reintroduced the mainstream public to "do-bop-shoo-bop." In 1987, I had the opportunity to meet and speak with founding members Jacob and Ezekiel Carey and watch them perform. Over the next several years, I would have the good fortune of discussing the history of the group and the music business with the Carey cousins on several occasions, in addition to seeing them on stage. One of my most cherished memories is an offer from Zeke Carey to consider booking the group as the entertainment for my own wedding reception in 1992.

The fact that the Flamingos continued to entertain audiences for nearly 45 years is a direct reflection of Zeke and Jake's dedication to their craft, their business, and their fans. Awed by the ethereal tones of Nate Nelson, I was truly saddened when I saw his wife, Angel, on a Boston television news broadcast in the spring of 1984, appealing in vain for an organ donor to prolong her ailing husband's life. While working on my first two books in the 1990s, my thoughts often turned to the Flamingos. As much as I wanted to write about them, I felt their story would be an epic undertaking, and that many of the performers whose stories I had already completed but not yet published ultimately wouldn't live to see the books go to print.

While some of those artists did pass away within a short time of publication, I was equally saddened when Sollie McElroy, Jacob Carey, and Ezekiel Carey all died within a period of less than five years. I felt that without their active participation, a detailed study of the Flamingos would be impossible, and any such attempt would be poorly received. Yet I felt that a significant part of their story remained untold. When the Flamingos were inducted into the Rock and Roll Hall of Fame in 2001, Terry Johnson took center stage. I must confess that I had never really understood his contributions to the group until he started to explain his role as writer, arranger, and vocalist that night. I guess I had always been led to believe that "Buzzy" was just the group's guitar player, and now I was understandably confused.

I am quite sure I'm no different from any other researcher in this field when I admit that a number of the folks I've interviewed over the years have probably taken a bit of an "artistic license" with me. Maybe some of that had to do with my wide-eyed approach to the subjects. After a while, though, I got to be pretty good at figuring out when the truth was starting to bend around the edges. My intent, in these situations, has always been to provide as much factual information as possible along with lengthy, detailed quotes, thereby allowing readers to decide for themselves.

In March of 2005, I received an e-mail from friend and respected collector George Lavatelli informing me that Terry "Buzzy" Johnson had previously been the lead singer of the mysterious Gotham label Whispers back in 1954. That night, I played "Are You Sorry?" and "Fool Heart" by the Whispers again and again. For the first time, I felt as though I was beginning to understand the part of the Flamingos' story that had never been told. Listening to those obscure, haunting R&B sides, I felt as though I could draw a straight line, following the progression of Terry Johnson's work from the Whispers to the Flamingos to the Starglows. At last, I understood the actual creative process that carried the Flamingos from R&B to the pop market. The next day, I contacted Terry and began the journey that led me to revisit a detailed study of the Flamingos. Tracking down and speaking with Fletcher Weatherspoon, the group's first manager, in early 2006, was both enlightening and inspiring.

While I had spoken and corresponded with the Careys and Sollie McElroy, my notes alone were not enough to sustain an accurate representation of their thoughts and words. As always, my goal has been to tell the stories through the words and memories of the artists themselves, as much as possible.

Through the assistance of respected Chicago R&B historian Robert Pruter and others, I was able to obtain copies of the vast majority of interviews and stories written about the group and its members over the past 65 years. I am indebted to all who have walked this road before me, and have listed every source in the accompanying bibliography. For the sake of brevity, and in an attempt to create a flowing, comprehensible biography, quotes are not repetitively attributed in detail to, for example, interviewer A, B, or C in the main text. Here and now, however, I must reiterate that this work would not have been possible without the efforts of Robert Pruter, Seamus McGarvey, Lou Rallo, Joe Mirrione, Wayne Jones, Jeff Tamarkin, Dave Hoekstra, Jack Sbarbori, Phil Groia, Eric LeBlanc, Earl Calloway, Carl Tancredi, Marv Goldberg, Mike Boone, Rockin' Richard Phillips, Billy Vera, Colton Thomas, Paul Power, and especially the online Red Saunders Research Foundation, dedicated to increasing our knowledge of the musicians who filled the clubs and recording studios of Chicago with great music during the two decades after World War II. Quotes not attributed to another source are the result of my own interviews.

Finally, I believe it is important to impress upon the reader that although Sollie McElroy, Nate Nelson, and Jake and Zeke Carey are quoted throughout this biography, it is obviously quite impossible for a researcher to enjoy the same kind of give and take he may experience with a readily available subject. Simply put, the essence of these now deceased artists can only be gleaned through the recorded words and deeds they've left behind. From there, it falls upon the researcher to try to create a balanced, accurate portrait. I offer my sincere thanks to my wife, Kristen, and sons, Kyle and Devin, for their support as I wrote this book. I am also forever grateful to my late father, Randy, whose love of the Flamingos and passion for writing continues to inspire me.

It is my sincere hope that this work, which I offer with gratitude and thanks to those who have researched them in the past, will provide readers with a definitive view of the pioneering Flamingos.

"Someday, Someway"

Jacob Andrew Carey, the elder statesman of the Flamingos, was born August 29, 1923, in Pulaski, Virginia, 90 miles north of Winston-Salem, North Carolina. Jacob was the fourth child of Isaac Carey, born in the tiny town of Whaleyville, Maryland, in 1878, and Elizabeth "Lizzie" (Curry), a Milford, Delaware, native who was two years younger than her husband. Married in 1906, the Careys lived in the equally minuscule community of Stockton, Maryland, where Isaac worked as a farm laborer. Less than two square miles, Stockton did boast a canning factory, a pair of sawmills, and barrel factories in the late 19th and early 20th centuries. Beginning in 1876, trains ran regularly through Stockton's Hursley Station, primarily transporting Chincoteague Bay–harvested seafood to Philadelphia and other commercial markets.

Isaac and Lizzie Carey had at least six older children. Census records note two sons: Samuel, born about 1907, and Lawrence Simon Carey, born in July of 1909. Eldest daughter Clara was 10, sister Mary was six, and brothers Paul and Daniel were five and two years old when younger brother Jacob was born. His middle name honored a paternal uncle, Andrew Carey, who lived with the family in Stockton before serving overseas with the United States Army in World War I. Isaac and Andrew's teenage sister, Elenora, who was employed as a domestic servant, also resided with the Careys in Stockton. With employment prospects dwindling in Worcester County, Isaac moved his family 60 miles northwest to Cambridge, Maryland, in 1919, where he found work as a carpenter. By the time of Jacob's birth four years later, the Careys had made the 375-mile journey southwest, settling in Pulaski, Virginia.

A key stop on the Virginia and Tennessee Railroad line, Pulaski was founded in 1886, and named for a Polish immigrant who came to America and died in the Revolutionary War. Located in the heart of mining country, the town had lost its premier employer in 1910, when advances in steam-shoveling forced the local Bertha Mineral Company out of business. The years that followed were difficult ones for the citizens of Pulaski, who often struggled to make ends meet. In fact, the section of town where the Careys lived was known as Needmore. Furniture and mirror production brought jobs back to the town just as the Great Depression dawned.

By 1930, however, Isaac and Lizzie had moved 55 miles to the north of Pulaski to the Beaver Pond district of Bluefield, West Virginia. Located in the southeastern tip of the state in Mercer County, Bluefield was home to an extensive railroad switching yard that served the region's ubiquitous coal-mining industry. At the time of Carey's birth, the city boasted nearly double the 11,000 citizens who reside there today.

It was in Bluefield, West Virginia, on January 24, 1933, that Jacob's paternal cousin, Ezekiel Joel Carey, was born to Silas Carey and the former Mariah Kelly. A gardener and laborer with only a third-grade education, Silas (1895–1984) had been born in Newark, Maryland. He and Mariah (1900–1979), born in Louisburg, North Carolina, were married in Mercer County in 1925. Ancestral records reflect that Isaac and Silas were half-brothers; both were sons of William Carey of Worcester County, Maryland.

In search of a better life, the Carey families moved to Baltimore during the Great Depression. In the 1940 Federal Census, seven-year-old Ezekiel was living on Baltimore's Whatcoat Street with his father Silas, age 41, mother Mariah, 38, and older siblings Solomon, 13, and Ruth, 10, along with 55-year-old Archie Baker.

Applying for his Social Security card in April of 1941, 17-year-old Jake Carey gave a Woodyear Street address, located in a neighborhood to the west of the present-day Route 83, and listed his occupation as private gardener. The clerk recording the data erroneously listed his birthdate as September 9, 1923. At the time, he declared his employer to be Charles Johnson in Ashburton, an upscale and predominantly African American neighborhood in northwest Baltimore.

"When we were children, we used to live in Baltimore, and Sonny Til used to live right down the street from us," Zeke recalled to interviewer Tancredi. "My oldest brother went to school with him. It wasn't until we left Baltimore [that we] began to hear his records." In 1943, Zeke and his family relocated to Portsmouth, in Norfolk County, Virginia. "I decided when I was about 14, that I was going to have a group one day. I told my mother I was. [Around 1949], I had gone to see Sonny Til and the Orioles, who I idolized, performing in a peanut warehouse up in Suffolk," Zeke told interviewer McGarvey. "The place was packed. I was just totally spellbound by Sonny Til's performance. He was with Cootie Williams's band and Willis 'Gator Tail' Jackson, the saxophone player."

Applying for his Social Security card in May of 1950, Zeke listed his employer and current mailing address as the Belleville Service Store on Route l in Portsmouth. After graduating from high school, Zeke moved to Gary, Indiana, 30 miles east of Chicago. It was there that Carey caught up with his cousin Jake, then 26 years old, who was living in the Douglas community on the city's South Side. Jake had been drafted into the United States Army in May of 1943. Standing five-feet-six and weighing in at 143 pounds, he served with the rank of private first class, and was discharged in February of 1946.

"Jacob was attending the University of Chicago," Zeke stated to McGarvey. "He wanted to be a gynecologist. I started visiting, and was caught up in the rhythm of that. I wanted to be a psychologist. We fell into a show business career, finally, because we could not afford college. At that time, they didn't have grants, so it was extremely difficult for us."

Uninterested in the small number of steel mill jobs that Gary had to offer, Zeke moved to Chicago in late 1950. "I stayed with some friends, and got a job delivering telephone directories. [I] finally got a job as a porter in early '51. At that time, being draft age, the factories wouldn't hire you, and being black also had its problems. The only jobs offered were janitor jobs." Zeke eventually found work in a Neisner Brothers five-and-dime store, and then as a porter in the Montgomery Ward warehouse.

Deeply religious, the Careys regularly attended services at the Judaic Church of God and Saints of Christ, located at 39th and State Street. "We are Black Jews, and nothing else can be used to designate us," Jake told a *Chicago Defender* reporter in 1961. "To call one of us a Negro is an insult. Of course, we have no objection to being called Afro-Americans. Our families have been followers of the Jewish religion for many years, long before I, my parents, or their grandparents were born." The minor chords so often utilized in Jewish music, with what historian Pruter described as their "overtones of sadness and darkness," would play a key role in the conception of the Flamingos' harmony patterns.

The Church of God and Saints of Christ, a Black Hebrew Israelite denomination, was established in Kansas by William Saunders Crowdy (1847–1908) in 1896. Born into slavery, Crowdy served with a United States Colored Troops regiment from Maryland during the Civil War. After completing his military service, he settled in Guthrie, Oklahoma, and was ordained a Baptist deacon. Crowdy relocated to the Kansas City area for several years in the 1890s before returning to Oklahoma.

Crowdy later explained that through a series of divine revelations, he received instructions regarding the establishment of the Church of God and Saints of Christ. Initially, he converted his followers by preaching on the streets of Guthrie. In the mid–1890s, he organized his first tabernacles in the Kansas towns of Emporia, Lawrence, and Topeka. Often met with opposition from authorities, he was arrested on 22 different occasions. Crowdy perse-vered, and began establishing tabernacles in Missouri, Chicago, and New York. In some newspapers, Crowdy was referred to as "the Black Elijah."

By 1899, he had relocated to Philadelphia. In 1903, as the congregation continued to grow, Crowdy purchased 140 acres of land in Belleville, Virginia, as the intended site for the church's headquarters. In 1921, one of Crowdy's hand-picked successors, William Henry Plummer, executed the move. By 1936, the Church of God and Saints of Christ had established more than 200 tabernacles, or congregations, and numbered 37,000 members, including the Carey families.

"In going to church services, we ran into a couple of other cousins that could sing," Zeke explained to McGarvey. "They were relatives to the friends I stayed with when I first came to Chicago, the Wilson family. Paul Wilson and Johnny Carter were cousins, and they could sing. Johnny Carter had a couple of nice sisters, and that was important, too. We used to go down there a lot."

"Johnny Carter is the real founder of the Flamingos," opines Terry John-son, who replaced Carter in late 1956. "They were all in church and Johnny said, 'Man, why don't we get a group together?'"

"We decided to form a group," Jake told interviewer Tamarkin, "and asked them if they'd be interested in being part of what we were talking about. They said, 'yeah,' and we started out doing house parties and things like that."

John Edward Carter, who pos-sessed a pitch-perfect soaring tenor, was 16 at the time, having been born in Chicago on June 2, 1934. John's father, Gressum Carter (1902–1992), a plasterer born in Richmond, Virginia, and mother, Geneva Joanne (Wilson) Carter (1906–2001), were married in Camden, New Jersey, in 1924 and lived there before relocating to the Midwest.

For several months, Juda Byrd, another member of the church choir who was the same age as Zeke and lived on nearby 40th Street, sang bari-

Johnny Carter in the early 1950s (Carter family photo).

tone in the group. When Byrd left, Carter's charismatic cousin, Paul Wilson, was brought in to replace him. Fifteen-year-old Paul R. Wilson, Jr., was the youngest member, having been born to Paul and Edwina Jackson Wilson in the city on January 6, 1935. Edwina and her three children (the others were Rita, two years older than Paul, and one-year-old Dennis) lived with the Byrd family at 764 East 40th Street. Wilson attended Gillespie Elementary and Calumet High School, participating in numerous dance and musical activities. He began singing at the age of eight in the church's Junior Choir, gradually working his way up to the Youth Chorus. Wilson usually sang baritone, one step below Zeke, who was installed at second tenor.

"We got a little group going, unofficially," Zeke explained. "One of Johnny Carter's sister's boyfriends became an adopted lead." Earl Lewis, no relation to the Channels' front man of the same name, served as the group's lead singer for nearly two years. "We started together about ... 1950, and were all just neighborhood guys who started singing," Lewis told Pruter. "That's how we got together. We used to sing, and man, we would have a big crowd around us. Every night we would sit around, just sitting out on the front steps, and all the kids would come around and listen to us sing. This was around 35th–36th and Lake Park on the South Side. We originally called ourselves the Swallows. We went under that name for six to eight months. Then, there was another group named the Swallows, and they started raising hell." Recording for King Records, the Baltimore-based Swallows, featuring the expressive tenor lead of Eddie Rich, became rhythm and blues stars in the summer of 1951 when their debut release, "Will You Be Mine," hit the top 10 on *Billboard's* R&B chart.

In the summer of 1951, Carter suggested the ultimate group name. "We had to get a name," Zeke recalled. "We said, 'Look, everybody come up with some names.' One of the fellows came up with the El Flamingos. El in Spanish means 'the.' We thought that was beauty. So, we started off calling ourselves the Five Flamingos. That name stuck. It sounded good to everybody, and the majority said, yep, this is it, forget about the rest of them."

According to Sollie McElroy, who replaced Lewis in early 1952, Carter's inspiration came from a venue where the group had performed. "We went to the Southtown Theater on 63rd Street, and they had a big old pond inside the theater," McElroy told interviewer Lou Rallo in 1992. "It had ducks and flamingos and different things in there. So we used to tease each other about our skinny legs. None of us had athletic legs. So we looked at the flamingos standing up [on one leg] and we said, 'That's what we're going to call ourselves.' We didn't think it was going to work. There were 'bird this and bird that' groups, and we really didn't think it was going to catch [on]. 'If it doesn't work, we'll change it.'"

"No one particular group influenced us," Zeke explained. "We greatly admired the Dominoes, the Orioles, and the Five Keys. We always thought that the Clovers, for instance, used to come up with great songs. We used to sing some of their things. But we always cared a lot about harmony, and they were not a very tight harmonizing group. As a child, I greatly admired Sonny [Til]. Sonny and the Orioles were before the Dominoes, before the Five Keys." Among the original compositions that Lewis remembered practicing with the Five Flamingos were "Someday, Someway" and "If I Can't Have You," which were eventually recorded at the group's first studio session in January of 1953.

(From left) Sollie McElroy, Paul Wilson, and Johnny Carter with an unidentified young girl, Chicago, 1952 (courtesy Sollie McElroy).

"It was pretty good back then," Lewis reminisced to Pruter, "because we could sound like any of the groups. Johnny Carter, Zeke, Jake and Paul, they were all from a Jewish church, [the] Church of God and Saints of Christ. They were all family. I wasn't any relation to them. I was the one who was not in the family, the outsider. So it was hard for me to fit in. In their church, the other guys had a choir of something like 60 people. They were part of this choir, so they pretty much specialized in singing. I would sing lead, and they would give a technically polished and perfect background which came from their musical training in the choir."

"The difference in the Flamingos was that the emphasis was on the harmony," agreed Jake. "In the average group, the emphasis was on the lead. We just reversed it."

"We concentrated on very basic harmony, as you would say, bass, baritone, tenor," Zeke explained. "We always had that. Then, on top of that basic harmony, once we got that right, we would color [it]. Sometimes, we used to sing three-part harmony; sometimes we would sing four, sometimes five. When the group expanded, we would sing six parts, always centered around that basic, fundamental harmony. Then, we used to take basic harmony and switch it around. Instead of the bass note being very low, we may take it high, and have the bass singer sing an octave higher. Or, he may start off an octave higher, and then go down. In the midst of tunes, in an instant, we used to switch parts. The bass singer would come up and switch to baritone. Maybe his bass note would be taken by two other guys singing together. There were just all kinds of things that we used to do. So, our harmonies used to be very basic in their structure, but with a lot of unique coloring. We would color that basic harmony. In the beginning, we were solely responsible for whatever we sounded like. We selected our own tunes."

The first individual to take an active interest in the career of the Swallows/Flamingos was Fletcher J. Weatherspoon, Jr. Ten months older than Zeke, Weatherspoon was born in Tuscaloosa County, Alabama, on March 18, 1932, and had graduated from Chicago's Wendell Phillips High School in 1950. "Zeke and I both worked at Montgomery Ward's warehouse, but we didn't really know one another well," Weatherspoon recalled. "We were at a picnic together. I happened to know somebody that knew somebody who knew about the picnic. Jake might have been there, too, because a lot of ladies had invited us out. In fact, it may have been their church picnic. Anyway, we were at the park. That's when I saw Zeke, and I told him, 'Hey, I know you from work!' He said, 'Yeah, we work at Montgomery Ward's together.'"

That day, Zeke and Fletcher struck up a friendship that would last nearly 50 years. "We realized

Fletcher Weatherspoon, the Flamingos' first manager and lifelong friend, Chicago, 1950 (courtesy Fletcher Weatherspoon).

that we worked together, and we started talking about different things," Weatherspoon remembered. "He told me that he had this little singing group, and that they sang in the church. One thing led to another, and we got to talking about Billy Ward and the Dominoes, and other groups, and they were saying they could sing like that. I wanted to hear what they sounded like. Zeke invited me to one of their rehearsals, and I liked how they sounded. Right away, they had that harmony."

"We were at a picnic," Jake confirmed for interviewer Gus Gossert in 1971. "We were kids, sitting around and humming a tune," Jake recalled. "This man came around looking for mosquito ointment. His ears caught our sound. He said, 'Let me hear you do something.' Fletcher said, 'Man, I like that harmony you've got there. You've got a very unique sound. I know someone who has a nightclub.'"

"The next thing I knew," Weatherspoon continued, "I was taking them around to different clubs and different parties, different talent shows, and we went from there." He added, "When they decided that they were going to start singing popular music, a lot of times they would rehearse in my mother's basement."

"We didn't know what it was to go and sing around microphones," Zeke admitted. "We never sang with music. We used to rehearse in basement apartments, never on the street corner. What we would do is take a stand-up lamp or a broom, and stand it up by a chair, and that would be our microphone. Then we would practice how we would move around it, how we would stand, where the lead singer should be. This is the way we would practice. We would see different groups on television or in theaters, and how they would move around microphones. We said, 'We can't afford to buy a microphone, so we'll use a broom or a stand-up lamp.' We just sang, man. We sang our little hearts out to that broom. This is the way we used to do it."

At first, Weatherspoon had a tough time interesting Zeke, who didn't drink or smoke, in the house party scene. "He would always invite me to parties," Zeke recalled to McGarvey. "I always turned him down. I didn't know he was heavily into the social thing among blacks—cabarets, rent parties. At the time, most of the Chicago blacks were migrants from the South, or descendants from migrants. The Southern folk tended to be pretty drawn together. Rather than going out to nightclubs, house parties used to be the thing to look forward to on the weekend. Let's face it, there weren't that many black nightclubs. At a house party, there was good, down-home cooking—fried chicken, chitlins, regular soul food."

Eventually, the Swallows consented to sing at a local neighborhood party. "Fletcher was our manager at the time," Zeke continued. "He went in there, stopped the music, we sang, and the people went crazy! Next weekend, he had two or three parties for us. [He] started getting requests. Suddenly it started to click. We sang very close harmony, and that was unusual at the time. We sang the hits of the day, and people got off on that. We had never sung that type of music in front of audiences before. We had sung in churches on Sundays, but this was a very unique experience for us. The feedback that we got gave us a second notion that maybe we should take singing a little more seriously."

Over time, the group used the neighborhood house party scene to hone their craft while building up a local following. "When we'd go out to these house parties, we would just have fun," Jake remembered. "We would do our little thing as far as harmonizing, and people would gather around in large crowds. We weren't getting paid anything, but it was just the enjoyment of singing, the thing that we enjoyed the most. That was the thing that we loved to do—sing."

"They were singing at house parties and little local clubs, whatever we could get," Weatherspoon confirmed in 2006. "A lot of times, we would do it for the money that the crowd would bring up and put in the hat. I've been giving parties for 56 years, and that was one reason I was able to get the fellows so many little local jobs. Back then we called them jobs. People would laugh at it now. But that's how I could get them so many little jobs, because a lot of the affairs my little club [the local Elks] would have, we would book them to do the show for us. And then other clubs I knew would book them."

In the early months of 1952, Earl Lewis was dismissed from the group. "My friend wanted to pay us to do a cabaret, $25 I think, so that night we rehearsed real hard," Zeke recalled. "We all showed up except the lead singer. He was with some chick, and we had to improvise. I took charge that night. We told him that was it."

"I was kicked out," Lewis admitted. "Girls, you know. Not making rehearsals, things like that. They were tired of my messing up."

Lewis did hang around long enough to meet his replacement, 18-year-old Sollie Sylvester McElroy, Jr. Born in Gulfport, Mississippi, to Sollie (1909–1978) and Alberta McElroy (1913–1978) on July 16, 1933, McElroy had come to the Windy City with his family at the age of 15, and he had attended Dunbar High School. Sollie had two older sisters, Ora and Betty Jean, and a younger brother, Herbert. "I had no one, really, to inspire me to sing," McElroy told interviewer Lou Rallo in 1992. "I started singing in church, and I didn't feel right there because it was [people] singing in the church and boozing in the joints. You'd go to church and sing, and you'd leave the church and go to a joint. So, I said, 'This is not for me.' So my mother sent me downtown Chicago to the Conservatory of Music for me to learn voice. I didn't like that, because it was taking away what we call soul."

At the age of 16, McElroy formed a trio with a Jewish man and female singer from nearby Gary, Indiana. "We started learning Jewish numbers," McElroy continued. "We would go to old folks' homes and things like that. We would sing 'My Yiddish Mama' and several songs I learned in Hebrew. I said, 'That's not for me, either,' and so I started singing in talent shows. You'd go to win five dollars, ten dollars, something like that."

"There used to be a theater off 51st [Street], the Willard Theater," McElroy told interviewers Pruter and Rallo. "I had gone there to perform in a talent show. I had been singing in church, but it wasn't a thing I felt. I never forgot the song I was singing, 'Cry,' by Johnnie Ray. I was so excited that when I got to the high part, I lost control of it. I got to the point where it says, 'if your sweetheart sends a letter of goodbye,' and when I got to that high part, nothing came out. This guy stuck the hook out and pulled me off the stage. The audience goes, 'No, no, no, let him go on again.' The orchestra started up, and I sang the complete song. I won second prize and I got five bucks."

In the Willard Theater audience that night was Fletcher Weatherspoon, who felt that McElroy would be a perfect fit for his group, who now called themselves the Five Flamingos. "I knew he had potential, but he just wasn't getting over that night," Weatherspoon explained. "He had gotten his feelings hurt. I asked him would he would like to sing lead for my group. He said, 'Yeah.' So, I took him with us one night. We were doing a party or something. They were singing, and he was sitting there. I said, 'Do you know that song?' He said, 'Yeah.' I said, 'Go ahead up there and sing with them.' He said, 'Would it be OK?' I said, 'Yeah.' I told Zeke to let him sing a little bit. Zeke brought him on and gave him the mike, and the crowd went wild. 'Have mercy, mercy baby, I know I've done you wrong.' He became the lead. At that time, they were singing all covers. They were doing, like, the Dominoes' and the Orioles' songs."

"We got hired for a birthday party, $10 or something," Zeke agreed. "While we were singing this song, a voice out of nowhere was singing with us. [It was] a song by Billy Ward and the Dominoes, and he sounded good. The guy's name was Sollie McElroy. He was our first legitimate lead singer."

"From there, we just [did] quarter parties, [singing] in doorways, on the corners, you know," McElroy explained to Rallo, referring to the informal gatherings where each of the guests would pay 25 cents to help cover the expenses. "We weren't trying to get any money. We were just trying to get established and let people know we were out there because you could go out there on a Friday or Saturday night, and see 30 to 40 groups on the corners or in doorways, subways, you know, and we just started going from place to place. We'd hear about a quarter party or something, we'd go, or a talent show, we'd go. We had a couple of [talent shows at] the Crown Propeller and the Green Door. These were night spots on the South Side."

Lewis, who still occasionally hung around with the group, related a bizarre tale to interviewer Pruter in 1979 about an early rehearsal that took place not long after McElroy joined. "Sollie showed up and sang 'September Song.' But he sang it so high and, you know, he put so much into it, he collapsed and just fell over and fainted. We all just stood there and stared, because we never saw anything like it."

"They were just a bunch of good guys, you know, and they heard me sing and they said, 'Well … maybe,'" McElroy explained. "And after I relaxed with them, heard what they were doing, how they would present themselves, I started blending in a little more, a little more … as we rehearsed. We rehearsed every day. That's all we did was rehearse. You see, Ezekiel and Jake were the head honchos of that group. They were in control of what went down, and they kind of supervised everything that went on, which was very, very good. We had fines if you didn't show [up]. Whatever money you made, if you made ten dollars, they might charge you a dollar. Because we would go on gigs and do a whole night show for 15 bucks apiece."

Before embarking on a full-time career in the entertainment industry, which would include singing on the Sabbath, Zeke and Jake considered it essential to obtain the approval of their religious leaders. "Four of them, Zeke, Jake, Paul, and Johnny, were all Black Jews," Weatherspoon explained. "They could not work sundown on Friday until sundown on Saturday, because that was their Sabbath Day. They had to go get their head Rabbi's permission to sing from sundown Friday until sundown Saturday. We all got into my little car and drove up to Indianapolis to see him. I'll never forget what he told them. After they had their little meeting, he told them, 'If this is the way in which you have chosen to make your living, just do not forget the Rock from which you were hewn, and may Allah go with you.' He got up and left, and they were all happy. They said that was his permission to do what they wanted to do."

"Jake and I were on a 4th of July picnic with Fletcher," Zeke explained. "Jake and I were humming 'The Glory of Love' and [a guy] heard us. He told us about a talent show going on at a black night club on the West Side of Chicago." The club was Martin's Corner, located at 1900 West Lake. "One of the most venerable black and tans in the city," according to researcher Pruter, Martin's Corner had first opened in the 1930s and regularly featured a diverse group of local entertainers from exotic dancers to comedians to rhythm and blues vocal groups. "I took them over to enter in the talent show that Thursday night, and they won," Weatherspoon recalled.

While both Zeke and Jake Carey remembered being the only act on the talent show that night, the likelihood that no other aspiring performer would have entered the competition at such a popular inner-city club seems unlikely. Weatherspoon himself recalled a much more plausible scenario. "They might have been the only group, but there was a lot of talent there. There were singers, female singers, tap dancers, a lot of different talent, because it was a talent show. I knew everything that was going on in the clubs, which clubs were having live entertainment and who was doing what, you know. One of the things we won at Martin's Corner was a weekend where they paid you to come back and work the next weekend. The star of the show was a singer by the name of Joe Williams. During those days, Joe Williams was the star, and they were opening for him."

"We were really good," Zeke remembered, "and the man said, 'Come back at the weekend.' We came back and performed."

"That was in the latter part of 1952," Jake recalled. "The people enjoyed us, and after we appeared on that Thursday night show, the guy said I want you to come back on Friday night when the crowd is larger. The people liked what we did in our little white buck shoes and towel shirts that we took our nickels and dimes to buy. Being the weekend, he had a better audience, and there was a fellow in the audience by the name of Jimmy Thurmond. He was one of the representatives of King Booking Agency. He said, 'You all want to be in show business?' And that was it. On Monday morning, Thurmond took us over to see Ralph Leon. He ran the agency."

The 20-year-old Weatherspoon, who had just received his U.S. Army draft notice, stepped aside in deference to 39-year-old Ralph Leon. Born Refuel Liszanski in Kiev, Ukraine, on January 22, 1913 (some documents claimed 1912), Leon emigrated to the United States through the port of Boston in July of 1923. Standing five-foot-eight and weighing a slight 135 pounds, Ralph married Lillian Harris in 1936. Soon after the birth of their son, Stanley, in 1941, Liszanski applied to become a United States citizen. Employed as an orchestra manager and residing at 4149 Wilcox Avenue in Chicago, Liszanski legally changed his name to Ralph Leon upon his naturalization.

"Fletcher Weatherspoon was drafted into the Army and that really concluded his managerial duties," Zeke explained. "Ralph Leon had limited knowledge of the business, but there was very little a young black man [like Weatherspoon] could do for a black R&B group. He had no money, no [record company] connections, so Ralph Leon took us under his wing."

"Fletcher Weatherspoon didn't have the managerial experience," Jake stated. "You could say that he just knew this was our chance."

Under Leon's guidance, the Five Flamingos shifted away from the house parties and gravitated toward theater and nightclub work. "He was new in the business," Zeke explained, "and unaware about what show business was all about. But he believed in himself, and when he saw some unique quality in somebody else, he believed in them, and he really pushed."

"Ralph Leon took over, and that's when the group started to roll," McElroy agreed. "We didn't start to entertain big until Ralph Leon took us over. He went into an agency, and he started to move us into places in Chicago." An advertisement in the *Chicago Defender* for a Saturday, October 18, 1952, midnight show at the Indiana Theater, located on East 43rd Street, noted the appearance of the "5 Flamingo Boys, the Harmony Kings," along with blues singer Lil Mason.

November and December found the group performing at the New Club DeLisa, located at 5521 State Street. As part of Sammy Dyer's "Yester-Daze," the quintet performed with the Co-Ops, China Doll, comic and emcee Allen Drew, and Red Saunders and his band, among others. "Our biggest break was the DeLisa," Jake recalled. "They used to have this Monday morning breakfast show, and everybody in town would come. They would be packed. The Red Saunders band was the house band."

"It was just to fill in temporarily," Sollie added, "but we stayed there two months because we were a young group, and people weren't familiar with us. We were something new. Then we started snowballing. We played the Crown Propeller, a very popular place on the South Side. We played the Little Squeeze over on the West Side. We did the Black Orchid. We did any place in the city at that particular time. There were a lot of clubs that you could sing in."

The group earned their first trade journal mention in the December 13, 1952, issue of *Cash Box* magazine, which touted "the Flamingos, new singing group, drawing raves during this, their first job, at Club De Lisa. Several recording companies [are] bidding heavy for their wax contracts. Personal manager, Ralph Leon, [is] being firm about the whole thing and holding out for the label of his choice."

Taking a Chance

In late 1952, Ralph Leon brought the Five Flamingos to audition for United Records, located at 5052 South Cottage Grove Avenue in Chicago. One of the biggest and most successful R&B labels in the city at the time, United was bankrolled by a tailor named Leonard Allen and handled by Lew Simpkins, an experienced A&R man who had worked at Miracle and Premium Records in the 1940s and early 1950s. Formed in the late summer of 1951, United struck gold almost immediately. Alto sax man Tab Smith's "Because of You" and Jimmy Forrest's tenor sax honker, "Night Train," both went to the top of the *Billboard* R&B charts for a combined nine weeks between December 1951 and May 1952.

"Ralph Leon took us to a record company after we had worked for a little while," Zeke explained to McGarvey. "He said, 'Gee, let's go to a record company. I think you should be recorded.' United Records had a few hits. They were strictly R&B. We sang, and we really thought we were saying something. We said, 'Well, the harmony is great, we sound good. We know we're going to get a contract out of this.' We sang a cappella, because that's the way we started out. The harmony was close and everything. So, after we sang, the guy from the record company told our manager Ralph Leon, 'Listen, they sang in harmony. They have a nice sound. They have a nice potential. I'll tell you all what you should do. Go back and rehearse for about a year, and then come back and audition!'"

"The thing that they thought about," Jake added, "[was] you had such groups as the Clovers and the Dominoes at that time. So, what did they care about the Flamingos? You know, for them, we were just another doo-wop. There was no uniqueness, because we were young. You could see the chlorophyll in us, we were so green. So, the whole thing is that they wanted us to go back and get something that was relevant to what was on the market at that time."

Undaunted, Leon took them less than a mile to the northeast, stopping in at Sheridan Record Distributors, located at 1151 East 47th Street. Formed by Art Sheridan, a 27-year-old city native who had begun his career building

Flamingos manager Ralph Leon, pictured with his wife and son Stanley at his bar mitzvah, October 1948 (Leon family photo).

pressing plants and distributing records, Sheridan Record Distributors was also the home of Chance Records. Established in September of 1950, Chance also focused its attention squarely on rhythm and blues. "I thought it sounded great," Sheridan told Pruter, "probably because I didn't know enough about music, per se, but I really liked the sound." Ewart Abner, Jr. (1923–1997), Sheridan's accountant, served as the company's general manager and book-keeper. Chance's earliest releases included tenor sax instrumentals by Cootie Williams band alumnus Schoolboy Porter, and the ubiquitous bluesman John Lee Hooker, thinly disguised as John Lee Booker for contractual reasons.

In January of 1953, Sheridan signed the group to his fledgling label, along with Bobby Prince, Chubby Newsome, Anita Brown, and Big Boy Spires. The group's initial session was held on January 28 at Universal Recording, unquestionably the premier studio in the city at that time. Established by Bill Putnam (1920–1989) in 1946, the original Universal studio boasted the country's very first echo chamber. By the time the Flamingos walked in the door, the studio had moved several blocks from North Wacker Drive to 111 East Ontario Street. With the assistance of pioneering audio engineer Emory Cook (1913–2002), whose company produced the first commercial binaural, or stereo recordings in 1952, and recording engineer Jim Cunningham, Putnam constructed two recording studios at Universal: one was 25 by 40 by 15 feet; the other was 15 by 20 by 12 feet. As researcher-writer Jim Cogan elaborated in *Mix* in 2003, Putnam also built two mastering rooms. One housed a Scully disc-cutting lathe with Grampian cutting heads. During this era, all major lacquer masters were cut on Scully-manufactured lathes. The other mastering room contained a "home-brew" belt-driven turntable with Olsen feedback cutting heads. In all probability, Putnam, who invented the modern recording console and is regarded as the father of modern recording, engineered all of the Flamingos' early masters.

Sheridan hired local trumpeter William "King Kolax" Little (1912–1991) and his band for the date. A 40-year-old Kansas City native, King Kolax had been working steadily since the mid–1930s, and at one time had employed jazz greats Charlie Parker and John Coltrane. "He was the greatest," McElroy explained to Rallo. "He had a band of his own. He was really popular in his day, and as things started to whittle down from the big bands, he had his little quintet. He was a big man in Chicago."

Tenor saxophonist Dick Davis, pianist Prentice McCary, bassist "Cowboy" Martin, and drummer Little Gates rounded out the group. "If I Can't Have You," one of three originals recorded at the four-song session, was the first tune committed to tape. "We had two leads," Zeke remembered of the Flamingos' initial offering. "Sollie sang the lead to the song basically. I think if you listen to 'If I Can't Have You,' and if you remember the Orioles, you will probably recognize the fact that we were influenced to some extent by the Orioles. You'll recognize how the second lead would come in, and he would sing a little part, and then the main lead would come back. Johnny Carter was the second lead singer."

Carter's smooth falsetto tenor flourishes and Jake's round bass notes highlighted the group's harmony, which was augmented nicely by Davis's smooth tenor sax riffs. Like many of the Flamingos' early efforts, "If I Can't Have You" was written by Charles Gonzales. "Charles Gonzales was a singer, and he used to write," Zeke recalled. "Truth be told, he was a better writer than he was a singer." Gonzales sang with the band of trumpeter Hot Lips Page for a year in the late 1940s before embarking on a solo career. Charles initially recorded for Gotham Records before moving on to Chance, where he was given the name Bobby Prince. Throughout the 1950s, Prince remained active, recording for RCA Victor and M-G-M in addition to his frequent club work with local bands, including Red Holloway's.

Gonzales also penned the up-tempo "Someday, Someway," led by Sollie. The group's performance, again featuring Carter's falsetto trimmings and

Jake's sturdy bass, turned a rather ordinary R&B jump into an above-average recording, with Davis taking a jazz-flavored solo over the group's handclaps. The second fast song, "Hurry Home Baby," credited to Kolax, featured a unison lead, followed by a call and response segment with Jake up front. Davis again filled the instrumental break with a 24-bar tenor solo. "Now, that guy had a beautiful [sax] voice," Sollie emoted. "It's bluesy. Not fast, but it has a little more groove. We had a lot of songs that King Kolax wrote, Red Holloway wrote. Different people did a lot of writing for us. We were with all those people right in Chicago."

Between the two up-tempo sides, the Flamingos delivered their own unique arrangement of "That's My Desire." Written by Helmy Kresa (1905–1991), Irving Berlin's principal arranger and orchestrator, and lyricist Carroll Loveday in 1931, "That's My Desire" was initially recorded as an upbeat dance number by John Firman and his Orchestra that year. The song remained largely forgotten until Frankie Laine scored a Top 5 national hit with his 1947 pop ballad rendition. In the years that followed, "That's My Desire" became an undisputed standard, with literally hundreds of versions being committed to wax. In the R&B field, Ella Fitzgerald and pianist Hadda Brooks cracked the charts with their own interpretations on the heels of Laine's hit.

"These songs started selling, and you heard them everywhere at that particular time, so we said, 'Hey, let's get that,'" McElroy recalled. "We were working in these clubs where these songs were in demand, so we had to know them. I like [that recording]. I always did."

After a unison opening of "da da-da da da da da" from the vocalists, McElroy again took the lead, as Carter perfected his trademark falsetto atop the group's harmony pattern. "We got a great argument from them when we did 'That's My Desire,'" Zeke confessed. "We wanted to do it this way, and we could only use about four or five musicians."

Jake vividly remembered the record company's disapproval of their arrangement. "'You're mutilating the melody! Oh man, why do you do things like that?' He said, 'The guy that wrote the tune would turn over in his grave to hear you doing this.' But the thing of it was, they found out that this sounded commercial for the rhythm and blues market. It may not have sounded like Frankie Laine, but it sounded all right for rhythm and blues, and it did very nicely."

"We were balladeers," McElroy explained to Rallo. "[We'd sing] anything that was popular on either side; on the black side, and the white side. We mostly would lean to anything that came out on the white side that was a ballad, like anything that Patti Page or someone like that [did]. [They were] very popular, and we would jump right on it and do it in a group version.

We didn't do too much blues, very little blues, because the houses that we were playing wouldn't accept blues. So, we had to be mostly like the Ink Spots. We would do things so the people would sit down with their lady friend, have a drink, candlelight, and things like that. We went into Canada and we did supper clubs."

While waiting for their first record to be released, the group kept busy in the nightclubs. On February 21, they appeared at Club Paris on the West Side at 1632 West Madison, billed as "Those Fabulous 5 Flamingos." The Claudia Oliver Revue also included Bobby Caston, Freddie Gordon, Mabel Hunter, the Claudettes, and the King Kolax Orchestra.

They also worked day jobs to make ends meet. Carter had married Barbara Jean Hogan in December of 1952. McElroy was married and would soon welcome the birth of a son, Sollie III, in August of 1953. "I was a busboy," he recalled, "and I hustled. Then I was a janitor, going out doing different stores where you would do the floors and the windows, and I'd go from one store to another. Then, I started to work in Marshall Fields, like in New York. You'd take clothes on a rack and run them down the sidewalk. I worked in a linen store, sold linens, curtains, towels, and things like that. I began to cook. I worked myself up from busboy to the kitchen, and I started to learn how to cook short orders, and I left there, and that's when I really started off with the Flamingos."

In early March, Sheridan issued "If I Can't Have You" and "Someday, Someway" by the Flamingos, removing the "five" from their name. Both sides received "very good" ratings from *Billboard* the week of the 14th. "A happy bounce effort, almost on a spiritual-type kick, is sung with life and spirit by the boys over a hand-clapping background and good orchestra work," the magazine's reviewer wrote of "Someday, Someway." In the March 21 edition of *Cash Box*, "If I Can't Have You" was given a B grade, with the reviewer remarking, "[T]he Flamingos chant with feeling as they dish up the romantic slow beat against an easy backing." On Saturday night, April 25, the group shared the stage at the Crown Propeller Lounge on East 63rd Street with "Aqua Tease Girl" Atlantis, comedian Danny Lee, and the bands of Eddie Williams and Red "Mr. Groovy" Klimo. By the time they began a mid–June engagement at Gleason's in Cleveland, the ballad side, "If I Can't Have You," had started to break in Philadelphia. The week of the 20th, *Billboard* selected it as its R&B Territorial Tip in the City of Brotherly Love.

After completing their first Eastern States tour, the quintet returned home for the 4th of July weekend, appearing at the Paris Club for four nightly shows on Friday, Saturday, and Sunday. Also on the "Star Studded Revue" bill were tap-dancers Leonard and Leonard, vocalist Dahl Scott, and Paul

YOUTHFUL QUINTET

Although they have been singing together for just a little over a year, the Flamingoes, five youthful Chicagoans (average age: 20) have swept the nation with their rollicking, zesty acting and smoothly-blended vocals (top disc: *Carried Away*). The quintet is already lined up for an engagement at the Windy City's swank Black Orchid.

The original Flamingos in 1953. Left to right: Paul Wilson, Jacob Carey, Sollie McElroy (top), Johnny Carter and Ezekiel Carey (from the collection of Richard and Eunice Tulimieri).

King and his Combo. One week later, *Billboard* selected "If I Can't Have You," the Embers' "Paradise Hill," and Roy Milton's "Early in the Morning" as Territorial Tips in the Los Angeles market. On July 28, 1953, the Flamingos joined Eartha Kitt, June Valli, Eddy Arnold, and others at the Chicago Recorded Music Association's annual gathering at the Southmoor Country Club in Palos Park.

Despite its regional successes, Chance #1133 failed to click on a national level. "'If I Can't Have You' was a big record in Philadelphia, and did fairly well in New York and other Eastern seaboard cities," Zeke remembered. "[It didn't sell] much in the South at all."

By this point, however, Sheridan had already issued the other two songs from the January session, pairing "That's My Desire" and "Hurry Home Baby" in June. Within weeks, "That's My Desire" began selling in key Midwestern cities including Chicago, Cleveland, Detroit, and St. Louis. *Billboard* proclaimed it a Best Buy on August 8, with additional hot markets noted to be Philadelphia, Pittsburgh, New York, and Nashville. Both sides received "excellent" reviews the week of August 15. One week later, the journal selected it as a Territorial Tip in Los Angeles. In the rhythm and blues market, the Flamingos were slowly establishing their reputation.

"Golden Teardrops"

In August of 1953, Sheridan brought the Flamingos back to Universal Recording for their second session. On this occasion, he hired tenor saxophonist James "Red" Holloway (1927–2012) and his band to provide the backing. The other musicians on the date were pianist Louis Carpenter, bassist Hawk Lee, baritone saxist Mac Easton, drummer Robert Henderson, and an unidentified trumpeter.

The first song completed was "Carried Away," an up-tempo offering from Charles Gonzales that borrowed the familiar Jimmy Forrest "Night Train" riff for the opening. The tune featured the familiar gospel-based call and response pattern popularized by Clyde McPhatter and the Dominoes, who served as a strong influence on the Flamingos during their formative years. "The girl we were singing about had gray eyes," McElroy remembered. "Her name was Geneva. She was on staff. She was running our fan club. We arranged this song. I didn't write any songs, but we all pitched in. A guy might come and bring us some lyrics and maybe a little bit of how he wanted it to go. Then, we'd set it in motion and create the song."

The Johnny Carter–penned and –led ballad, "Plan for Love" was next, followed by "You Ain't Ready," essentially a reworking of Gonzales's "Someday, Someway." The new version was done at a slightly faster tempo and featured Sollie in the lead, a 24-bar solo from Holloway, and a dual falsetto tenor segment after the break. "We had a little routine for 'You Ain't Ready,'" McElroy recalled. "This is a song I really liked, too."

The fourth and final song of the session was "Golden Teardrops." An ethereal ballad which has grown to legendary status among record collectors and vocal group harmony fans through the years, "Golden Teardrops" was brought to the Flamingos by Bunky Redding, who had served as the emcee at Martin's Corner the night the Flamingos won the talent competition. Born in Columbus, Ohio, Edward Lee "Bunky" Redding (1928–1975) was a singer-songwriter and guitar player who had moved to Chicago and recorded a trio of singles with Red Saunders's All Stars for Aladdin and its Score subsidiary label in late 1947. An additional 1959 Apex single, subsequently leased to

Edward "Bunky" Redding (1928–1975), composer of "Golden Teardrops" (Historic Images photo, from the author's collection).

Chess, and an obscure 1960 disc on Dempsey Records, completed the sum of his recorded output. Redding's heroin addiction led to incarcerations, and ultimately his death at the age of 47. "He was a junkie," Zeke confirmed to McGarvey. "He brought us that song, and wanted us to record that so bad. It had something to do with his girl. That's a song we worked on at least three months before we went to the studio, first [by] ourselves, then with a piano player, Mr. McKesick, to get the chords right. We used to go over to his house."

The group's a cappella introduction, featuring the silky tenors of McElroy and Carter, came about after hours of diligent practice. "I've never heard a beginning on a song like that, ever," McElroy recalled nearly 40 years later. "Bunky Redding wrote the song, but we added a little bit here and there. We started rehearsing that song at my mother's apartment on 46th and Langley. I never will forget it. We rehearsed and we rehearsed and we changed it and changed it and we began to put the song together like a puzzle. It took us about three months to do that song. Then, we finally got it. If you listen to the background, there is very little music. It was almost a cappella. You could hear the singing. You could hear the notes, the blending of voices. We rehearsed a long time on that song. In fact, we were almost ready to give it up."

Carter wafts over Sollie's impassioned lead and the group's soulful, tight harmony in seemingly effortless fashion throughout, finishing the song an octave above the lead singer. "We couldn't get it like we wanted to, and Johnny started to bring in that tenor, and it started fitting in, and so when we felt like we were comfortable with it, we recorded it," McElroy explained. "I was very relaxed because I liked this song. It's about a girl. He's asking her not to cry, because her tears are golden. They're precious to him. It wasn't like they were hurting tears. They were sweet tears. He's asking her not to cry over him."

Despite their tightly crafted vocals, Zeke Carey was disappointed with the overall sound of the final product. "In my opinion, the recording should have been musically far better than it was. You can hardly hear the music. It's all vocals. But [Chance] didn't know. You come up with something left-field, [and] they don't even know what it is. We were many years ahead of our time."

On Labor Day, September 7, 1953, the Flamingos appeared in concert at the Park City Bowl with the Coronets and sax great Sonny Stitt and his

Chance Records advertisement, 1953 (courtesy Joe Mirrione).

Orchestra. Before month's end, Sheridan had paired "Golden Teardrops" and "Carried Away" as the group's third release. Redding and Johnny Carter were listed as the songwriters on the original Chance label. Through the years, Redding's name was inexplicably dropped from the credit on subsequent LP and CD reissues. "Carter gets a lot of credit on these albums, but truthfully, these are misprints," Zeke asserted. "For instance, on *The Flamingos Meet the Moonglows on the Dusty Road of Hits*, he's down as writing 'Golden Teardrops.' Bunky Redding wrote 'Golden Teardrops.' Johnny had nothing at all to do with 'Golden Teardrops' as far as lyrics were concerned."

In mid–October, the group joined the Five Royales and Willie Mabon at Detroit's Graystone Ballroom. By this point, Chance was advertising their latest release as an "overnight hit." The week of the 31st, it was reviewed in *Billboard*, with "Carried Away" actually receiving a higher rating. Apparently, the record sold fairly well in areas where it was promoted and distributed. A full two and a half months after its release, in the first week of January 1954, *Billboard* selected "Golden Teardrops" as its R&B Territorial Tip in New York.

"Art Sheridan didn't know anything about music, neither did Ralph Leon," Zeke stated to McGarvey. "He was a businessman. The records we gave him, if he had had better distribution, we would have had much bigger records. 'If I Can't Have You,' most of them, all of them, were regional hits. Chicago, oddly enough, wasn't a big record-selling area for us when we were on Chance. 'That's My Desire' did fairly well in Chicago and a few other areas. 'Golden Teardrops' was a big New York record. It didn't do well in Chicago. There were people on other stations in the country [that played it], but you need power."

"A lot of our music, at that time, wasn't played on white stations," McElroy affirmed. "It was like underground for the white media, and I didn't think a lot of our stuff reached them. But we got better work because we sang those types of songs."

With "Golden Teardrops" still gaining ground in some markets, Sheridan went ahead and issued another disc, "Plan for Love" and "You Ain't Ready" in November. The pairing received a tepid response. "Over the even backing by the group, the lead singer wails a convincing blues," *Billboard*'s reviewer remarked when "Plan for Love" finally appeared in the trade journal on February 20, 1954.

Hoping to acquire better-paying and higher-profile jobs, Leon signed the Flamingos on with the Associated Booking Corporation in November. Their first big gig was a week of shows at Chicago's Regal Theater with Duke Ellington and his Orchestra, beginning Christmas Day. On Christmas Eve 1953, the day before the engagement began, the quintet returned to Universal

FLAMINGO'S

EXCLUSIVE
CHANCE RECORDING ARTIST!

Chicago studio portrait, 1953. Clockwise from top right: Ezekiel Carey, Johnny Carter, Jacob Carey, Paul Wilson, and Sollie McElroy (Maurice Seymour photo, from the author's collection).

Recording for another four-song session. Al Smith (1923–1974) organized the band, with Red Holloway on tenor sax, Mac Easton on baritone sax, trumpeter Hobart Dotson, pianist Horace Palm, drummer Vernel Fournier, and Quinn Wilson, whose bass playing easily eclipsed Smith's rudimentary skill on the instrument.

The first song attempted was the bluesy "Listen to My Plea," with Carter in the lead. "That song dragged a little," McElroy confessed. "I wanted it a little faster. So I didn't sing it."

Johnny also fronted the group on his own ballad, "Blues in a Letter." "He sang it because I wouldn't touch it with a ten-foot pole," Sollie admitted. "It wasn't my type of singing. That was a B-side. They had to throw something in."

For "September Song," the third tune of the date, Palm switched from piano to celeste, augmenting the horn-laden backing nicely. The real stars of the performance, however, were the Flamingos themselves. Though their rendition lacked the power of the two Ravens versions, which featured the soaring tenors of Maithe Marshall and Joe Van Loan respectively, the simple beauty of McElroy's restrained delivery and Carter's delicate falsetto runs made the Flamingos' "September Song" a favorite with audiences and fellow performers alike. "'September Song' was one of our finest," agreed Zeke. "It was never released [at the time]. I never will forget that when we worked with Lionel Hampton, he literally cried when he heard that song."

The session concluded with a traditional blues rave-up called "Jump Children," alternately titled "Vooit Vooit," for the nonsensical phrase used by the background singers. For the better part of a decade, the song would serve as the group's traditional closing number, featuring wild choreography conceived by Paul Wilson. "We had the green suits for that," McElroy recalled. "That was one of our most popular songs. Now, this kind of blues, I didn't mind. Scat was pretty hot then, [so] that was something I tried to pick up and do in between there. I had to fill in. I didn't have any lyrics, so I just tried to scat."

Although Chance credited Carter with the composition, the song dated back to at least the World War II era. "Johnny Carter had nothing to do with that, nothing at all," Zeke insisted. "'Jump Children' was an old blues tune." Indeed, "Jump Children" was first recorded by the International Sweethearts of Rhythm with vocals by Tiny Davis for Guild Records, a New York–based jazz label, in 1945. Later that fall, a second version, titled "Voo-It! Voo-It!" by Marion Abernathy, was issued under the moniker "The Blues Woman" on the Jukebox label.

From a commercial perspective, the Christmas Eve session, on the whole, was less than successful. For the first time, however, recording engineer Bill Putnam seemed to strike an ideal balance between voices and instruments. "The final outcome depends largely on the engineer,

78 RPM pressing, 1953 (author's collection).

the musicians, the arrangers, [and] whoever is A&R'ing the date," Zeke explained. "We discovered a lot of things. We found that when you go into the studio, there are certain things that you can do, and harmonies that would sound a lot different when you put an echo on it, or put certain kinds of instrumentation around it. So we began to experiment with sound. As we recorded, and continued to record, we would come out of the studio feeling very bad because it didn't come out like we thought it was going to come out. You know, after you rehearse, man, you rehearse, and you say, 'All right, I've got it now.' You go into the studio and you hear the playback and you say, 'Wow! Who did this? This doesn't sound like what we were doing.'"

"In those days, they didn't have tracks like they have now," Sollie explained in 1992. "You'd rehearse, and they'd have take one, take two. We've gone as high as 26 takes. The musicians are getting tired, throats are getting rough. Nowadays, you sing to a track. But in those days, you just stayed in the studio and started over again. They'd say, 'Pick it up from here.' It was rough. It could be 26 takes on one song before you got ready to try and do the other song before your voice ran out. And time was money."

After concluding their Christmas week obligation at the Regal, the Flamingos had time to take a January 9 gig at the 2,500-seat Rainbow Arena with Mugsy Spanier and Dinah Kaye. They made their local television debut on a March of Dimes show later that month. On Friday night, January 29, 1954, they appeared with 10 other acts, including the 5 Echoes and 5 Thrills, for disc jockey McKie Fitzhugh at the Corpus Christi Auditorium on the city's South Side. Singing first tenor for the 5 Echoes that night was Earl Lewis, who had joined the group after being expelled from the Flamingos two years earlier. Second tenor Tommy Hunt, who began his career with the 5 Echoes before moving to the Flamingos in 1956, had recently been drafted and was not with the group on this night.

Before heading out on their longest tour thus far, the quintet was called back to Universal in mid–February for a two-song session. The task at hand was an R&B cover of Patti Page's current hit, "Cross Over the Bridge." Written by Bennie Benjamin and George David Weiss, Page's Mercury label version had entered *Billboard*'s national pop chart that week. The record would spend 23 weeks on the list, peaking at #2. Smith rounded up Holloway, Easton, Wilson, Fournier, and pianist Willie Jones for the date. Opening with a tenor lead from Holloway over Easton's baritone sax fills, the song simply swung from start to finish. Carter handled the main lead with McElroy adding falsetto overlays throughout. For the B-side, the Flamingos rerecorded "Listen to My Plea," which had been cut in December but deemed unsatisfactory. Holloway and Easton again featured prominently in the mix. Chance rushed the sides into record stores that month, but aside from some scattered airplay in Chicago and other regional cities, the Flamingos' cover of "Cross Over the Bridge" failed to make a dent in Page's sales. A similar R&B rendition by the Chords was dwarfed by their blockbuster flipside, "Sh-Boom," in the late spring and summer.

With their recording obligations completed, the Flamingos headed off to Washington, D.C., to begin their first swing through the major black theaters on the eastern seaboard. "With Chance, Ralph pushed us as much as he could in the crossover direction," Zeke explained, "not on the strength of records, because we didn't get the distribution. He got us with the big booking agent. When 'Golden Teardrops' came out, not on the strength of it, our first date in a big theater was with Duke Ellington at the Howard Theater [in] Washington. Then, we went to the Apollo. We were well-liked, fortunately, by all of these guys because they appreciated the fact that we liked to sing in tune."

"We played with the big bands, I mean like the Woody Hermans and the Duke Ellingtons," agreed Jake. "We had our part there, and the people enjoyed it."

"We went to New York with Duke Ellington," McElroy recalled. "[After rehearsing "September Song," owner] Frank Schiffman at the Apollo said, 'We don't want that song!' We had a week there. He said, 'If you sing that song and it doesn't go over, you're out of here! You won't even make the week!' We sang that song, and we stood them up! Five standing ovations and we were in!"

During their Apollo stint with the Ellington band, "Plan for Love" was reviewed favorably in *Billboard*. By April, they had worked their way back home, and appeared at Martin's Corner, the site of their initial talent show victory. On July 2, 1954, the Flamingos began a week-long run at Detroit's Broadway-Capitol with Lionel Hampton and His Orchestra. Hoping to add to their appeal, Leon saw to it that his act was seen by as diverse an audience as possible, booking them with everyone from gospel giant Mahalia Jackson to country and western pioneer Eddy Arnold. "I don't think we ever got paid for it, [but] he wanted us to be seen by [audiences] other than just blacks," Zeke explained to McGarvey. "With Eddy Arnold in a little place on the outskirts of Chicago, he had to make the commitment to the people [that] he would lead us in and lead us out. There was a place in the white section of town, owned by a boxer, and the deal was he would take us in, either the back door or side door, never in the front. We go in, wait in the dressing room, go on, come off, and we'd leave, never mingle. We did a song or two at a wrestling match one time with [jazz trumpet player] Mugsy Spanier in between matches. We had to get all around one mike, but that was done a lot then, no accompaniment of our own."

Although the group never performed a cappella, they may have preferred working that way when they found that most backing bands were incapable of reading the music charts they provided. "We worked with Muddy Waters, Little Walter, Eddie Boyd, Lowell Fulson, Jimmy Reed, great blues guys," Zeke recounted. "We'd take out our music and they'd say, 'What's that for? You might as well put that back where you got it!' Sometimes, if we were really lucky, one cat could read. Sometimes they'd butcher us, wipe us out. I started learning early that these were keys I was singing in. I'd ask musicians, 'When I go to a band, what do I ask for? What key is this?' 'Look, you ask for a G-flat arpeggio' or a bluesy shuffle in whatever."

"The furthest South we got when I was with them was Louisville, Kentucky," McElroy recalled in 1992. "We played a lot of burlesque houses, too. We sang in boxing rings during intermissions over on the North Side. We went to a place that had the longest bar in Chicago. They had peanut shells and sawdust all over the floor, spittoons, the brass rail where you put your foot on, and we would go there and make a few bucks and I might come home with five dollars in my pocket."

Throughout their career, the Flamingos' stage performances regularly included hits made popular by other artists in addition to their own recordings. "We would do our little records, and we always picked the popular tunes," Zeke remembered. "What we used to like to do was take a song that was done by a single artist. We would sing it as a group, and put a group arrangement to it. We used to do a wonderful arrangement on Johnnie Ray's 'The Little White Cloud That Cried.' 'You Belong to Me' by the Orioles was another, [and Joni James's] 'Why Don't You Believe Me.' We wanted to record these things, but at the time, the rhythm and blues companies would say, 'No, you can't cut that because it won't sell in the rhythm and blues market. It's a white tune. It's a pop tune.' But we used to get a great response on that."

"[Our audiences] weren't into rock 'n' roll as yet, so we had to do such things as 'How Much Is That Doggie in the Window,'" agreed McElroy, and "some other things by Patti Page, 'September Song.' In other words, this was quiet music. I had a little zircon ring. My mother gave it to me, and we would get up there, we had a couple of songs [by the Ink Spots] that we did. The one that was really popular [was] 'We Three.' You know how Bill [Kenny, tenor lead of the Ink Spots] used his hands and everything [flashing his diamond ring]? Well, this is what the people wanted to see. You stand up clean. You had your makeup on. You had your hair done. Your shoes were perfect.

And you had one guy on a mike, four on another, so everything was blending together. You sang, you used your hands to express [like Kenny], and that's how we became known as balladeers, and that's how we got into the better clubs. We didn't play juke joints. The only time we played small clubs in the city was in between gigs for some little pocket money."

Parrot Records

After a year and a half with Chance Records, Ralph Leon opted to take the group to the powerful and influential black Chicago disc jockey, concert promoter, and label owner Al Benson (1908–1978). Born in Mississippi as Arthur Leaner, Benson gained fame over the airwaves at WGES, initially with a gospel program in 1943, and then a rhythm and blues show in late 1945. Acknowledged as the Godfather of Black Radio in Chicago, Benson partnered with Egmont Sonderling, owner of Master Records and the United Broadcasting Studios, in founding Old Swingmaster Records in 1949. The label name came from Benson's on-air moniker, but the company was essentially a vehicle for Sonderling to release jazz and R&B masters that Chicago independent Vitacoustic Records had recorded at his studio. Vitacoustic had later filed for bankruptcy, leaving their bills to Sonderling unpaid. Old Swingmaster issued only a scant dozen and a half discs before folding in June 1950, when Sonderling decided to separate himself from the music business.

In November 1952, Benson made preparations for launching his own record company, Parrot. He had been cutting sessions at Universal and shopping masters to other companies, primarily Chess and Checker Records. Beginning with Willie Mabon's "I Don't Know," Benson brokered a deal with Leonard and Phil Chess that would allow him to take some of his masters that were being released on Chess/Checker, and press them on Parrot to sell strictly in the greater Chicago area. Gradually, he began releasing more product on his own. Mabel Scott, Jo Adams, J.B. Lenoir, Jimmy Rushing, Joe Williams, and Coleman Hawkins all recorded for Parrot Records or its Blue Lake subsidiary. In the fall of 1953, Benson purchased a stack of masters from Jack Lauderdale's California-based Swing Time label, thereby adding sides by Lowell Fulson, Playboy Thomas, Marvin Phillips and others to his catalog. Obscure vocal group gems by the Pelicans and Five Thrills, now highly sought-after collector's items, were issued on Parrot in 1953–54.

In June of 1954, Benson relocated his essentially one-man operation from South Parkway to 750 East 49th Street. About that time, Leon sold him on the Flamingos. "Ralph Leon was thinking, if I get on a label with a big disc jockey, I'm going to automatically get played," Zeke explained to McGarvey of the move. "That would have been good for just Chicago, but he didn't realize the record business extended far beyond Chicago. You don't have any distributing powers."

The 46-year-old Benson booked the Flamingos into Universal Recording in July of 1954 for their first Parrot session. Again, bassist Al Smith was contracted to organize the band. William "Lefty" Bates was brought in to play electric guitar, while Paul Gusman occupied the drummer's chair. It is likely

A rare 1954 portrait of the Flamingos. Left to right: Sollie McElroy, Jake Carey, Johnny Carter, Zeke Carey, and Paul Wilson (Maurice Seymour photo, from the Billy Vera collection).

that either Cliff Davis or Lucius "Little Wash" Washington played tenor sax and were joined by Norman Simmons on piano and celeste.

Simmons's stabbing piano opened the first song they recorded, the mediocre up-tempo "On My Merry Way." Written by Chicago nightclub entertainer and recording artist Walter Spriggs, the song featured both Sollie and Jake at the lead mike and a 12-bar tenor sax solo that Holloway told Pruter was played by either Washington or Davis.

The second tune committed to tape, the Gene Rowland composition "Dream of a Lifetime," had originally been recorded as "You're the Dream of a Lifetime" by Bill Johnson and his Musical Notes, with vocal refrain by Gus Gordon and Trio, on RCA Victor in 1947. The key elements found in the finished product—McElroy's impassioned lead, Carter's soaring tenor, and the group's exquisite minor chord harmonies—framed effectively by Simmons's unobtrusive celeste, elevate "Dream of a Lifetime" to the rank of undeniable classic.

"That was another record we worked on, [but] not as long as 'Golden Teardrops,'" Zeke stated. "[It had] beautiful harmony. The piano player and arranger was Norman Simmons."

"That was a very difficult harmony pattern," Jake admitted. "This is where our practice had come into perfect use, when we used this type of difficult harmony pattern. 'Dream of a Lifetime' was one of those types of tunes. The fifth voice, the top tenor, would go up above the rest of them."

"My singing was kept down, my octave was kept down to a certain point," Sollie told interviewer Rallo in 1992. "My octave was higher than I was allowed to sing because of certain notes that Zeke in particular couldn't make. So we had to keep the balance for him to blend in. But if I got my octave a little too high, they couldn't blend in with me. Johnny was the only one who could keep up with me because he had that high tenor. They always kept me at a limit. I could have expressed myself better, but I couldn't because of the range of their voices. That song has a really nice bridge. Johnny does a really nice job. I think Johnny and I could have carried the group alone … with *anyone* else."

Sollie and the group gave their best effort to "If I Could Love You," an unremarkable R&B ballad that had been written and recorded by Danny "Forty Cups of Coffee" Overbea (1926–1994). Overbea's original was never released. The Flamingos' rendition remained unreleased until 1976. The group concluded the session with their own version of Eddy Arnold's recent #2 country and western chart hit, "I Really Don't Want to Know." Written by Don Robertson and lyricist Howard Barnes, the song had also been recorded the previous year by Les Paul and Mary Ford. With McElroy and Carter in the spotlight, the Flamingos' rendition transformed the song into an infectious, swinging R&B tune.

"We used to rehearse an awful lot," Zeke explained. "A lot of times, when you would go to a [recording] date, you had to get it right on the spot. No overdubbing. No several different tracks—one track. Three-hour dates, you had to do four songs, not one song. That's the only way they thought. You were dealing with small record companies who had small budgets. They didn't have the money to go in and stay in for all day or several hours getting one tune. So you had to be ready when you got there."

"I was told what to do," McElroy confessed when discussing how the group's material was selected. "Zeke and Jake would mostly pick out the songs that we would sing, and if I could sing it, and it fit my voice and do it justice, then we would sing it. If I didn't, then we wouldn't do it. I wasn't a blues singer. I was a balladeer."

Benson released "Dream of a Lifetime" and "On My Merry Way" on Parrot in August and immediately found a receptive ear in Alan Freed. Freed, who transferred from Cleveland's WJW to a $75,000-a-year position at New York's WINS in September of 1954, had the power to make or break a potential hit singlehandedly. "I knew that Parrot was never going to happen," Zeke recalled, "We had 'Dream of a Lifetime,' [and] Alan Freed went out of his mind [over it], and it was a worse disaster than 'Golden Teardrops.' Alan Freed was playing it, and they couldn't find the record in New York, because Al Benson had no money to press records!"

With "Dream of a Lifetime" making a little noise, Chance issued "Blues in a Letter" and "Jump Children" in October to try to grab a little cash. Poorly promoted and distributed, it sold lightly. "[Benson] was one of the biggest things in Chicago as far as a deejay was concerned," McElroy admitted. "But he wouldn't pay people. He would do unorthodox things. He would record you, but he wouldn't want to pay you. He'd want you to do shows, but he wouldn't want to pay you. He'd say, 'If you do a show for me, I'll give you free play on the air.' I needed some money in my pocket."

While singing with the Flamingos, McElroy maintained a day job in the restaurant industry in order to support his family. "I had to be at work at six o'clock in the morning, because that's when the kitchen started rolling, taking the food in," he remembered. "I would leave a club ... I'd been up all night long, drinking. I would go to work and do my job and get off at three o'clock, and then I'd go to sleep. The only thing that was really bad for me was going to work Monday morning, because I had supper club shows [on Sunday nights]. All the bands and trumpet players and saxophone players would meet at a place called the Flame on 39th Street. All the entertainers would

Nate Nelson (top left) joins the Flamingos. Clockwise from center: Jake Carey, Zeke Carey, Johnny Carter and Paul Wilson (Maurice Seymour photo, from the Billy Vera collection).

come down there and have a [jam] session, sometimes until two or three o'clock [in the morning]. The city was booming as far as entertainment was concerned."

That fall, the Flamingos began courting Nathaniel Joseph Nelson, a 22-year-old Navy veteran with a smooth, silky tenor who was singing locally in a group called the Velvetones. The quintet, which consisted of Nelson, Donald Blackman, Lee Diamond, Roy Flagg, and Winfred Veal, plied their trade on the corners of Washburne Street on the city's West Side, in the city's clubs, and at local amateur talent shows. It was at one such event at Martin's Corner where Nelson met the Flamingos. "You have to understand that in those days, there were no outlets for teenagers, whether it be clubs or dances," Nelson explained to interviewer Jones. "The only thing the teenagers had were talent contests. So this is how we started with the talent shows."

Born in Chicago on April 10, 1932, Nelson was only two years old when his father, John, died. He enlisted in the Navy at age 17 in June of 1949, and was discharged in April of 1953. A distant cousin of Sonny Til, Nelson was invited to join the group and, for a time, he and McElroy sang together as part of a six-man unit. By the time of the group's November session, however, Sollie was gone. "Sollie left not too long after Nate came, while we were on Parrot," Zeke summed.

"There were money problems," wrote Jack Sbarbori after interviewing McElroy in 1975, "yet the strongest factor may have been that Sollie considered himself an outsider. Not only were the other four members of the group related, but they were also of the Jewish faith, and Sollie was not. When there was talk of a new lead singer, Sollie decided that it was time to make a move." Others, including Carter, have stated that McElroy became jealous after Nelson was invited to join the group, and after problems developed, Sollie was subsequently let go.

McElroy himself set the record straight for interviewer Rallo less than three years before his death. "I never knew exactly what we were getting paid. That was one of the reasons I left the Flamingos. I don't know if the others knew or not, but they kept a lot of things from me. They were listening to our manager and weren't so much interested in the money part of it, and that's what I was in it for. We had a station wagon to travel in. We never did finish paying for the station wagon. We had clothes tailor-made at Fox Brothers over there on 12th Street. We were still paying for them."

Road trips were notoriously tough and often less than profitable. "I would go to New York [with the Flamingos], and come home and wouldn't have a dollar in my pocket," Sollie stated. "We didn't live in the best of any kind of hotel. At the time, they didn't have too many hotels for black people anyway, so we would go to these homes where they would rent out rooms, and you'd be like in a bunk. There would be rows of beds. Even in New York, we stayed in a flea house. We didn't eat the best food. We'd be on the road where blacks couldn't go in certain places. My manager being Jewish, he was in as much trouble as we were, you know. He went into several places and they found out who he was and where he was carrying the food, and they wouldn't give it to him. It would be bagged up, and they'd say, 'Hey, keep on moving!' Right there in St. Paul, Minnesota, it happened. You'd go to a gig and eat peanut butter sandwiches and drink pop and eat greasy hamburgers and didn't have a decent place to lay your head down. The only time you were clean was when you were on stage."

The final straw, according to McElroy, came in December of 1954, when he learned that the Flamingos were working jobs without him. "King Kolax told me that they were taking Nate out on gigs behind my back, breaking him in, and I didn't know this. So, they got ready to do a New Year's Eve show at the Pershing. So, I said, 'Hey, you got Nate, do the show … 'bye!' And I never came back. They thought I'd get over it and come back. I got me a job and went to work. They didn't fire me. I don't know if they had an inkling [that] I was going to do it or what, because I always asked, 'Where's the money?' Every time we go out on a gig, there's no money! I was ready to take the group higher, but I was broke. When I say broke, I mean I didn't have any money. I wanted to dress nice, and I couldn't buy the clothes I wanted to buy and look the way I wanted to look with the compensation I was getting from my singing. Now, if they had turned some money loose, I'd probably be with them today."

The late baritone George Prayer recalled to Pruter how McElroy ended up joining his South Side group, the Moroccos, in late 1954. "Our manager [United Records President Leonard] Allen knew the Flamingos' manager. At that time, Sollie was having problems within the group. They were trying to oust Sollie or something. Allen said to us, 'I know this dude, Sollie, from the Flamingos. I'll have him come over.' Sollie showed up. He was much older than us. We were kids. Sollie was a man. Anyway, that's how we got him, and we liked him."

"Once I left the Flamingos, the Moroccos knew it, and were looking for someone to [join] them," Sollie agreed. "They were all young gentlemen, too. I still liked to sing, so I went to see what they had to offer. The Flamingos had five voices, but they only wanted four. They weren't strong enough to drop a man. So, I had four young men, and I was the fifth, and I was able to join them because I was well-known."

"I never had the pleasure of meeting Sollie," Flamingos veteran and long-time Nelson friend Terry Johnson states. "I feel he was treated really badly, though, and I have to blame that on Jake and Zeke. After Earl Lewis messed up and they put Sollie in the group, he did the recordings. Then they heard Nate, and they had Nate and Sollie in the group at the same time, sharing leads. Then they kind of kicked Sollie out, and forced him out of the group, for Nate. That was dirty, because he was there first. I fell in love with his voice."

Nelson made his first trip to Universal Recording with the Flamingos in November for their second four-song Parrot session. Al Smith again brought in the reeds of Holloway and Easton. According to Pruter, the rest of the band likely consisted of trumpeter Sonny Cohn, trombonist Harlan "Booby" Floyd, Quinn Wilson on bass, Paul Gusman on drums, and Horace Palm on piano and organ.

Walter Spriggs gave the group "I Found a New Baby," an up-tempo tune that inexplicably went unreleased until 1976. Despite numerous LP and CD reissues in the 1980s and 1990s, the song remains unjustly overlooked by vocal group harmony collectors and fans. With the exception of a brief solo by Nelson, "I Found a New Baby" was sung in unison, and provides listeners an ideal example of the group's proficient five-part harmony structure. "Walter Spriggs was a lot of help in our group," McElroy recounted to Rallo. "He used to sing blues, too."

"Get With It" was another upbeat offering from Spriggs. The song boasted a lead opening from Nate, unison singing, bass flourishes from Jake, and a 24-bar baritone sax solo from Mac Easton that borrowed a melody line from "Stormy Weather." The take Benson selected, however, contained several obvious mistakes.

Benson also had the Flamingos put their stamp on "Ko Ko Mo," a current noisemaker which had been recorded by the Los Angeles–based duo Gene and Eunice. Nelson and Carter sang a smooth duet lead over minimal vocal backing and appropriate calypso-flavored accompaniment. Again, Benson selected a take with a glaring blown note from Holloway in the introduction as the master.

The fourth song recorded was the ballad "I'm Yours," penned by Ukrainian-born composer and publisher Robert Mellin (1902–1994), best known for co-writing "My One and Only Love" and the Ames Brothers' "You You You" in the early 1950s. "I'm Yours" had been a national pop hit for both Eddie Fisher and Don Cornell in 1952. Over the group's pleasing "doo wop" chants and Palm's pounding piano triplets, Nelson delivered a romantic and impassioned lead. Despite the fact that Nate's voice cracked 70 seconds into the take that Benson chose as the master, the quintet's version of "I'm Yours" remains a collector's favorite today. In 1995, vocal group harmony enthusiasts selected the song among their all-time top 25 favorites of 1955 in a survey conducted by the New Jersey–based Relic Record Shoppe.

"We got pop tunes," Jake explained, "tunes that people understood. We gave them our treatment or rendition on it. A lot of times, it might not have been the way it was written, but it was just another way you were injecting your personality into this thing, and this is the reason why it was accepted."

"Golden Teardrops" and "Dream of a Life-time" each ranked number one in similar Relic Record Shoppe surveys held for the years 1953 and 1954.

On November 20, 1954, the Flamingos performed at Martin's Corner for show producer Chuck Johnson, along with blues singer Rocky Brown and exotic dancer Rosemary. The show was billed as the "Five Flamingos' last appearance" before going on tour. "I Really Don't Want to Know" and "Get With It" were paired and released on Parrot in December, followed quickly by "Ko Ko Mo" and "I'm Yours" in January 1955. Due to Benson's lack of promotion and distribution, the

Rare disc jockey 78 RPM pressing, 1955 (author's collection).

Parrot releases failed to draw much attention. By this point, however, the group had more serious issues to deal with.

"I'll Be Home"

Ralph Leon was quietly negotiating a deal that would bring the Flamingos to Leonard (1917–1969) and Phil (1921–2016) Chess's Chess/Checker empire, home to national hit makers Muddy Waters, Howlin' Wolf and, most recently, the Moonglows, when he died unexpectedly at age 41 on December 1, 1954. "A sudden heart attack," Zeke recalled with sadness. "It was a total shock to us. Turmoil existed as a result of bills that had been made. We had cars and clothes to pay for. This was two years he had spent building, including that year rehearsing before recording. We were tied into contracts when he died. We had [unpaid] uniforms, station wagons, a lot of things to take care of."

Years later, Zeke Carey was quick to credit the contributions that Ralph Leon made and the profound influence he had on the Flamingos. "Ralph Leon's philosophy was the basic philosophy that we use today. You have to give. He'd say, 'Listen, I know that we're taking a beating now. We're recording and we're not getting statements, etc., but let's get big. Let's get hot. Let's work hard and become in demand. Let's become somebody, and once we grow to a certain stature, then we can start making certain demands. Right now, we're small.' This was his philosophy. He knew what the other people were doing. Although he was new in the business, I mean green as grass, he knew what the record companies were doing, and what they would do. But he had a plan for the group. He knew the barrier breaking over from rhythm and blues into pop. He would insist on us not doing songs that were strictly rhythm and blues that wouldn't be appreciated by a pop audience." Leon was buried in Waldheim Jewish Cemetery in Forest Park, Illinois. His wife, Lillian, survived him by nearly 40 years, dying at age 80 in 1994.

Five months after its release, a promo copy of "Dream of a Lifetime" finally made its way to *Billboard*, which reviewed it the week of January 15, 1955. One week later, *Cash Box* tabbed the tune "a slow, dreamy, pretty ballad that has a lot of sales potential. The lads blend well and the lead is good." On Sunday, January 23, the group appeared in a special 2:30 p.m. matinee at the Circle Theatre on East 105th Street in Cleveland. Also on the bill were Danny

The classic Checker lineup, 1955–56. Clockwise from top left: Jake, Johnny, Paul, Zeke, and Nate (Maurice Seymour photo, from the author's collection).

Overbea and Bea Booze. Advertisers apparently confused the Flamingos with the Harptones, billing them as "Those Sunday Kind of Love Boys." Despite Leon's death, the group followed through with a tour of the western states and Canada in the early part of the year, as arranged by booking agent Joe Glaser. The trip included an engagement at the Flamingo Hotel in Las Vegas.

Zeke Carey painted a frustrating portrait of life on the road for black entertainers in the 1950s. "The hotel accommodations were major problems because of the time. You'd go into a town and have to find your kind of hotel on the other side of the tracks. This was happening even in Las Vegas in the late 1950s. We played the Flamingo on the strip in Las Vegas. We came off the stage, and if we wanted to have something to eat, there was a certain spot in the restaurant [for us]. We had to go over to that corner. We had our own waiter assigned to us. I mean, we had privacy, that's for sure. They definitely gave us privacy. We were restricted. When it was over with, our accommodations were on the other side of town. They weren't interested in how you got to the other side of town, as long as you got there. It was pathetic. Even then, we used to look at it and say to ourselves, 'How can they like our music so well and put these kinds of restrictions on us?'"

Billboard and *Cash Box* reviewed "Ko Ko Mo" by both the Flamingos and the Charms the week of February 5, one month after the original. Exactly one month later, Gene and Eunice's version, which reached #6 on the national R&B chart, was selected as *Billboard*'s Territorial Tip in both the New York and Chicago markets. The Flamingos' Parrot cover shared the honor in the Windy City.

For Zeke, Jake, Paul, Johnny, and Nate, however, it was too little, too late. While some sources state that the Chess brothers approached the group directly after Leon's death and signed them to their label, Zeke Carey told McGarvey that he was the one who initiated the deal. "I elected to take the reins. I was only about 21. I found a way to break the contract with Al Benson. If he had elected not to play our records, forget it, so I said, 'How can I get out of this contract and still keep this man a friend?' I found an agent that nobody knew that wanted the Flamingos. I knew I was never going to sign with [him, but] I knew he could get us out of that contract, and I could make him the bad guy. I learned those kinds of things from Ralph Leon."

In March of 1955, the quintet signed with Chess's Checker subsidiary, headquartered at 4750 South Cottage Grove, just one block north of Benson's Parrot/Blue Lake operation. The Flamingos' initial session for Checker took place at Universal on Monday, March 21, 1955. The up-tempo "Chick-A-Boom (That's My Baby)," written by Carter and Nelson, kicked things off. The superb, swinging arrangement featured Carter leading, a five-part "chime" effect, tight harmony, and standout vocal performances from bass to tenor. "I give Johnny Carter a lot of credit for what he contributed to the original Flamingos," Zeke admitted. "He's one of the few fellows I've ever met who had a keen ear for music. He never sang out of tune, no such thing. He always had a great ear for music."

Opening with a baritone sax run, "When" sported harmony patterns that harked back to the days of the pop-flavored sides of the late '40s and early '50s. The song was credited to Levi McKay, manager of various local groups including the Five Chances, the Fortunes, and the Clouds. It is likely that McKay was in attendance at the date, as Checker recorded the Fortunes singing another of their manager's compositions, "My Baby's Fine," immediately following the Flamingos' three-song session. Despite a stellar lead from Nelson, "When" was woefully out of date when compared with what teenagers were buying in 1955.

"Need Your Love," a much more contemporary-sounding ballad written by Nelson, rounded out the proceedings. With tight harmonies, falsetto runs from Carter, another tasty lead from Nelson, and enduring piano triplets in the backing accompaniment, "Need Your Love" was arguably the strongest of the three performances captured on tape. All were assigned to the Chess brothers' Arc Music publishing firm. "I wrote 'Need Your Love,'" Nelson told interviewer Groia. "They gave me credit, but I just didn't get paid." In later CD reissues, Zeke Carey's name surfaced in the credits as a co-writer.

"Chick-A-Boom" and "When" were coupled as the Flamingos' initial Checker offering in April. "The boys warble 'When,' a poignant ballad, with appealing warmth and a relaxed charm," *Billboard* noted in its April 30, 1955, issue. "'That's My Baby' has plenty of drive, both on the vocal and instrumental sections. Watch this one. It could be a two-sided hit." While the record did earn some spins, it failed to leave a significant impression on record buyers.

On Wednesday, June 15, the quintet was back at Universal with four more tunes on the agenda. "Please Come Back Home," a ballad written and led by Nelson, was followed by "Just for a Kick," a Zeke Carey–credited tune that featured two distinct tempos. Nelson led the dreamy intro and ending of the song while Paul took the lead on the up-tempo segment. The soulful "I Want to Love You," written by Nelson, featured the group singing in five-part harmony with Jake and Johnny showcased prominently in the mix. "Whispering Stars," another Nelson-led ballad, opened with a distinctive whispered, "Does she love me? Will she come back?" "I wrote a couple of tunes with Johnny," Zeke recalled. "Johnny and I wrote 'Whispering Stars.'"

Phil Chess took to the road in July, traveling to Detroit and Cleveland to plug the Flamingos' latest coupling, "I Want to Love You" and "Please Come Back Home," and Chuck Berry's debut, "Maybellene." While the overwhelming interest in "Maybellene" forced the brothers to shift their attention away from "I Want to Love You," *Billboard* didn't forget the record, giving it a four-star review the week of July 30. "The Flamingos move smoothly through an unusually appealing ballad here, backed with strong combo support," the reviewer stated. "The material is specially tailored to the warm sound of the lead. Flip is also strong, 'Please Come Back Home.'" *Cash Box*'s review that week was equally glowing, remarking that "the Flamingos perform expertly on a very strong piece of material ... an impressive side."

In July of 1955, the group played Las Vegas again, appearing for four weeks at the Moulin Rouge Hotel with Toni Harper, the Hines Kids, Stump and Stumpy, and the Benny Carter band. A string of Midwestern appearances followed, filling their calendar through September.

As the popularity of rhythm and blues and rock 'n' roll began to swell, hundreds of vocal groups began springing up, literally overnight, from coast to coast. Dozens were signed to equally eager independent storefront labels hoping to earn some quick cash. Some of the more seasoned performers, like the Flamingos, felt quality would win out in the end. "I'll never forget we worked in Houston, Texas, once," Zeke recalled. "It was an R&B crowd. There was a lady from one of the big record companies, and she talked to us and she said, 'You know, there's one thing wrong with you all. You have one big problem.' I said, 'What's that?' She said, 'You guys like to sing in tune.' The groups were coming and going. Ninety-day wonders we called them. They'd cut a record and 90 days later you'd wonder would they be around. They would just cut a tune and didn't care anything about the harmony being in tune. They were just making noise and putting the music and the beat around it. The lead would get up and do his little thing and that would be it. But then 90 days later, you would never hear anything more about these kinds of groups."

On Tuesday, November 1, 1955, NBC-TV's cameras captured huge crowds at the Apollo Theatre waiting to get in to see an R&B stage show produced and hosted by WWRL disc jockey Tommy "Dr. Jive" Smalls. The show starred Howlin' Wolf, Bo Diddley, the Flamingos, the Jacks, the Harptones, the Heartbeats, Dakota Staton, Etta James, Bill Doggett's Trio, and Gator Tail Jackson's Band. "That was one of the greatest experiences that I have ever had," the Jacks' lead singer Willie Davis (1932–2011) recalled. "The Apollo could be rough. If you made it at the Howard in Washington and the Apollo, you were all right." Broadcast on that night's 11 p.m. news, the footage caught the attention of Ed Sullivan, who arranged for Smalls to bring an R&B revue including Diddley and Jackson to his national television program on November 20.

By this point, the Flamingos were back in Chicago, working on a new song idea titled "I'll Be Home." "I wrote the song," Nelson told Groia two and a half years before his death. "Leonard Chess came to me. All he had was the first line and the first-line melody. I took the thing home and worked on it because I just came out of the service myself. I came out of the Navy in June of 1953. I wrote the entire second verse, the bridge, the melody for the bridge, and the third verse. It was nothing but an idea. But I didn't know anything about copyrighting. I was just doing something for a song. Leonard Chess ended up owning it with someone named Washington."

In a 1991 interview with McGarvey, Zeke Carey also claimed to have been given the song by Leonard Chess. "The song was given to me personally by Chess, nowhere near what it was when we recorded it. You wouldn't believe the way we turned it around. We worked on that song [for] hours, [into the] wee hours of the morning,

Disc jockey promotional copy, 1955 (author's collection).

tape recorded ourselves, just vocally. It was mainly me, the lead singer, Nate Nelson, and Johnny Carter. I remember bringing it to them. They had their own little apartment. I worked on the lead with Nate, and he sang it the way I thought he should. The talking part was an idea I thought would work."

Veteran Flamingos tenor Terry Johnson dismisses Carey's claims as an embellishment of the truth, and credits Nelson with authoring the majority of the song. "Nate really told more of the truth," Johnson asserts. "Zeke made sure nobody knew what was happening because he wanted to take all the credit, which wasn't really fair. Everything that Zeke talked about was the Flamingos this, the Flamingos this, and of course the Careys. He always made sure that he and Jake were put out there. He didn't really mention anybody else, including Nate, which was so cold."

When Chess assigned the copyright of "I'll Be Home" to Arc, he listed the songwriters as Fats Washington and Stanley Lewis. "Fats Washington was a disc jockey from Shreveport, Louisiana, and he would write songs," Zeke explained. "He actually wrote [the first line and melody for] 'I'll Be Home.'" Born in 1928, Ferdinand "Fats" Washington, a paraplegic African American, hosted a nightly show on KTNT in the city and was also a gifted lyricist. Among the 160-plus songs in Washington's catalog is "Pledging My Love," to which Duke label owner Don Robey assigned himself a 50 percent share. Issued immediately following the untimely death of its originator, Johnny Ace, "Pledging My Love" spent 10 weeks atop the *Billboard* R&B chart in the early months of 1955.

Stan Lewis (1927–2018) was the owner of a popular record store located on Texas Street in Shreveport called, appropriately, Stan's Record Shop. Having opened for business in 1948, Lewis was also a successful R&B distributor in the South, and worked regularly with labels including Atlantic, Chess-Checker, Modern-RPM, Imperial, and Specialty. By purchasing advertising time on the powerful WLAC late night R&B programs, Lewis developed a lucrative mail-order business, selling records to listeners all over the country. His relationship with the Chess brothers also extended into the country and western market. For about a year, from the spring of 1954 to the spring of '55, Lewis leased or sold C&W masters to Chess that he had produced or purchased himself. "Stan Lewis got credit for half-writer simply because he had the money," Zeke stated. "He had a record outfit down there. He was a white fellow. Stan got this as a compensation for exposing and getting the tune [from Washington] to Chess. That was done an awful lot."

Before sinking their teeth into "I'll Be Home," the group tackled "Chickie-Um-Bah," a mundane up-tempo song credited to local disc jockey Nathaniel "Magnificent" Montague, which featured Johnny Carter and Jake Carey.

Opening with a piano glissando, "I'll Be Home" established Nelson as one of the premier balladeers in the vocal group field. His echo-drenched lead, reportedly captured inadvertently through a triple feedback process, brimmed with an ideal blend of romanticism, skill, and raw emotion. Equally effective was Paul Wilson's recitation, done over a four-part harmony structure featuring Carter's glorious falsetto. "We recorded the song twice," Zeke explained to McGarvey. "First time, Leonard Chess wanted to go downtown to one of the big studios, Universal Studios, because he believed in the song so strong. He thought it came out too clean. He went back into his office where he cut a lot of his hits, set up, put us around a couple of mikes, made a few takes. He liked that over the clean sound."

Nelson recalled a similar setup to interviewer Jones in 1979. "It was nothing but a small storefront on Cottage Grove in Chicago. Besides the Flamingos, Bo Diddley, Chuck Berry, the Moonglows, Muddy Waters, Howlin' Wolf, and others recorded there. We did all of our recording in the back room of this two-room storefront on a big tape recorder. There were only two microphones, one for the band, and one for the group. I sat there and watched many of the blues greats record as well as our group, and not get paid, of course."

Although the Chess brothers did open a small studio in the back of the company office in the spring of 1954, researcher Pruter explains that it was essentially used to record demos. "Any recordings that were done there and used for release would have had to be done on the sly, as the studio soon got the attention of Local 208 of the Musicians Union. And the sound quality would have fallen well short of Universal's standards."

Whether or not the actual master of "I'll Be Home" was recorded at Universal or in the back room on Cottage Grove, it was assigned master U7950, the letter designation that usually meant it had been recorded at Universal. Chess, however, apparently applied this prefix to all of its releases, irrespective of whether or not the session was held at Universal. Still, it is also unlikely that the crisp sound of "Chickie-Um-Bah," master U7948, was captured in the back of the Chess offices.

Later that month, the group traveled to New York to appear with Dr. Jive for a week of shows at the Brooklyn Paramount, beginning on Christmas Day. Also appearing on the bill were the Turbans, Shirley and Lee, the Five Keys, Ruth Brown, the Cheers, Bo Diddley, Willis "Gator Tail" Jackson and his band, and Pat Boone. On stage at the Paramount, the Flamingos debuted "I'll Be Home," which was already being pressed.

In early January 1956, Checker released "I'll Be Home" and "Need Your Love." On January 15, as the group began a week of personal appearances in Hartford, *Billboard* selected "I'll Be Home" as a spotlight pick of the week. "The boys blend smoothly and sweetly on a pretty ballad with a relaxed romantic tempo and a standout performance by the lead singer," the reviewer noted. "This one should grab off plenty of attention from jocks, jukes and cross-counter buyers."

Heading back to the Midwest, the quintet appeared for a week in Saul Korman's chain of five theaters in Detroit, beginning at the National on January 27. Patrons paid $1 to see the Flamingos, along with Sonny Til & His New Orioles, the Charms, the Sweethearts, Nolan Lewis, Nolan Strong, and Dakota Staton. *Billboard*, meanwhile, selected "I'll Be Home" as its Buy O'The Week, stating, "[T]he past two weeks have seen this disk moving up at a very brisk pace. It is now rated good to strong in New York, Baltimore, Philadelphia, Buffalo, Chicago, Milwaukee, Detroit, Nashville, Durham, and St. Louis." "We knew within the first month that we had a hit," Zeke recalled. "I was excited."

The group's excitement quickly turned to anger and disgust when a cover version by Pat Boone appeared on the powerful Dot label. Boone had cracked the pop top 20 in 1955 with his renditions of the Charms' "Two Hearts," Fats Domino's "Ain't That a Shame," and the El Dorados' "At My Front Door." He had also been on the Brooklyn Paramount bill with the Flamingos when they debuted the song. "About two weeks after the [Paramount] show closed, they flooded the market with Pat Boone's 'I'll Be Home,'" Nelson recalled.

"I was devastated to see how an industry could do what they did," Zeke disdainfully recounted to McGarvey. "Pat Boone did a carbon copy of our record. At the Brooklyn Paramount, Pat Boone was ... in the wings, listening [at] every show. Within weeks, the radio was blasting Pat Boone's recording of 'I'll Be Home.' I had worked so hard, and to get a hit you create inroads into the industry, only to be struck down because some guy makes a carbon copy. He's on Dot Records, top quality, and gets all the chart action. It should have been a top 10 crossover hit for me. We wound up having to be forced on rock 'n' roll shows with Associated Booking [Corporation]."

On February 4, *Billboard* selected the Flamingos' original as its Territorial Tip in the New York market, but the Boone cover was already breaking nationally. That week, it spent the first of 22 weeks on the national pop chart, peaking at #4 and earning the 22-year-old crooner his second gold record.

A pair of unpublished photos of the Flamingos on stage in 1956. Left to right: Johnny, Jake, Zeke, Paul, and Nate (Billy Vera collection).

In the process, Boone and Dot Records thwarted the Flamingos' first legitimate attempt at reaching white listeners on a national level.

"It's horrible to say it, but it was just a matter of race," Zeke opined. "They were racists. The establishment said, 'All right now, that's a black station, and this is a white station.' It's funny, man, but the youth then, are the ones that forced the change. What happened was, the little rhythm and blues companies began to make a lot of money, and they began to be a thorn in the big companies' sides. The little companies that had these R&B groups were cleaning up. The big stations wouldn't play their records. But the kids used to turn to the R&B stations because that was what they wanted to hear. They would get the fresh sounds, and they would get a combination of music. They would hear records that they loved, that they had heard about, and then they started going out and buying. The little companies started getting rich. They started getting fat.

"When he was in Cleveland, Alan Freed discovered that there were big bucks in rhythm and blues music. He said, 'Wow. This is my thing.' Money knows no color, just like music knows no color. The real basic things in life know no color.

"[Freed] was a scapegoat. He was involved [in payola], but so were all of them. In those early days of rhythm and blues and small companies, the bookkeeping and records were not kept that well. Many gimmicks and different means by which to expose and promote had to be used. There were a lot of them, and they just picked on the biggest guy. He knew he was big, and he let it be known. A lot of people wanted to see him removed. His removal hurt, to a great degree, what was really happening with music. But it had to happen, because everyone was taking. You may hear it said that the big companies don't do this and don't do that, but in their own quiet way, they were taking care of a lot of business, [too]."

The week of February 17, *Billboard* selected the Flamingos' "I'll Be Home" as its Territorial Tip in Chicago as it reached the national R&B list. In eight weeks on the chart, the Checker original peaked at #5. It also reached #5 on the R&B Juke Box chart, #10 on the R&B Best Seller, and #15 on the R&B Disc Jockey charts. "We got very hurt by that song," Zeke summed. "We had worked so hard to get through, and we knew that it was going to be a bona fide hit. His record came out and swamped ours. It was a devastating, painful experience."

Still, the Flamingos persevered. On February 10, the quintet began a one-week stint at the Howard in Washington, along with the Ravens, Priscilla Bowman, Danny Overbea, Joe Tex, and Jay McShann and his Orchestra. From there, they traveled to Harlem, spending seven days at the Apollo working with Little Richard, Guitar Slim, and Linda Hopkins. The group missed a one-nighter stop with Bill Haley and his Comets in Omaha on March 6, having been trapped in another city during a heavy snowfall.

By mid–March, they had worked their way back to Chicago to prepare for a two-song session which was held at Chess's South Cottage Grove studio on the 28th. The first tune recorded, a mid-tempo number called "Cry," employed the familiar vamp used several years earlier in the Spaniels' "Baby It's You" and Marvin and Johnny's "Cherry Pie." With the exception of a fine bridge with Nelson up front, the bulk of "Cry" was sung in unison. Chess apparently didn't see any potential in the song, and it remained unreleased until 1997.

The second tune recorded, "A Kiss from Your Lips," was another stellar ballad, and an ideal follow-up to "I'll Be Home." "A Kiss from Your Lips" was credited to the songwriting "team" of Roquel Davis and Russ Fratto. Twenty-three-year-old Roquel "Billy" Davis (1932–2004), who had recorded with Detroit vocal groups the Thrillers and the Five Jets, had attended Wayne State University and the Maurice King School of Music before beginning an association with Chess Records.

Davis had brought his cousin Lawrence Payton's group, the Four Tops, to the company, and would provide the Moonglows with a top 10 R&B hit called "See Saw" later in 1956. Long before he began a successful alliance with Berry Gordy, Davis submitted "A Kiss from Your Lips" to Chess. Later, using the pseudonym Tyran Carlo, Davis co-wrote hits including Jackie Wilson's "Lonely Teardrops" and "To Be Loved" and Marv Johnson's "You Got What It Takes," among others. He served as Chess's A&R director in the 1960s, writing, arranging and producing. His production credits included Billy Stewart's "Summertime," Etta James's "All I Could Do Was Cry," and Fontella Bass's "Rescue Me." After leaving the company in 1968, he produced many of Coca-Cola's memorable 1970s television commercials.

Fratto (1911–1969), owned the stationery store next door to the Chess offices. In payment for services rendered, the Chess brothers periodically assigned Fratto a songwriting credit. Fratto's biggest payday came when he was given a ⅓ share in Chuck Berry's "Maybellene," an act it took Berry 29 years to resolve. "The whole bridge of 'A Kiss from Your Lips' and the melody of it, I wrote it," Zeke maintained. "I wrote it. I took the whole tune and completely overhauled it and I wrote the whole bridge. I got no credit for it. But if we were under contract with Chess when the album was released, it would have been a different story. So, when I did it, and arranged it, I got a promise."

A romantic rock 'n' roll ballad featuring brilliant echo-soaked harmonies and an effective, pleading lead from Nelson despite a key selection that the singer felt was too high, "A Kiss from Your Lips" was yet another first-rate effort.

The Flamingos spent Easter Sunday, April 1, 1956, in New York City, where they would appear as part of Alan Freed's Rock 'n' Roll Easter Show at the Brooklyn Paramount. The ten-day engagement, where shows ran continuously from early morning until late night, also included the Platters, the Teenagers, the Willows, the Rover Boys, the Royaltones, Dori Anne Gray, Ruth McFadden, the Jodimars, the Valentines, the Cleftones, Cindy and Lindy, and Freed's band. On screen, patrons saw John Lund and William Bendix in "Battle Stations." Tickets cost $1.25 to $2 per show. The event netted over $240,000. "Ten days, morning, day and night," remembered Joe Martin of the Willows.

"At the Paramount, they'd rip your clothes," remembered fellow Willow Ralph Martin. "They'd tear your clothes off, or rip them off your back. We couldn't leave to go out and get lunch, the block was so filled up. They'd want to tear your clothes off."

On Friday night, April 20, the Flamingos joined Irvin Feld's "Biggest Rock 'n' Roll Show of 1956" package tour, a nationwide 45-day one-nighter tour. The troupe included Bill Haley and the Comets, Frankie Lymon and the Teenagers, the Platters, Clyde McPhatter, LaVern Baker, Joe Turner, the Drifters, the Cleftones, the Teen Queens, Bo Diddley, the Colts, the Red Prysock Combo, and emcee Harold "Stumpy" Cromer. The kickoff concert, held in Hershey, Pennsylvania, grossed $19,000, the largest take in the city theater's history. In its first week, the tour hit Atlantic City, Richmond, Norfolk, Scranton, Philadelphia, and White Plains, New York. On April 28, they appeared at the 8,000-seat Onondaga County War Memorial in Syracuse, New York. Tickets ranged from $1.50 to $3.00.

"The only way we really got on the tours," Zeke admitted, "is that [Joe Glaser, our ABC booking] agent had the Platters, and Irvin Feld, the big promoter, wanted the Platters. The guy said, 'If you want the Platters, you have to take the Flamingos.' He made us open the show, but we toured seven weeks and five days. We put the record up in the top 10 R&B and paved the way for 'A Kiss from Your Lips' to make it."

On May 11, the Flamingos played before a hometown audience, as the show rolled into Chicago's International Amphitheater. A week later, they were entertaining fans at the Loyola University Field House in New Orleans. "I would say the most unusual [tour we did] was probably the first real big rock and roll show to ever go on the road," Nelson recalled. "I think it had everyone who had a record in the top 40 at the time, everyone from Bill Haley to the Teen Queens. I think that tour was the most exciting one." Crisscrossing the country in buses with hundreds of miles between shows, the artists, Nelson recalled, bonded together immediately. "I can only speak from my point of view and the people that I knew," Nate told interviewer Jones. "We were all extremely close friends. There were so few entertainers in our age bracket, you see, and also, you were limited as to where you could work, which was only theaters and dances. There were no clubs or that sort of thing. Everyone pretty much helped each other out, and most everyone had their own style. If you think back to the 1950s and early '60s, every group had their own sound. No one sounded like anyone else. In most cases, when a song came out, you could tell from the first five bars as to who the group was without ever hearing the song before."

Life on the road for a young black vocal harmony group in the 1950s was a difficult one. "On that tour, especially across the Mason-Dixon line, we could not stay at regular hotels," Zeke told *Chicago Sun-Times* writer Dave Hoekstra in 1987. "We had to stay in black hotels or rooming houses. You knew where you had to go. I always saw [Bill] Haley on the bus, but never in the hotel. The other thing was when you went to a concert, you would look out at this massive audience, and it was split in half. One side of the auditorium was black, and one side white. It was as if you painted it that way. It used to baffle me."

Although the tour was an overwhelming success, grossing over $1 million by the time it concluded on June 3, appearances in some Southern cities were fraught with danger. In Birmingham, Alabama, the White Citizens Council picketed the Municipal Auditorium in protest of black and white performers being in the same cast. "We had a lot of problems when we appeared in the South," agreed Nelson. "There were kids picketing and the Ku Klux Klan, too. There were also a couple of bomb scares where we had to clear out the auditorium."

"It was every bit as bad as you've always heard it was, and probably worse for many," Zeke related. "A lot of it I didn't have to deal with, by choice. A lot of these tours I just didn't take. Maybe it was a mistake. Had I taken a lot of the tours, maybe some of the records would have been bigger. The promotional aspect would have helped, [but] who knows whether I'd have lived through it or not, 'cause many of them didn't. The percentages weigh heavily out of your favor, the road conditions, [and] the dangers of it. If it wasn't with the traveling, then it could have been with the other [racial] conditions."

On the road, Jake Carey was selected to handle the group's finances. "Someone [had] to handle the money, and [that] fell on the most mature person, Jake," Zeke explained. "Way back, he used to carry a big old wallet with a chain on it!"

In March of 1956, John "Lawyer" Burton, an attorney and music publisher, bought the Parrot and Blue Lake companies from Al Benson. Burton was also the attorney for Chess, and therefore began leasing and selling Benson's old masters to the Chess brothers. His initial transaction involved the Flamingos' "Get with It," which was issued as the B-side of "A Kiss from Your Lips" in late April. "We had moved from Parrot to Checker, and after Parrot went out of business, Chess bought out the catalog," Zeke confirmed. While the Parrot original was credited to Benson and Spriggs, the Checker reissue listed Zeke Carey as the songwriter.

"Though the material on both sides is below par for this fine group, the renditions should carry them into the money," *Billboard* remarked in its review of "A Kiss from Your Lips" the week of May 12. "This one's a ballad with an especially tender voice handling the lead throughout." One week later, the journal selected "Kiss" as its Buy O'The Week, stating, "Out just a short time, [this] disk has already gone a long way toward establishing itself. New York, Philadelphia, Baltimore, Buffalo, Chicago, Detroit, St. Louis, and Nashville are among the territories reporting brisk action."

Returning to Chicago in early June after completing their grueling tour, the Flamingos found their latest release in the top 10 on local station WAAF. On June 9, "A Kiss from Your Lips" made its debut on the national Rhythm and Blues chart. In two weeks on the list, it peaked at #12.

In July 1956, another four-song session was taped on South Cottage Grove. Johnny Carter led and likely authored "Stolen Love," a mid-tempo R&B tune which remained in the can until the group's 1959 Checker LP. Re-recordings of two earlier efforts suffered a similar fate, languishing in the vaults until the act gained crossover status with "Lovers Never Say Goodbye."

Recorded at a brisker pace, "Dream of a Lifetime" was technically more proficient than the Parrot original, with a smooth and pleasing lead from Nelson, but somehow lacked the emotional impact of the McElroy rendition. "Nobody's Love," a new version of "If I Can't Have You," surpassed the original in both style and tempo, with Nelson soaring to Joe Van Loan–like heights in the ending.

The real focal point of the session was "The Vow," another romantic ballad that the Chess brothers hoped would follow the group's two previous releases onto the national charts. "The Vow" was credited to George Motola, Horace Webb, and Zeke Carey. The sales manager at a Los Angeles Lincoln-Mercury dealer, Motola (1919–1991) also penned Jesse Belvin's 1956 monster hit, "Goodnight My Love." "George Motola was deaf in one ear," recalls Jacks/Cadets baritone Thomas "Pete" Fox. "He was a songwriter, and he played piano and sang a little. He always said, 'I can't hear out of that ear. Go to the other one.'" Webb had previously shared authorship on Big John Greer's 1954 Christmas release, "We Wanna See Santa Do the Mambo."

"'The Vow' was not written by the three names on the label," Zeke admitted. "They have my name on 'The Vow,' but that came about simply because when we received the songs, you should have heard them before we got them."

"We arranged it," agreed Jake, "because they came to us in the roughest form. When I say rough, I say crudely rough. We had to sit down and spend many hours. We burned a lot of midnight oil and used a lot of brain power to bring these things together, to build these tunes that you listen to on record, the tunes that other people wrote their names to."

While back in Chicago, the Flamingos repaid a debt that had been outstanding since manager Ralph Leon's death in December of 1954. "Hal Fox had a tailor-made clothing store at 712 West Roosevelt Road that made clothes for many show-biz folks, and practically all the musicians in the name bands," jazz drummer Marty Clausen explained in 2004. "On any given day you could run into people like Lionel Hampton, Stan Kenton, Dizzy Gillespie, Louis Jordan, everyone. It was very hip to have a Fox Brothers suit. It took me about five years before I could afford one, even though they only cost about $55. At Fox Brothers Tailors, in addition to Hal Fox, were Hal's brother Victor, their mother, and the manager, Morris. They were all like an extended family to us youngsters. Hal Fox was also 'Jimmy Dale' of Jimmy Dale and his Orchestra. He bankrolled the band with some of the profits from the store."

The Flamingos had obtained a set of uniforms from Fox Brothers in 1954. Ralph Leon signed for the clothes, but the bill had gone unpaid since his death. Made aware of the problem, one member of the group, likely Zeke or Jake Carey, walked into Fox Brothers in late July and paid off the note in full.

On July 21, 1956, a press release was issued announcing that Vanguard Productions would begin shooting the film *Rock Rock Rock* in New York City on August 6. The movie would be shot over a period of two weeks and include performances by Chuck Berry, the Moonglows, the Flamingos, and Frankie Lymon and the Teenagers, among others. Independently produced by Milton Subotsky and Max Rosenberg of Vanguard, the film starred disc jockey Alan Freed, who also owned ten percent of the film. Freed also owned Snapper Music, which published 15 of the 21 songs heard in the movie, which filled 60 of the film's 85 minutes.

Songwriter Glen T. Moore penned several of the tunes used in the soundtrack, including the Moonglows' "I Knew from the Start," The Teenagers' "Baby Baby," the title song, performed by Jimmy Cavello and the House Rockers, and "Would I Be Crying (If I Were Lying to You)," which was given to the Flamingos. "That song had a lot of soul in it," Jake Carey recalled in 1987. "That was the time when you made records that had soul. We recorded it for, and performed it in the movie." Led by Nelson, "Would I Be Crying," and the up-tempo Carter-led "Shilly Dilly," another Motola-Webb creation, were recorded at the Chess studio in early August, just before the group traveled to New York to perform for the motion picture cameras. The Flamingos were headed for the silver screen.

Greetings
from Uncle Sam

One member of the quintet who did not make the trip to New York was Zeke Carey, who had just received his draft notice from the United States Army. Johnny Carter's official greeting from Uncle Sam followed a month later. He left on September 19. "We were in Las Vegas at the Flamingo, heading for the really big time. We had worked hard and made it," Zeke lamented to McGarvey. "[Then] two of us were drafted. Jake had to hold it together."

In his search for a replacement, Carey selected 23-year-old Tommy Hunt, who was dancing and singing second tenor in a local group called the Five Echoes. Born in Pittsburgh on June 18, 1933, Charles James "Tommy" Hunt had been living in Chicago since the age of 12. "Mom was traveling the country as a chorus line dancer, and so from a young age, we all went to live with our elderly grandparents in the small country town of Perrysville, Pennsylvania," Hunt wrote in his 2009 autobiography, *Only Human*. "When I was about five, she came and took us back to the city." After serving a stint in a Pennsylvania reform school due to chronic truancy, Tommy rejoined his family in Chicago.

Influenced by the Ink Spots, the Mills Brothers, the Orioles, the Dominoes, and balladeer Roy Hamilton, Hunt began singing with four South Side friends in late 1952 or early 1953. Hunt, Constant "Count" Sims, Herbert Lewis, Jimmy Marshall, and Earl Lewis, who had recently been kicked out of the Flamingos, comprised the Five Echoes, who all lived in the vicinity of 35th to 39th Streets and, according to historian Pruter, hung around the Morocco Hotel at 39th and Cottage Grove.

After their initial release, "Lonely Mood" and "Baby Come Back to Me," which was issued on Art Sheridan's Sabre subsidiary label in September of 1953, Hunt enlisted in the Air Force, hoping to find a place in special services as an entertainer. He was replaced by future soul and funk star Johnnie Taylor, who had been singing gospel in the Highway QCs.

Although he didn't participate in the group's second release, Hunt joined the group for their final Sabre session in 1954, singing second lead on "Why Oh Why," a ballad which would remain unreleased until a 1964 LP. By this point, Hunt had gone AWOL. "The boys knew I was AWOL from the Air Force and became very protective towards me," Hunt wrote. "I continued working gigs with the Echoes, and enjoyed every minute of it. By now, I'd been AWOL about seven months. We were doing a gig close to my mom's house one night, and after the show, I snuck around to see her. But the police were waiting to swoop. I was grabbed, handcuffed, and pushed to the floor of their vehicle. The military police took over, and they sent me straight to the stockade to await court-martial." Sentenced to five years in Kansas' Leavenworth Prison, Hunt was subsequently released after serving less than half his scheduled time.

By the summer of 1956, Tommy was back on stage with the Five Echoes. "Shows started coming in real [*sic*] slowly," Hunt wrote. "Money was tight, but we didn't give up hope. We used the time for rehearsing and trying to get a record deal, but that seemed almost impossible. Finally, after months of virtually no work, a decent job came in." The gig was a week's engagement in a Chicago supper club called the Beige Room, located in the Pershing Hotel on 64th and Cottage Grove in Chicago.

"On the Friday night after the show, a gentleman approached me, asking if he could speak with me in private," Hunt wrote. "We went to the bar in the hotel where he bought me a drink. My immediate thought was, 'Is he gay?' He said, 'My name's Zeke Carey. I'm with the Flamingos. The reason I'm here is to offer you a deal if you're interested.' I was staggered. 'What kind of deal?' 'Would you like to be with the Flamingos? It's only a substitute job. It'll only be for two years.' 'Why do you want me?' I asked once I'd come down to earth. 'Two of the group [members] are going into the Army soon, and we need replacements. We heard about you, and that's why I wanted to see what you can do. I liked what I saw tonight. You're a good dancer, and you've got a nice voice. Not the best, but good enough to make you some serious money. Do we have a deal?' I shook his hand, 'It's a deal.' He passed me his card, which I put carefully in my pocket."

Although Hunt was not with the Flamingos when they traveled to New York to film their cameo in *Rock Rock Rock*, Johnny Carter, who was home on leave from the Army, was. "Johnny came home on leave from the service, I think it was in August, and they shot 'Would I Be Crying' for the Alan Freed movie, *Rock Rock Rock*, and then Johnny went back in the service," Terry Johnson explains. "What was really deep about it was it was just Johnny, Nate, Paul and Jake, just the four of them. Tommy didn't get to do the movie."

"Making those rock and roll films was just like working on television,"

Nelson recalled. "It was nothing, really, just a couple of cameras and you. I remember we did them in huge warehouse-type studios in New York. They were spliced and put together in California."

While they were in New York for the early August filming, the group also taped performances of "A Kiss from Your Lips" and "The Vow" for the CBS radio show, Alan Freed's *Camel Rock and Roll Dance Party*. In the broadcast on Tuesday, August 28, between 8:30 and 9 p.m., listeners were treated to performances by the Flamingos and fellow *Rock Rock Rock* participants Chuck Berry and Frankie Lymon and the Teenagers, along with Freed and his house band. The recordings, along with dozens of others culled from Freed's radio show, were issued in 1978 on a series of five LPs on a WINS label. The Flamingos' harmony is strong on both cuts, showcasing Carter's beautiful falsetto, Jake's authoritative bass, and Wilson's romantic recitation, to the delight of shrieking females. Nelson delivers soulful leads but finds the key a little too high on "Kiss," which causes his voice to crack on the "nothing went right until that night" lyric line.

Back in Chicago, Nelson, billed as "Nate Nelson of the Flamingos," performed for local disc jockey and concert promoter Sam Evans at a Trianon Ballroom gig that included Ray Charles, Chuck Willis, J.B. Lenoir, Jimmy Binkley, and the Calvaes on September 1. On October 12, the group began a week of appearances at the Apollo with the Dells, the Channels, Robert and Johnny, the Solitaires, the Pearls, Ruth McFadden, Titus Turner, and the Velours, promoting their latest release, "The Vow" and "Shilly Dilly." "The group intones a slow, fervent recital of devotion with some mighty fancy wailing by the lead man [on 'The Vow']," *Billboard* enthused in its review that month.

On the road, the act formed friendships with many of their contemporaries. Teddy Scott of the G-Clefs vividly recalled that the Flamingos would wait until just before they were called on stage to dress for the show. Since practical jokes were the norm, one group was always trying to outdo the other. "They would come running back into the dressing room to change, and find that we had tied their pants in knots!" Scott laughed.

In late October 1956, Hunt joined the Flamingos as they began a tour at the Casino Theater in Toronto, Canada. "You won't be singing for the first three or four days—not until you take my place as second tenor," Hunt recounted Zeke explaining to him. "I want you to use the time to listen and watch. Take in all our movements so they stick in your head. We can rehearse you in the hotel during those first few days anyway, before you take over for me."

The group made the 525-mile journey together in the group's green station wagon with Zeke doing much of the driving. "The trip gave me a good chance to familiarize myself with the rest of the guys, and by the time we got there, I felt I knew most of them quite well," Hunt wrote. "Paul and I got on real well straight away. Jake was a very strange person, a real oddball. To me, he looked like a black version of Grumpy in Disney's *Snow White*. When I spoke to him, he just grunted. Nate and Paul indicated to me not to pay any attention to him. When we arrived at the hotel, Zeke and Jake got out and went in, leaving me with Paul and Nate to empty the car. I found I could easily relate to Paul and Nate. Zeke was simply too busy organizing things, but I admired the way he took care of the group so well and seemed really on top of everything. After a while, Zeke came over to us with our room keys in his hand. He and Paul were in one bedroom, Nate and I were in another, and Jake had a room to himself."

"'[Jake's] the oldest member of the group and he expects us all to look up to him,'" Hunt recalled Nelson explaining to him. "He chuckled, 'Actually, he tries to be older than he really is. Basically, he just wants you to think he knows all the answers. He's a miserable ass, but a great bass singer.' 'Doesn't he ever smile?' I asked Nate, and he replied, 'Yeah … when he sees money.'"

In the days leading up to opening night, Nelson taught Hunt some of the basic harmony patterns, and Tommy and Paul began talking over new dance routines as the Flamingos thoroughly rehearsed their stage repertoire, which included "Jump Children," "I'll Be Home," "A Kiss from Your Lips," and "Ko Ko Mo." "I watched in awe and fascination and carefully studied the routines," Hunt wrote of that first week. "Their movements were very slick, but they'd be no problem for me. The whole act was real [*sic*] smooth, and I was hugely impressed."

By week's end, Zeke had left to fulfill his military obligation, and Hunt had stepped into the second tenor role. "The week had ended successfully, and everyone was delighted with the group's performance, especially me," Hunt wrote. "I was over the moon that the guys were pleased with the way I'd fitted in. They didn't seem to miss Zeke or Johnny Carter. Even Jake was kind of complementary as we came off stage. 'You're OK,' he grunted. 'You're gonna be all right with us, man.'"

Heading back across the border, the Flamingos returned to the Apollo, kicking off a string of theater dates. "Every night as we left the theater, droves of screaming girls were at the stage door waiting for us," Hunt recalled in his memoir. "It felt great signing autographs. The girls kept touching me and running their hands through my hair. I can't say I liked that too much, but there was nothing I could do. Paul became the most popular in the group because he had enormous dimples and girls flipped over them. I had my share of girls, too. We all did. Even Jake had a few. He was a different character when he was busy impressing the ladies. He'd be all smiles and used to giggle a lot."

Continuing their East Coast tour, the group appeared on stage at Baltimore's Royal Theater later that month. In the Royal audience was 17-year-old Terry Johnson, an aspiring singer, songwriter, and guitarist. "Zeke and Johnny were in the service, and I went to see them," Johnson recalls. "I was sitting in the audience, and I saw Tommy Hunt and Paul Wilson and Nate Nelson and Jake. The four of them were on stage, and I swear I saw a halo around the group, and I saw myself. Like I left my body and I was on that stage with them, playing guitar and singing. I saw it. It was like, 'woah,' it scared me for a minute. I went backstage to tell them what I saw, and Nate laughed and then said, 'Well, you say you play guitar. You know anybody else that plays guitar and sings tenor?' I said, 'I sing tenor.' He said, 'Can you read [music]?' I said, 'Yeah.' He said, 'You mind auditioning tomorrow?' I said, 'I'd be glad to. I can read.'"

Armed with his guitar, Johnson met the Flamingos backstage at the Royal the next day. The group handed him the sheet music to several of their songs and listened as he played. "They put the music in front of me, and I zipped through it," Johnson explains. "I played 'A Kiss from Your Lips,' 'I'll Be Home,' 'The Vow,' and I think 'Would I Be Crying,' and 'Jump Children.' Nate and Paul were doing 'Jump Children' with the dance. I was strumming the guitar [mimics a fluid rhythm pattern] on 'Jump Children,' and they really liked it because it was different than the chunk-chunk-chunk [mimics a staccato down-stroke pattern] like everyone else was doing at the time. Jake said, 'OK, I'll let you know.'"

On December 5, *Rock Rock Rock* debuted at Lowe's Victoria Theater in New York before a packed house that also got to see Alan Freed, Chuck Berry, and Connie Francis, who voiced the songs that Tuesday Weld mimed in the film, live on stage. A promotional soundtrack album was pressed and issued to disc jockeys. Checker coupled "Would I Be Crying" with "Just for a Kick" that month.

Two months went by before Johnson heard another word from the Flamingos. But on December 24, 1956, Jake Carey called Johnson's Baltimore home from Philadelphia. "On Christmas Eve, Jake called me and said, 'Buzzy, you still want to be in the group?' 'You know I do,' I told him. 'You have to be here tomorrow, on Christmas Day in Philadelphia. We're going to be going to New York.' I said, 'I'll be there.' It was so exciting."

Johnson, who had just turned 18, was by far the youngest member of the group. Paul was nearing 22, Tommy was 23, Nate was 24, and Jake was 33 years old. Despite his youth, Johnson had already written and recorded a pair of R&B ballads that are fondly recalled by R&B vocal group harmony fans and collectors today.

The Whispers

Isaiah "Terry" Johnson, also known to his friends as "Buzzy," a nickname his sister gave him when she had trouble pronouncing Isaiah, was born in Baltimore. Although some reference books have listed his year of birth as 1935, he was actually born three years later. "When I got in the Flamingos, I wanted to be older like them, so I put my age up three years," Johnson confesses. "I was really born on November 12, 1938. Now, you can believe, I don't like those three years."

Johnson grew up in the 1300 block of Whatcoat Street in Baltimore, along with Earl Hurley of the Swallows, four years older than Johnson, Sonny Til of the Orioles, and "J.R." Bailey (1937–1985), who found success with the Cadillacs, and later as a songwriter and producer with groups including the Main Ingredient. In the early 1940s, Zeke Carey lived on Whatcoat and Jacob Carey lived at 808 Woodyear Street, just six blocks away. "It was great because down the street, on the same side of the street that I was on, was Earl Hurley of the Swallows," Johnson fondly recalls. "They would always come and rehearse at Earl Hurley's house. As a matter of fact, I even went on a few jobs with them. I played guitar and sang a few songs with them. Money [Johnson, no relation to Terry] got sick, and it was really in the process of the group breaking up. Dee Ernie Bailey was leaving, and a few other people were there. They got me to go with them because Earl Hurley and Money really taught me to play the guitar."

Hoping to learn to play tenor saxophone, Johnson had gone to a local music store to buy one. When the store didn't have any in stock, the 14-year-old settled on the guitar. Unquestionably the most inspirational figure to aspiring vocal group harmony singers in the late 1940s was Sonny Til. The Baltimore native and his group had rocketed to the top of the R&B charts in the fall of 1948 with their debut effort, "It's Too Soon to Know."

Thirteen years older than Johnson, Earlington "Sonny" Tilghman (1925–1981) was a neighbor who lived directly across from him on Whatcoat Street. "I loved Sonny Til," Johnson declares. "I would always go to the Royal Theater and just watch him. I would say, 'Mom, please give me more money. I've got to go see him again.' I watched his style, the way he bent and hunched over when he was singing. It looked like he was singing from his gut. I loved him, and I also knew him. I would go down the street and talk with him. I told him I wanted to sing like him, and he said 'Well, keep trying. It's an easy thing, but you have to just keep practicing and keep trying,' words that I still respect. Up the street from me was a good friend of mine, we grew up together, Junior Bailey. He and his brother were friends of mine. They grew up right up the street from me. J.R. was my buddy. We had dreams of being in a group. Then the Flamingos happened with me. The next thing I knew, J.R. picked up the saxophone and got with the Cadillacs and moved to New York."

"I was inspired for guitar when I first heard Les Paul and Mary Ford," Johnson states. "Little did I realize that he was using three or four different tracks when he was playing his solos. I said, 'It's impossible for someone to be playing that fast!'"

In addition to Earl Hurley and Frederick "Money" Johnson (1934–1998), several other local guitarists taught Terry to play guitar and read music. "Earl Hurley showed me my first notes, doing that little pick thing," Johnson remembers. "Money showed me some heavier duty chords. Another friend, Bunty Rogers, he's dead now, but he really showed me a lot of Johnny Smith's jazz guitar. He was an excellent teacher. That's how I really got my soul. Guitar is my soul. Guitar speaks what I feel inside. So, when you hear me strumming those six strings, man, you're touching my very soul. You're hearing it. Then, there was a guy who was in love with my sister. I forgot his last name, but his first name was Grady, and he was with the Ink Spots. On the right-hand side of the street, they would come and rehearse a lot. That whole block was just filled with real entertainers, people that were in show business and the recording industry. That's why it was so easy for me to get into it."

Although Johnson would draw experience and motivation from the local R&B acts, his initial inspiration came from pop artists he heard over the airwaves. "My roots were Arthur Godfrey, the McGuire Sisters, Julius LaRosa, Andy Williams, all the white artists back in the day. That's all my parents would let me listen to, because that's what they would listen to. If I tried to change the radio, they'd say 'Leave the radio alone, Buzzy!'"

In addition to honing his skills on the guitar, Terry Johnson also developed a smooth baritone and falsetto tenor singing voice. In early 1954, Billy Thompson, Terry's best friend and schoolmate at Douglass High, suggested they form a singing group. "I told Billy Thompson I didn't even know what rhythm and blues was," Johnson confesses. "Billy and Ronnie Thompson and I had a club called the Don Juans. Everybody was light-skinned with nice hair, pretty boys, if you know what I mean. We had our own jackets that said Don Juans on them. Billy played piano, and I played guitar. I just started writing songs and said, 'Let's get a group together.' I said, 'Who do you know, Billy?' He said, 'Well, I know Bill Mills.' I knew Eugene 'Lump' Lewis, and it all just kind of jelled together."

Bill Mills, who possessed a high tenor voice, had previously approached Terry and Billy about joining the Don Juans. "He didn't look the part, but he was friendly and made everybody laugh, so we let him in." Second tenor Eugene "Lump" Lewis and bass Eddie Rogers, the brother of guitarist Bunty Rogers, joined Bill, Billy, and Terry in rounding out the quintet. "Billy was about three or four years older than me," Terry explains. "I was always the youngest guy. I couldn't hang around with people my own age. I didn't get anything from them."

A photograph was taken of the five singers with Johnson holding his ever-present guitar. Before long, however, Rogers was expelled from the group. "Eddie made love to my girlfriend," Johnson admits. "I hate to say it, but he did, and that was the end of his butt. I never wanted to sing with him anymore. He was a dog. So, we got James Johnson, who was Bill Mills's roommate, and also sang bass."

They began calling themselves Terry Johnson and the Rhythm Kings until a female admirer inspired the ultimate group name. "The girls always loved us. We were ladies' guys. I remember girls were saying, 'You all sound so good, you could even whisper and sound good,' and that kind of stuck. I thought, 'Whispers, yeah, Whispers.' So, I presented it to the guys and they said that's nice."

The Whispers practiced songs popularized by the Swallows, Orioles, Dominoes and Drifters, in addition to writing and arranging their own material. Mills wrote "Don't Fool with Lizzie" about a girl he was dating at the time.

The Whispers in the spring of 1954. Left to right: Billy Thompson, Bill Mills, Terry Johnson, Eugene "Lump" Lewis, and Eddie Rogers (courtesy Terry Johnson).

Thompson authored another up-tempo song, "We're Getting Married." In addition to arranging the group's harmony and writing the music, Johnson wrote and led two ethereal ballads, "Are You Sorry?" and "Fool Heart." Perfecting their craft daily, the Whispers were regulars on the local talent shows, never failing to capture top honors. "We had done quite a few talent shows, and we won every show," Terry proudly recounts. "We had our sky-blue suits with white shirts and blood-red ties and blood red puffs in the pocket of the suit and white shoes. We were sharp, and we looked good. I just had an ear for harmonies. Everyplace we went we just sounded so good that we won. That's really how that went down. They had these shows at all different places, some nightclubs. I remember one was at a roller-skating rink. We were doing some of our own songs and other people's songs. I would be playing the guitar on stage."

In the latter part of 1954, Eugene "Lump" Lewis began contacting record companies, hoping to secure an audition and, ultimately, a record deal for the Whispers. "I have to give Eugene credit for that, because Eugene was really a hustler," Johnson explains. "He was making the phone calls. He asked me, 'Do you have those songs that we've been singing and practicing?' I said, 'Yeah, of course I have those songs.' He said, 'I talked to Mr. Ballen in Philadelphia, and he said if we sound good, he'll record us.' I said 'Well, OK,' and everybody said 'All right.' Lump had the car, so we got in his car and went for it. It was great."

Although Terry had never heard of Ivin Ballen (1909–1978) or Gotham Records before, the company had been in business since 1946. Originally founded by Sam Goode in New York City, Gotham was acquired by Ivin and Morris Ballen in January of 1948 and relocated to Philadelphia. Ballen eventually acquired the Miltone, Pacemaker, and Adventure catalogs, and branched out with several subsidiary labels, including Apex and Music Master. Ballen Record Company also served as a distributor for a handful of small East Coast labels into the early 1950s.

By the time the Whispers came calling, Gotham had issued over 300 records, from jazz instrumentals by alto sax giant Earl Bostic to the blues of pianist Champion Jack Dupree, under the colorful alias Meat Head Johnson. Coincidentally, Charles "Bobby Prince" Gonzales, writer of "If I Can't Have You," also recorded for Gotham. The firm's strongest sellers, however, had been in the gospel field. In the early 1950s, Ballen's roster included the Harmonizing Four, Clara Ward, and the Dixie Hummingbirds. In the fall of 1954, Gotham had scored moderate sales on both coasts with "God Only Knows," a simple, effective ballad by a local R&B group called the Capris. When Lewis called Ballen to offer the services of another vocal harmony group with original material, the label owner was all ears.

Impressed with their harmony and original material, Ballen recorded the Whispers immediately. The four original songs they had been rehearsing were all recorded in one three-hour session. Bill Mills led the up-tempo "Don't Fool with Lizzie" and joined Billy Thompson at the lead mike on the mid-tempo "We're Getting Married."

The real gems of the date, however, were the delicate ballads written and led by 16-year-old Terry, who also played guitar on all four songs. The haunting arrangements and harmonies Johnson created for "Fool Heart" and "Are You Sorry?" were direct precursors of his later work with the Flamingos on End Records. Johnson opted to sing "Fool Heart" in his falsetto tenor voice. "I loved Clyde McPhatter singing in that high voice," Johnson explains of his inspiration. "He had just left Billy Ward and the Dominoes, and he had recorded a few songs with the Drifters, and I really liked it. I liked that style." Mills's floating falsetto tenor atop the group's backing harmony was inspired by Alexander Sharp, who perfected the concept with the Orioles.

The opening line of "Are You Sorry?," "I'm through with old love, I'll never fall again," sung in unison, harked back to the Harptones' "A Sunday Kind of Love" in both lyric and approach. "It is, it is," agrees Johnson. "I was very inspired by the Harptones. I loved that song." The remainder of the song, however, was unique and original. Johnson sings the lead in his natural romantic baritone and delivers the recitation, utilizing a style that is strikingly similar to his self-penned 1958 effort, "Lovers Never Say Goodbye." Bass James Johnson, inspired greatly by Jimmy Ricks of the Ravens and the Drifters' Bill Pinkney, complemented Terry's recitation with a Ravens-like bass lead segment. The chime-in concept, where each member of the group follows Terry and James by echoing the word 'sorry,' was suggested by Thompson. "That was Billy that had that funny sounding voice, [doing the last 'sorry'], too," Johnson laughs.

Ballen sat on the sides for several months before pairing "Fool Heart" and "Don't Fool with Lizzie" in early April 1955. "It was nice. It was exciting," Johnson admits. "They had released 'Fool Heart,' and I remember I heard it on the radio a few times. Hot Rod Hulbert played it on WITH, you know, and I said, 'Mama, mama, listen, listen, that's me, that's me!' Then I didn't hear it anymore. That kind of broke my heart. It was like, 'What happened?' I waited and waited and it finally came out, and I heard it two times. Then I didn't hear it anymore, and I got very discouraged."

After "Fool Heart" failed to entice record buyers, Gotham issued the final two Whispers recordings in June. Ballen's meager promotional effort and limited means of distribution doomed the group and their records to obscurity in the 1950s. "We never heard from him again," Terry recalls of his relationship with Ballen. "I don't think he paid us for the session, either."

The group occasionally worked at local hotspots like Sparrow's Beach and Carr's Beach, but their activities were limited since both Terry and Billy Thompson were still in high school. "I was a kid, but I always carried myself like I was older," Terry explains. "People never asked me for any cards or anything." Eventually, Mills and the other members got into a disagreement that resulted in the tenor's departure, and the Whispers called it quits in late 1955. Nearly 50 years would pass before Terry Johnson would hear the songs or discuss the Whispers again.

Before auditioning for the Flamingos in October of 1956, Johnson kept himself active, working an occasional gig with the Swallows and performing with a new band that he had formed. "Through my guitar playing with Earl Hurley and Money Johnson and Bunty Rogers and a few other fellows, I started getting in bands and formed my own band, Terry Johnson's House Rockers. I was working on Baltimore Street at that time. I was still under age, but carried myself like I was grown. I had a good band and was making money. At that time, it was kind of unheard of for a black group to be downtown on the strip, at the Diamond Club on Baltimore Street in Baltimore. But we were doing so well that we were constantly being booked. But when Jake called, I couldn't wait to leave." One regret that Terry does harbor is dropping out of Douglass High to join the Flamingos. "I had left school when I went with the Flamingos. I didn't finish school. I'm sorry about that now. What I would tell kids today would be first, get your education and finish school. Music is a very rewarding, self-gratifying thing, but first, finish your schooling. Get that degree if you can, and then dabble in music."

On Christmas Day, Terry arrived at Jake and Leah Carey's home, ready to join the Flamingos. "I went to Philadelphia and stayed at Jake's house with him and his wife. The next day we were on a train or a bus and went to New York, up in Harlem. I was scared. I had been to New York. I had aunts and cousins there. I had gone with my father, but not like that. Tommy had just gotten in the group before me. They had just gotten Tommy made up, so I didn't get uniforms made up right away. I had to wait. We had to do a lot of rehearsing."

"Jake was handling the money and gave us an allowance," Johnson recalls of his first weeks in New York. "I can remember Jake would give us 35 cents apiece a day. Up there in Harlem, 35 cents would get me a fish and chip dinner and a lime soda, and you know, you'd have bread with the fish and chips, and that would last me. That would be my meal for the day, thirty-five cents a day." After nearly three months of rehearsing, the reformed Flamingos were ready to hit the road and return to the studio.

Decca Records

Johnson states that by the time he joined the Flamingos, they had already broken away from Checker Records. Despite a pair of nationally charted hits, the group had become disenchanted with the reimbursement they had been receiving from the Chess brothers. "We stayed with them a few years," Nelson recalled to interviewer Jones, "[but] our group [did] not get paid. There was no income tax paid. There were no royalties paid. There was just nothing."

"Our first international hit, which sold all over the country, in Canada and other parts of the globe was 'I'll Be Home,'" explained Zeke Carey. "That was the first one that we can remember collecting some bucks as a result of. A lot of that has to do with ignorance on the part of the artist, too. We were young and knew nothing about the record business, really. We loved singing. We loved the idea of going into the studio and recording, hearing ourselves on the air, going before an audience and maybe the little girls were screaming. We couldn't care less at that time about royalties or statements. We weren't interested in that. We were concerned about singing, as it was with [many] artists. We didn't know. So, as long as we didn't know, the companies had a field day. Oh, this was great. They couldn't care less. Even today, as years went on, when you leave a company, you're still supposed to get royalty statements, etc. No such thing! They operated on a small budget. They were understaffed. They came up with these ridiculous contracts. They would just tie you up and guarantee you nothing. That's how they grew. That's the reason why so many small companies grew into giant corporations today. They stepped on and they stole."

"Slave clauses," summed Jake Carey. "You're a kid and you're coming from a very poor family, or a very poor environment, and all of a sudden, people are waving at you. People you've never seen before in your life. People want you to sign autographs. You're working here, and you're getting a little bit more. You've been able to work in this little place over here, and people are clambering just to talk to you, or people want to be around you. These things had never happened. So, your mind is not tuned in to what the economics are, or what business is about. Only after a few years of these misses or these hits, you find you wake up and say, 'Hey, man, there are such things as dollars and cents, and they go along with this, too. They help to keep up the wardrobe. They help to keep the cars going over the road. They help to keep you doing and having the things that you want.' So, all of this happened, and we said, 'Hey man, why didn't you get this?' You were unaware. After a while, when you became aware, you started saying 'Hey, man, we have to travel another route.'"

The Decca lineup, 1957. Top row, left to right: Paul Wilson, Tommy Hunt, Nate Nelson. Front row, left to right: Jacob Carey and Terry "Buzzy" Johnson (James Kriegsmann photograph, courtesy Terry Johnson).

In March, Jake Carey brokered a deal for the Flamingos with the powerful Decca record label. After buying out the bankrupt United Kingdom arm of Brunswick Records in 1932, Decca gradually grew into one of the largest and most powerful recording companies in the world, inking a wide variety of artists including crooner Bing Crosby, the big bands of Guy Lombardo and Count Basie, country stars Webb Pierce and Ernest Tubb, rhythm and blues stalwart Louis Jordan and his Tympany Five, and universally appealing artists like Louis Armstrong and the Andrews Sisters. During the rock 'n' roll era, Decca sold countless discs by Bill Haley and the Comets and, on their Coral and Brunswick subsidiaries, Buddy Holly and the Crickets, and Jackie Wilson.

During the transition from Checker to Decca, the group shifted their base of operations from Chicago to New York. "We were based in Chicago when I started," Hunt recalls, "but when we went to New York, the boys decided that that's where it was all happening. We moved to New York for that reason."

"I guess they would be able to get more work in the New York area, and the record companies were there," Terry adds.

"The guys moved when I was in the Army," Zeke explained. "We were working New York a lot anyway after 'I'll Be Home.'"

The Flamingos' first Decca session took place on Friday, April 19, 1957, at the famed Pythian Temple, a 30-year-old 11-story building located at 135 West 70th Street in New York City. Literally hundreds of seminal sides were recorded at the Pythian Temple's acoustically renowned third-floor studio, including Haley's "Rock Around the Clock." The label paired the quintet with Sid Bass (1913–1993), a 44-year-old New York–born composer, arranger, and producer who had previously served as the A&R director for Jubilee Records. The first of three tunes to be attempted was Clint Ballard Jr.'s pop-flavored ballad, "The Ladder of Love." The Texas-born Ballard (1931–2008), who brought the Kalin Twins to Decca later in the year, co-authored Jimmy Jones's million-seller, "Good Timin'," and wrote the oft-covered "You're No Good," originally a hit for Betty Everett, as well as the Mindbenders' #1 smash, "Game of Love," in the early 1960s.

Over a simple yet effective instrumental backing, Nelson delivered a dreamy lead, culminating in a dramatic finale that showcased his power and range. Wilson handled the recitation. "They would all come to my room at the Cecil Hotel on 118th Street and 7th Avenue in Harlem, New York," Johnson explains. "I would have my amplifier there and my guitar. They would come to my room as a group, or individually. Nate loved to just have me play the guitar, and he would sing the songs. He would hear my chords as he sang, and it would inspire him to do certain things with his voice. So, I would say that the chord changes on 'The Ladder of Love,' which I changed from what the original version was, made him sing those notes. I didn't give him those notes. It was the chord structure. He had to go where the chords were taking him."

The backing harmony was a departure from the group's previous efforts, with the sound taking on more of a crossover feel. "It was more pop," Johnson agrees. "I'm not trying to take all the credit, but I was the only one who played an instrument at that time, and so I was showing them harmonies. I had a structure of what to work with, because the tenors of 'A Kiss from Your Lips' and 'Golden Teardrops,' I knew that structure, so it was easy for me to arrange the voices and keep those tenors out there. But I can't take all the credit. God gave all us voices. He just gave me a knowledge of how to change the harmonies around and make the harmonies ring a little more. That was a beautiful song with a nice message."

Utilizing a similar harmony pattern, the group recorded "That Love is You," another stellar ballad written and led by Nelson. For reasons unknown, Decca never released the song. Although the Flamingos would later re-record "That Love Is You" at their first End session in 1958, the original version remains unreleased to this day. Rounding out the date was another Nelson composition, "Let's Make Up," an up-tempo rocker featuring Hunt singing lead for the first time, along with a crisp tenor sax break.

Decca released "The Ladder of Love" and "Let's Make Up" to a full-scale promotional effort in June, staging a gala media party in Washington, D.C., where the group performed for a week at the Howard. Also on the June 21–27 show were Solomon Burke, the Spaniels, and the Sensations. Almost immediately, "The Ladder of Love" began breaking out in key territorial markets. In England, the record was issued on the Brunswick imprint.

Soon, Leonard Chess reentered the picture, producing a personal artist pact he had signed the previous summer with lead singer Nate Nelson. During the period of uncertainty when Zeke and Johnny were drafted, Chess, apparently fearing the group was reaching its end, signed Nelson to a one-year deal, but never recorded the singer. Nate, as previously noted, had appeared solo, billed as "Nate Nelson of the Flamingos," in a Sam Evans show in September of 1956.

When it appeared that Decca was going to cash in on "The Ladder of Love," Chess came calling. "That song, 'The Ladder of Love,' was a smash," Terry agrees. "Leonard Chess still had Nate under contract for a little more time, and Decca tried to buy it out, but Chess just wanted to play hardball. Chess wasn't doing anything, and Chess had kept us in the rhythm and blues market as well. But they didn't want to give Nate a release, which was a drag."

With the group unable to return to the studio until Nelson's Chess pact lapsed and the label unable to promote "Ladder," the Flamingos spent the summer performing extended engagements at Harry Roesche's Beachcomber Club and Jake Diamond's Martinique in Wildwood, a seaside resort town located on a barrier island at the southeastern tip of New Jersey.

By this point, the group had perfected a diversified stage show that captured the attention of both nightclub audiences and the so-called "chitlin' circuit" theatergoers. When Johnson, the youngest and newest member of the group, suggested broadening their base to gain crossover success, he was initially met with resistance. "They did not understand where I was coming from at first," Terry admits. "Because my upbringing was Arthur Godfrey, the McGuire Sisters, Steve and Eydie, Andy Williams, all white artists. Our first job was in Miami, Florida, and we needed more songs. I had Paul singing, 'Singing the Blues.' That was a white song, but Paul liked it. He said, 'Hey, I don't mind it,' but everybody else was looking at me like, 'Man, why are you singing that song?' Then Paul and I sang 'Bird Dog,' and we did the Everly Brothers. I played the guitar, and they looked at me like I was nuts. They said to me, 'Man, why are you bringing this kind of stuff into the group?' I said, 'Because we need a variety.' They weren't hard to steer in the right direction, you know, because they liked good music. At first, they were kind of like, 'I don't know about this stuff,' but once Nate gave his approval, it was OK. Nate had a motor mouth. He never stopped talking. They called him 'Lips.'"

"For each song, we had a different routine," Tommy Hunt explained to interviewer McGarvey. "I believe the group was very good for routines because Paul was the choreographer, and he had a very good imagination for routines."

"Paul was the charisma of the group," agreed Jake. "This guy was charm."

"Paul Wilson was the best dancer, had the most charisma, finesse, and was elected choreographer," Zeke added. "Everything was choreographed within the group. We never hired anyone to stage the act or anything like that."

"Tommy Hunt came in in '56 and Terry Johnson in '57," recalled Zeke. "Terry was a guitar player, an excellent singer, and a good writer. Tommy was an excellent singer and an excellent dancer. [He] danced well with Paul Wilson. Those guys brought a lot of energy. [They] produced a high-profile group, a more energetic group than the 'I'll Be Home' group."

On Thursday, August 15, the Flamingos were back at the Pythian Temple for another four-song session. Following a trend that Capitol had recently employed with the Five Keys, and Atlantic had used with many of their R&B artists, Decca added a female chorus to the mix. In retrospect, Atlantic pro-

Left to right: Tommy, Paul, Jake, Nate and Terry in a 1957 promotional photo (James Kriegsmann photo, courtesy Terry Johnson).

ducer Jerry Wexler admitted he could "kick myself in the ass" for doing that to R&B. Atlantic historian Peter Grendysa states, "The deadly-dull chorus and arrangements by Ray Ellis that are heard on so many Atlantic records from the late 1950s adroitly alienated the R&B audiences for the Clovers, Lavern Baker, Ruth Brown, Joe Turner, and Clyde McPhatter, without making a place for them on the pop charts." In the case of the Flamingos, the results were no less abominable.

The first song tackled was "Helpless," another Clint Ballard, Jr., ballad. Nelson's smooth delivery was hampered by the chorus that echoed the last word of each lyric line. Occasionally, Jake Carey's bass could be heard in the mix, but the rest of the group was essentially washed out by the female chorus. Up next was "My Faith in You," penned by songwriter-arranger-producer Jesse Stone. Delivered at a brighter tempo than "Helpless," "My Faith in You" again featured Nelson in the lead with Wilson delivering a spoken recitation. While the male and female voices were balanced a little better, the absence of the Flamingos' full, rich harmony relegated the song to mediocre status.

The up-tempo "Jerri-Lee," written by David "Baby Cortez" Clowney, a pianist-organist and tenor singer who had recorded and performed with the Pearls and Valentines and as a soloist, fared much better. With the chorus sitting out, Nelson and the group delivered an enjoyable performance, backed effectively with wood-block percussion.

"Hey Now!," another rocker written by Nelson, rounded out the date. A rave-up with squealing tenor sax riffs, the song featured Hunt on lead, accompanied again by the Flamingos without choral backing. Although the latter two arrangements have held up better than the ballads through the years, there was little in this session to distinguish the quintet from the day's current chart toppers. Unaccustomed to recording vocal harmony groups in the R&B-rock 'n' roll vein, New York's Decca representatives failed to tap into the originality, creativity, and power of the Flamingos.

On September 13, 1957, Nelson sat in on a New York recording session with Steve Gibson's Red Caps, singing lead on their cover version of the Rays' "Silhouettes" for ABC-Paramount. "We had worked with the Flamingos at Martinique in Wildwood, New Jersey," baritone James "Jay" Price of the Red Caps recalled. "We were there for the summer, and they were one of the groups that rotated in. So, we knew them, and Steve was impressed with Nate's voice. For that record, Steve decided he wanted a teenage sound. Nobody in [our] group had a teenage sound. So, Steve got Nate to come in and do that one song with us. That was the only song he sang."

"We were at the Beachcomber when they were at Martinique, and we used to go over to see them," Terry Johnson recalls of the Red Caps. "After he had done the recording, Nate told me, 'Buzzy, between you and me, I did a recording session with Steve.'"

Featuring Nelson's commercial lead, "Silhouettes" by Steve Gibson's Red Caps was released by ABC-Paramount in late September. "Nate never appeared with our group," Price explained. "George Tindley would sing it at every appearance." Although the record failed to surpass the popularity of the Rays' original, Nelson's participation makes the record a subject of interest among collectors today.

On September 21, the Flamingos began a week at the Apollo, where they were teamed up with Johnny Mathis, who had the current #1 record in the nation with "Chances Are." "When we first went to the Apollo Theatre before we did 'Lovers Never Say Goodbye,' I was singing the song, 'Boney Moronie,' and we did little dance routines, and I would move my legs like Elvis Presley and shake my shoulders like Elvis, and it was a heck of a show," Terry recalls. "Paul would do his little white songs. Tommy Hunt would do 'Everybody's Got a Home but Me.' We wound up putting that one in an album. We did a little bit of everything."

"We all sang lead," agrees Hunt. "Everybody took their turn and swapped, but Nate Nelson was the main lead voice."

Billboard reviewed "My Faith in You" and "Helpless," their latest Decca single, the week of October 7, giving both sides a "very good" rating. Despite Decca's considerable promotional and distributional power, the choral-laden sides, not surprisingly, failed to find an audience.

The group continued performing at nightclubs for crossover audiences into the early months of 1958, occasionally latching on to a theater date as well. On April 4, they began a week at the Apollo, where they appeared with Fats Domino, the Dells, and the Spaniels. On April 17, 1958, Isaac Carey, Jake's 80-year-old father, fell into a spring and drowned in Portsmouth, Virginia. He was buried in nearby Belleville on the 25th.

On Tuesday, May 6, 1958, the Flamingos were back at the Pythian Temple for another four-song date. The first master produced, "Kiss-a-Me," was penned by the professional songwriting team of Guy B. Wood and Albert Askew Beach. Born in Great Britain, Wood (1911–2001) was a saxophone player with various dance bands and had also worked for the Columbia and Paramount motion picture studios. He had collaborated on a number of hits including "Till Then," "Shoo-Fly Pie and Apple Pan Dowdy," and "My One and Only Love," which had been written with Robert Mellin. Coincidentally, Mellin had composed "I'm Yours," which the Flamingos had cut for Parrot.

Beach (1924–1997) had collaborated on several songs with Wood, including the Three Suns' "Haunted Guitar" in 1956. Their best-known collaboration came in 1958, with "(Here I Stand) The Wedding," recorded by June Valli on RCA. Beach's most recognized effort was "I Wish You Love," using a 1943 tune by the great French pop composer and singer Charles Trenet.

"Kiss-a-Me" was a typical ballad of the period, which gave Nelson a chance to shine on the bridge. The syrupy chorus was back, arranged and conducted by Sid Bass, obscuring all but Jake's bass vocal behind the lead singer.

Arguably the most interesting of all the Flamingos' Decca sides was "Where Mary Go," written by lyricist Diane Charlotte Lampert and composer John R. Gluck, Jr. Previously, this partnership had produced "Can't Wait for Summer" for Steve Lawrence and "So Nice to be Wrong," recorded by Carmen McRae in 1957. Later, the duo collaborated on Eddie Fontaine's pop hit "Nothin' Shakin' (But the Leaves on the Trees)." After going their separate ways, Lampert co-wrote the Del Satins' "Feelin' No Pain" and the theme to the 1972 film *Silent Running*. Gluck (1925–2000) scored his biggest success co-writing "It's My Party," a #1 hit for Lesley Gore in 1963.

Opening with an Indian-styled tympani drum beat, "Where Mary Go" gave the group an opportunity to lay down some unique minor-chord unison singing and harmonizing as Nate took a brief solo. Wilson again delivered the recitation segment.

Lyricist Gerry Teifer, who wrote "A Full Time Job" for Eddy Arnold in 1952, collaborated with Bobby Sharp on Arnold's "I Need Somebody," and the Flamingos' "Ever Since I Met Lucy," the third song taped. With Hunt singing lead, a "tra la la la la la la" background, and a Fats Domino-inspired piano accompaniment, "Ever Since I Met Lucy" was passable, but hardly hit material. The session concluded with "The Rock 'n' Roll March," written by television pioneer Steve Allen (1921–2000) and his singer-songwriter friend, Bob Carroll. Literally a rock and roll song set to a marching beat, the tune gave bass Jake Carey a rare opportunity to sing lead.

"Where Mary Go" and "The Rock 'n' Roll March" became Decca's third Flamingos release in July. Both sides again received "very good" ratings from *Billboard*'s reviewer, but the songs didn't affect record buyers the way their Checker releases had.

At some point between 1956 and 1960, the Flamingos lent their talents to a Bo Diddley recording session, backing the singer on a fine ballad side, "You Know I Love You," which remained unissued until the 1990 release, *Bo Diddley—The Chess Box*. The song features a strong floating tenor throughout that likely belonged to Johnny Carter. "I wasn't with them then," Johnson asserts. "That was so weird. It sounds like my voice when I listen to it, but I don't remember it. Bo remembered it. He said, 'Yeah, you were in there. You were in the studio. You don't remember it?' I said, 'No.' It didn't make sense that we would have [recorded for a Checker artist] after leaving the label." After listening to the recording, Zeke Carey also stated that he was not involved in the session. The absence of Carey and Johnson suggests that "You Know I Love You" was likely made around August or September of 1956.

The group continued to tour during the summer months. On June 20, 1958, they appeared at Palisades Park in Northern New Jersey, a now-defunct 38-acre amusement park a half-mile south of the George Washington Bridge, along with Fats Domino and Dion and the Belmonts. August 16 found them back in Washington for a week at the Howard with Bo Diddley, the Danleers, the Pearls, and Arthur Prysock.

To maintain bookings, the Flamingos needed a hit record. Despite the resources available from the major industry player, their association with Decca can only be deemed a failure. The group's rich, soulful harmonies had been homogenized into the chorus-drenched pop of the day. Record buyers—indeed, even the group's most ardent fans—weren't buying it. Jake Carey knew they needed a change.

End Records
and a New Beginning

After a disappointing 18 months with Decca during which only three singles were released, the Flamingos began to look elsewhere. "They had a little manager doing nothing," Zeke explained, which "had them in trouble business-wise. They weren't recording. The Decca contract had gotten screwed up in legalities between Chess and Decca. All of the [Decca] records were ballads and in the nightclub scene, being a rhythm and blues group, you couldn't work the chitlin' circuit. You've got to have records or be definitely bluesy to work that. So the only place would be the crossover white circuit."

Competition among the artists seeking to cross over into night spot and supper club engagements was fierce, requiring an exciting, polished, and self-contained act. "You had to be comparable to the Treniers, the Dominoes, Steve Gibson and the Red Caps, high on excitement," Zeke continued. "[The Flamingos] still played those theaters, but you can't make a living on a theater here, a theater there. They had to go to work in Miami Beach, five or six shows a night. They wound up working for low money, and it had to be self-contained. They all picked up percussion instruments, hired a drummer. To make up for what they didn't have, they developed routines, unique and exciting choreography, and all types of singing. Tommy and Paul were doing splits and flips on those small stages."

"The work was flowing in, but strangely our income never got any bigger," echoed Hunt.

"I encouraged Nate to pick up the drums," Terry explains. "He said, 'How am I going to play drums?' I said, 'Well, look, we're like a corporation anyway. We'll put the money together and get you some drums,' and he was like, 'Yeah, yeah, yeah.' He got inspired and he got the drums. I was like an organizer. I was always thinking. I had talked to Tommy, and he was practicing on the piano. Eventually, we were self-contained."

Although Zeke Carey often told interviewers he had mediated an agreement between Leonard Chess and George Goldner that allowed the Flamingos

82

to transition over to End Records in 1958, Johnson vehemently denies the assertion. According to Johnson, it was Jake Carey, who handled the group's finances and served as their spokesman, who brought the Flamingos to End. "We were performing on 'The Biggest Show of 1956,' and we did a show in Newark," Jake told interviewer Tamarkin in 1981. "George Goldner, who owned the label, came backstage. He'd wanted the Flamingos for quite a while. He made it known. He asked us how long we had on our contract because he wanted the privilege of recording the group. He pursued it."

"Richard Barrett saw Jake walking down Broadway near 57th Street," Johnson explains. "Jake said, 'Hey, Richard, what's happening? I want to talk to you. You've got some good groups.' He had Little Anthony and the Imperials, the Chantels, and Frankie Lymon and the Teenagers [all recording for Goldner labels]. It just happened out of the clear blue sky. Jake met Richard walking down the street. 'Hey man, do you think George would be interested in recording us?' Richard said, 'I can talk to him for you, man. You know, I don't know why not. You guys have a sound altogether different from everybody else. I'll talk to George.'"

"Richard Barrett asked us to come talk to George, so that was what we did," Jake encapsulated. "George had a meeting with Jake and Richard Barrett," Johnson adds. "Then Jake came back to the hotel and told us about it. Jake made the deal with Richard Barrett. As a matter of fact, I have the original contract, and everybody's name was on it except Zeke's. It was already signed and notarized and everything, and you can see where Zeke kind of forced his name in there at the very end. Zeke wasn't even there. He did a lot of lying. He wanted to take a lot of credit."

Beginning with Latin music in 1948, the New York–born George Goldner (1918–1970) was one of the most prolific hit makers among 1950s independent record producers and label owners. As the head of the Rama-Tico-Gee empire, he had consistently produced chart toppers and quality regional noisemakers by the likes of the Crows, the Wrens, the Valentines, the Cleftones, and Frankie Lymon and the Teenagers, which helped to catapult his company into one of the strongest independent R&B operations by the mid–1950s. "He was good," affirmed composer-producer and Harptones founder Raoul J. Cita. "He had an ear, and he knew how hits ought to sound. He used a top-grade studio in Bell Sound, and had a great engineer in Al Weintraub."

Goldner's gambling losses forced him to sell the entire organization to his partner, the notorious Morris Levy (1927–1990), linked by the FBI to the Genovese crime family, and partner/music publisher Phil Kahl, in March of 1957. Levy's main interest soon became their recently activated Roulette label.

But Goldner emerged again, creating the Gone and End labels from his office in the Brill Building at 1650 Broadway, and enjoying hits with the Dubs, the Chantels, the Channels, and the Imperials. "George Goldner personally supervised all the recordings," Zeke stated. "He was a great producer, great promoter, and had an ear for hits." An integral member of Goldner's production team was Richard Barrett. A Philadelphia native, Barrett (1933–2006) had begun as the lead singer of the Valentines, who enjoyed success with "Lily Maebelle" and "The Woo Train" on Rama in 1955–56. By 1957, he was Goldner's Artists and Repertoire director at Gone/End and writing hit songs for other artists. "End Records, at that time, was a new company," Nelson summed. "Richard had just put the Chantels together and was working with Little Anthony and the Imperials. It sounded good, so we joined them."

Even before their first session with Goldner, the Flamingos began to make their presence felt. Nelson contributed one side of the Chantels' September 1958 release, "If You Try." "Nate Nelson of the Flamingos wrote 'If You Try,'" Chantels vocalist Lois Harris Powell explained to historian Charlie Horner. "Then he played it for Richard, who thought it would be good for us. In the same way, Richard had a demo of 'Congratulations' that he played for us. He told us we were going to record it. We worked on it and did our own background. We would make it up as we went along. Richard would get a demo and play it for us. If we liked it, we'd say OK, we'll do it. If we didn't like it, we'd say, 'We don't like it.' Sometimes he'd say, 'Too bad!'"

At the same time the Flamingos signed with End, both Johnny Carter and Zeke Carey were being discharged from the Army. According to Johnson, both wanted to return to the Flamingos, but were met with a mixed response. "When I got with the group, Jake was the boss," Terry states. "I wanted to get Johnny in the group. They said, 'Well, no, no, no, because Johnny has too many problems. He had too many women and too many babies, and the police were looking for him when he got out of the service. No, we can't let him back in the group,' and I couldn't fight it."

Sixty years after the fact, Terry Johnson remained upset by the fact that Carter, who arranged the vast majority of the Flamingos' harmony during his tenure with the group, was not allowed to rejoin. "All this stuff about how they got the melodic haunting sound from the Black Jewish Church, in my opinion, is such bullshit," Terry opines. "I don't mean any harm, but that's such bull. Johnny Carter is the real founder of the Flamingos. Johnny Carter was there before all of them. Johnny Carter came up with the name. So, I thought it was so dirty that they wouldn't let him back in the group. He was really one of the founding members."

"I was just at home," Carter admitted to interviewer Jack Sbarbori in 1976. "I couldn't get myself together. I got a job working for a plastering contractor, [but] I couldn't get used to not being on stage. So, I was out of work one day, and I came into this tavern, and the four of them were sitting there."

The four—Chuck Barksdale, Verne Allison, Mickey McGill, and Marvin Junior—were founding members of the Dells, the R&B unit that had hit the national charts with "Oh What a Nite" on Vee-Jay Records in 1956. After a serious auto accident en route to a 1958 gig in Philadelphia had sidelined McGill with a badly broken leg, the group disbanded. When they decided to reunite in 1960, lead tenor Johnny Funches, who had taken a job in a steel mill, could not be persuaded to return.

"Johnny Funches didn't want to go back on the road," Carter confirmed. "I'd heard of the Dells, but I was getting kind of disgusted, too. They asked me to go, but I said there was no way I could go right then. Plus, I had been thinking of going as a single. I had talked to Chess a couple of times, and, as a matter of fact, I had a few songs, and I told them I didn't want to go back with no more groups."

Barksdale and the others, however, were not deterred in their quest to add Carter to the Dells. "We just picked him up, and the next day we were

The Dells, ca. 1970. Clockwise from bottom left: Johnny Carter, Verne Allison, Chuck Barksdale, Michael McGill and Marvin Junior (Bruno of Hollywood photo, from the author's collection).

leaving town," Barksdale reported to Sbarbori. "We went to Philadelphia, and he started learning our tunes from the time we picked him up until the time we got on stage. He was learning songs all the time."

Carter, Barksdale, and Los Angeles vocal group stalwart Cornelius Gunter (1936–1990) comprised three-fifths of a quintet known as D's Gentlemen, backing Dinah Washington for several months before the career of the Dells took off once again. The group eventually signed with the Chess brothers, recording for their Cadet subsidiary. Carter and the Dells remained a cohesive unit from that point forward, scoring over 40 national R&B chart hits including the #1 smash, "Stay in My Corner." "I can attribute that to luck, determination, and God's will," Carter told a television reporter from Chicago's Urban Street in 1992. "I hate a quitter. The guy I replaced had quit. That's one of the reasons I went along with the guys. I was going to sing."

Diagnosed with lung cancer while the group was appearing in Las Vegas in August of 2008, Carter battled the disease for a year before succumbing in the early morning hours of August 21, 2009, at John E. Ingalls Memorial Hospital in Harvey, Illinois, at the age of 75. He was buried in Abraham Lincoln National Cemetery in Elwood, Illinois. A two-time Rock and Roll Hall of Fame Inductee, honored for his work with both groups, the singer was interred under a standard military issue headstone inscribed simply with his birth name, John Edward Carter, his United States Army rank, private second class, dates of birth and death, the Star of David, and the words "beloved father."

When Zeke Carey was discharged in August of 1958, the Flamingos similarly balked at his return. "Zeke was in the service, and they weren't going to let him back in the group," Terry states. "I didn't know Zeke at all. Not really, you know, not one on one. But I fought for him, because they weren't going to let him in. No one, including Jake, wanted him back."

When he arrived back in New York, Zeke met with the group in Johnson's room at the Cecil Hotel. "We always rehearsed in my room because that's where I kept the amplifier," Terry recalls. "We were having a meeting with him concerning his return to the group. They all agreed that he had a weak voice at best, and Jake was fighting not to have to pay a sixth person when we didn't really need him. I felt sorry for him. He looked so sad, because they were all saying these things to his face. I got emotional and wanted to help him. They said, 'No, we've already got five. We don't need anyone else. What are we going to do?' I said, 'Well, I can teach him how to play bass, and make him more valuable, and teach him another note. I can structure my guitar and get five-part harmony.' That's what we had. The Flamingos had five-part harmony. And plus, we can let Zeke help Jake, because Jake was always carrying this big stuffed wallet with this big chain in his back pocket, and it looked so stupid. We were always like, 'Jake, that's not the way. You don't carry money like that.' I thought that Zeke could help Jake with the business. So, Zeke got back in the group. Everybody was dead set against it, but I guess they went for it because we were just coming off the success of 'Lovers Never Say Goodbye,' which I wrote, and they respected my opinion. That was probably the biggest mistake of my life. I taught him how to play bass and gave him the parts."

In his 2009 autobiography, Hunt maintained his belief that Carey's return was imminent and his own role in the Flamingos was transitory. "We were back in New York again when Zeke came out of the service," Hunt wrote. "He joined us there. I'd never met Johnny, the other Flamingo, but I figured he'd be back soon, too, and I guessed there'd be no room for me. Knowing that Zeke had arrived, I went to my room and had started packing when a knock came on the door. In walked all the guys with Zeke. 'What time's your train?' he asked. 'Where are you gonna go?' asked Paul as they all lounged about in my room. 'Home, I guess. I've had a great time. Thanks for having me. I learned a lot from you guys. This experience has been something I'll never forget.' For a moment I felt like crying. 'You won't forget it man, 'cause you're not going nowhere,' said Nate, grinning at me. 'What do you mean? My time's up, and Zeke's back. There's no place for me now.' Zeke laughed. 'Why not? We can both be in the group. Look, all this time you've been doing three-part harmony. There's room for four.'" Carey invited Hunt to remain with the group "for as long as you like" and informed him that Carter would not be returning due to "a family matter." Soon, the new lineup was ready to record.

While researching session tapes for a CD reissue project in the late 1980s, Boston disc jockey "Little" Walter DeVenne discovered the Flamingos' initial End rehearsal tape of "Lovers Never Say Goodbye," backed only by Johnson's electric guitar. The fascinating performance was included on Collectables' 1992 double CD set, *The Flamingos—For Collectors Only.* "That was the first time that Paul had really heard the song," Terry remembers. "I didn't even do the repeats with him. It was an audition. We had gone into the studio and done something else, and George said, 'What's that new song you said you had, Terry?' And I said, 'Come on, Paul.' I showed it to Paul, and we did it on the spot. And the guys, they did 'shoo-do-do-doop,' 'shoo-do-do-doop,' and everything just fell into place. You can hear me counting it off and Paul clearing his throat or coughing before we started.

"When I wrote 'Lovers Never Say Goodbye,' I wrote it for a girl in Atlantic City. Her name was Elsie. As a matter of fact, she even came up with the title, because she was crying, and I said, 'Hey, don't cry, don't cry. We'll say so-long.' She said, 'Yeah, lovers never say goodbye.' I said, 'Oh, I like that.' So, even while she was [still] there, I started playing my guitar and I got the melody, and I started getting the lyrics together. I never saw Elsie again.'"

While arranging "Lovers Never Say Goodbye" for the Flamingos, Johnson selected Wilson to sing the duet lead with him, and also assigned him a co-writer credit. "I chose Paul to sing it," Terry explains. "When I presented it to the guys, I wanted Paul to sing it with me, because Paul was my friend, and we had done the Everly Brothers and a lot of other duet songs together. Paul was my best friend in the group. He taught me how to be suave and debonair with the girls. He taught me so many things. Paul was really my friend. Paul and I would drink vodka, you know, get a shot of vodka before we went on stage. We'd get fined $50 if Jake ever caught us drinking. So, we would drink vodka and Coca-Cola or vodka and orange juice so he couldn't smell the vodka. Because he was my friend, I gave him 50 percent of the song. He never wrote one word. He never wrote any of the melody. I mean, he was just my friend, and I gave it to him."

On Friday, September 26, 1958, the Flamingos shared a split session with Little Anthony and the Imperials at Bell Sound Studios, located at 237 West 54th Street. Opening with six solo guitar notes from Terry, "Lovers Never Say Goodbye" featured Johnson and Wilson singing a well-crafted duet lead in harmony, with Nelson, Hunt, and the Careys providing stellar four-part backing. In the bridge, Paul's solo baritone-tenor was echoed effectively by Terry's smooth falsetto tenor. Driven by Johnson's steady rhythm guitar strumming, utilizing minor and 7th chords, "Lovers Never Say Goodbye" was innovative, creative, and universally appealing.

"My natural voice when I sing is a baritone," Terry explains. "I had a low voice, but I just kind of liked singing up there. It gave me another style. That's why when I got with the Flamingos and all the songs that Paul and I sang, I did the baritone, the low part. Paul did the   Original 45 RPM pressing, 1958 (author's collection).

high part, and I would do the repeat in my falsetto. I played guitar on everything we did. That's my guitar. I would be strumming chords as I sang."

The echoed "kiss" sound heard on the finished product was an engineering trick created by Goldner and his engineer, Al Weintraub. "That was George Goldner's idea," Terry explains. "Nobody was making a kissing sound. That was some kind of a sound effect that he did in reverb or echo, and it made it sound like that."

In the search for a B-side, Goldner settled on Nelson's original "That Love is You," which Decca had passed on a year and a half earlier. A&R man Richard Barrett reworked the song for the session with Nelson and Johnson. "I remember Nate called me, and we went into the office," Terry recounts. "Richard was at the piano, and I had my guitar, and I added some chords and some background. I remember the background tenors were my idea." In October, Goldner paired the songs as End #1035. *Billboard* reviewed the disc the week of October 27 and actually gave "That Love is You" a higher rating than "Lovers Never Say Goodbye." Initial pressings, issued on both End's gray and multi-colored labels, erroneously listed the title as "Please Wait for Me." A pristine gray-label copy of "Please Wait for Me" can be expected to sell for $200 on the collector's market today.

Goldner quickly learned that the Flamingos were a unique entity—creative, innovative, and commercial, capable of tapping into mainstream tastes. He'd waste no time in mining and marketing their talent. The group's brightest days were finally on the horizon.

Doo Bop Shoo Bop

On Halloween, October 31, 1958, the six-man group returned to Bell Sound for another two-song session. The two songs selected were old standards: "Without a Song," written in 1929, and "I Only Have Eyes for You," which debuted in 1934. "George Goldner called me into the office by myself quite a bit, because he knew I played the guitar, and he knew where my background was from," Johnson explains. "He would call me Terry. He said, 'Terry, we need to do something different. 'I'll Be Home' is nice, and 'The Vow' is nice. 'A Kiss from Your Lips' and all that stuff is nice, but that is keeping you locked into this black market. Now, what I would like to do is do things like the Platters.' The Platters were on fire at that time. They had about four or five super smashes. So, he and Richard Barrett called me in the office and said, 'Look, we're going to pick out some songs. I want you guys to do an album.' We had done 'Lovers Never Say Goodbye,' but we hadn't done 'I Only Have Eyes for You' yet. That's when George said, 'You know, you guys have another kind of sound. Why don't we do a takeoff on the Platters and do some old standards? Let's just pick out some old standards, and, Terry, you know how to change the music and the chords around. Put a little bit more 'white flavor' in it. You know what I mean?' So, I was a little embarrassed to hear, white music, you know, even though it was my roots. I said, 'Well, OK, I'll do the best I can.' And we were on the trail of the Platters. That's how it really started off."

Between 1956 and 1958, the Platters successfully revived three songs dating back to the 1930s and early 1940s, "My Prayer," "Twilight Time," and "Smoke Gets in Your Eyes," turning each into a #1 hit record.

"Without a Song," written by Billy Rose, Edward Eliscu, and Vincent Youmans, had been in a musical play called *Great Day*. A #6 hit for Paul Whiteman in 1930, the song proved a winner for Perry Como in 1951 and Roy Hamilton in 1955. Apparently unhappy with the finished product, Goldner chose to keep "Without a Song" on the shelf. It has never been released.

"I Only Have Eyes for You" was a different story altogether. Written in 1933 by Harry Warren (1893–1981) and lyricist Al Dubin (1891–1945), "I Only

Have Eyes for You" was originally included in the movie musical *Dames*, star-ring Joan Blondell. Born Salvatore Guaragna in Brooklyn, Warren is undoubt-edly one of America's most prolific composers. With a catalog of over 500 titles including "Lullaby of Broadway," "We're in the Money," "September in the Rain," and "Chattanooga Choo," his songs have appeared in well over 100 films and earned him a pair of Academy Awards. The Swiss-born Dubin, a Songwriters Hall of Fame inductee, had begun his career in 1916 and first teamed with Warren to work on the musical *42nd Street* in 1932.

The romantic ballad had been a #2 hit for Ben Selvin in 1934. Dick Powell also scored with the song, which he introduced in the 1934 musical motion picture *Dames*, in a long number in which he crooned the romantic lyrics to misty-eyed Ruby Keeler. Although Johnson was aware of the smooth 1952 R&B rendition done by his hometown friends, the Swallows, his arrangement was completely unlike theirs, or any of the others. Consumed by the need to provide Goldner with something tangible, Johnson found the ultimate arrangement in a dream. "It came from me," he asserts. "It was in a dream. What I heard in my dream, I got right to my guitar and started playing it. I remembered everything that I heard in my dream. I taught it to the guys."

Both Tommy Hunt and Zeke Carey have claimed a share of the credit in various interviews. "We were rehearsing it in the Cecil Hotel, 118th Street in New York, and we were sitting there wondering what kind of ideas we could put to the song," Hunt recalled to McGarvey in 1985. "I'd heard another song. It was by a group. I can't remember their name. It was a fast song, and they had a little phrase in it that went 'do-do-do-do doo-bop shoo-bop,' and I said, 'Hey, I got an idea. Let's put in the 'doo bop shoo bop,' and they said, 'Yeah, yeah, it sounds all right.'"

"'I Only Have Eyes for You' was a result of Goldner's idea for us to do an album of great love songs," Zeke stated, "all ... well-known standards. George came up with the concept. It was the only album we ever did that he picked every single song. He chose 12 songs, and we decided we didn't want them to sound alike. We wanted all 12 to have their own unique arrangement. We decided to go really out in left field with that song, and it was one of the most left field things that we did. It had everything working for it. I'm proud I insisted on doing it that way."

Reading Hunt and Carey's accounts sixty years after the fact, Terry John-son vehemently disagrees. "Zeke and Tommy both lied about their partici-pation on 'I Only Have Eyes for You.' They didn't have any ideas for the song. The only person who gave an idea in the beginning was Nate Nelson. I was struggling with changing the chords and Nate was playing around and being silly. He said, 'You're the chord master. To really make it different, make it sound like the Russians' "Volga Boatmen,'" and then he laughed. I told him to get out of my room, because he was clowning around, but it stuck in my head." "Song of the Volga Boatmen" is a traditional Russian folk song sung by barge-haulers along the Volga River and published as early as 1866. Known in Russian as "Ey, Ukhnem!" (translated as "Yo, Heave Ho!"), it became a #1 hit for Glenn Miller and his Orchestra in the United States in 1941.

"After I finished with the song, Nate was the first one to my room when I called them all, and I played if for him and he was still clowning around and I had a certain background idea and he said, 'Why don't you try, "shoo fly pie and apple pan dowdy"'! Then I said, 'No, let's do the "shoo" but make it "doo bop shoo bop,"' and we both looked at each other and said, 'Yeah, that's it!'"

According to Johnson, he had originally planned on singing the song himself until Nelson goaded him into handing over the lead. "Nate was a talker," Terry recalls. "He made fun of everybody, and that's how he got 'I Only Have Eyes for You' from me. I was singing it. I was supposed to record it, and when I first put the chords together, everybody was looking at me like, 'What the hell is this?' I said, 'No, do the "doo bop shoo bop," and try to do this....' That was the only time they gave me a hard time. But when they finally did it, and heard what was happening, Nate really took a liking to it, and Tommy Hunt liked it. Paul said, 'Hey, Buzzy, that's haunting.' When we went in the studio, I sang it down one time, and George Goldner liked it. But Nate said, 'Man, you're not singing the song right. Look at you, listen to your voice.' Nate had a thing he would do with everybody. He knew how to needle you and discourage you and make you give up. He laughed at me, and made everybody else laugh at me, and I was so embarrassed. It was deep. He made me so mad. I said, 'Oh, you think you could do better?' He said, 'Any-body could do better than you, Buzzy!' and he laughed. I said, 'Well you sing it, damn it, you sing it!' And man, God bless Nate, he had that golden voice. He was Sonny Til's cousin. He had that voice. I can't knock it, but I was singing the song first."

Following three introductory chords from Johnson's guitar, Nelson's vel-vety "voice of champagne" opened with "My love must be a kind of blind love," over a repetitive piano triplet figure. The echo-heavy "doo bop shoo bop" harmony, and Johnson's floating falsetto backing provided the ideal counterpoint to Nate's romantic lead and the sparse instrumental backing. The three-minute-and-20-second recording, one of the Flamingos' longest to that point, was hauntingly romantic, distinctive, and commercially appeal-ing. Still, it would be six months before "I Only Have Eyes for You" would be released as a single.

By mid–November, "Lovers Never Say Goodbye" had begun to turn up on play sheets and bestseller lists around the country. *Billboard* selected the song, along with LaVern Baker's "I Cried a Tear" as its Territorial Tips in the St. Louis market the week of the 24th. In its November 1, 1958, review, *Cash Box* declared that "the Flamingos, who've had numerous hits through the years on various labels, bow in under the End banner with a pretty rock-a-ballad that could make it big. Group has excellent harmony and a dramatic love tune to work with here. Smooth."

At that time, the Flamingos saw success, according to Zeke Carey, as "what young people were listening to, not what people were drinking to. [We] started thinking 'records' and got back into the theaters. We started performing with the current groups that were making hits. It had gotten that the hot dee-jays weren't looking for the Flamingos on their shows. Now, with 'Lovers Never Say Goodbye,' they were playing something. That first show in Philadelphia was Georgie Woods.' 'Lovers Never Say Goodbye' was no hit yet, just being played, but we were singing. When we went on that show a second time, it was a hit."

From December 24 through January 3, the Flamingos appeared at Lowe's State Theater in New York City as part of Alan Freed's Christmas Rock 'n' Roll Spectacular, which grossed over $200,000. Also on the bill were Frankie Avalon, Jimmy Clanton, Eddie Cochran, Jackie Wilson, Harvey and the Moonglows, the Cadillacs, Baby Washington, the Crests, Chuck Berry, Bo Diddley, Jo Ann Campbell, Gino & Gina, Ed Townsend, the Nu Tornados, Dion and the Belmonts, and King Curtis. Johnnie Ray started at the top of the bill, but was subsequently replaced by the Everly Brothers. Zeke eventually hired a manager named Charlie Lavigna to handle some of the group's business affairs, but his association with the group was relatively short-lived.

"We did club work, concert work, theaters. We did practically everything," Hunt told McGarvey in 1985. "I think the theater work was the hardest because we had to start at 12 o'clock in the day until 12 o'clock at night. We were only doing four shows. But sitting around in between shows when the movie was on was a little bit tiring. You always had eight, nine, or 12 acts. But with club work, you went in, you did three shows a night, you did an hour, you came off, [and] you had about 20 or 30 minutes to relax and then you got ready for the next show. So, at least you kept moving. At the theater, you'd have to wait almost an hour and a half to two hours, or one hour and 45 minutes before you did the next show. Then, we were nearly always starring the bill, so we had to wait for six, seven, or eight other acts to go on, so it was waiting more than anything else that was the hard part."

On January 16, 1959, the Flamingos began a week of appearances at the

Apollo with Little Anthony and the Imperials, Jerry Butler and the Impressions, Wade Flemons, the Crests, the Quin-Tones, and Doc Bagby's Combo. On January 19, "Lovers Never Say Goodbye" cracked *Billboard's* national pop chart, the group's first appearance on the list. In 10 weeks on the chart, it peaked at #52. Following their stint at the Apollo, the Flamingos, the Impres-

Billboard magazine trade advertisement, April 1959 (Galen Gart collection).

sions, the Quin-Tones, Flemons, and the Bagby troupe traveled to Washington for a week of shows at the Howard.

From there, the Flamingos headed home to New York for a February 2 recording session. The first song taped was a faster version of "Jump Children," the 1954 Chance cut that they had been using as their show-stopping closer. Paul Wilson and Nate Nelson handled the lead vocal chores. According to Johnson, the re-recording was done so that they could feature it, and the eye-popping dance routine that accompanied it, in the motion picture *Go, Johnny, Go!*

"The *Go, Johnny, Go!* movie routine was actually developed in the night clubs, as a closer, a show-stopper," Zeke explained. "Getting girls, competing for girls, was always a part of that, and they would take this excitement to the theaters. The other acts would see the Flamingos and go, 'Wow!', but had no idea how and why this came about."

"We were the first ones that were doing that stuff," Johnson adds. "I think Tommy and Paul got that from the Step Brothers." An African American dance group established by Maceo Anderson at Harlem's Cotton Club in 1925, the Step Brothers pioneered acrobatic dancing on stages, television shows, and in motion pictures for nearly 40 years. In 1949, comedian Milton Berle refused to appear on his live NBC-TV show, *The Texaco Star Theater*, unless the show's sponsor allowed the Four Step Brothers and their "eight feet of rhythm" to break an unwritten color barrier. "The Step Brothers would do those kinds of dances and would do the splits," Johnson continues. "Tommy had his own style of dancing, and Paul had his own style, and they put it together that way. That was our show-stopper."

From the George and Ira Gershwin songbook, Goldner selected "But Not for Me." Another powerful lost-love ballad, the song had been written for the 1930 musical *Girl Crazy*, which was made into a motion picture in 1932 with Busby Berkeley directing. Also featuring the Gershwin chestnuts "Embraceable You" and "I Got Rhythm," *Girl Crazy* was remade in 1943 starring Mickey Rooney and Judy Garland. Johnson and Wilson again shared a smooth duet lead while Nelson anchored the background harmony as top tenor. Two completed master takes were produced, the latter of which remains unreleased.

Tommy Hunt delivered a confident and heartfelt lead on "I Shed a Tear at Your Wedding," which featured smooth harmony and organ accompaniment. The ballad was written by composer-producer-arranger Alphonso Higdon, who later penned songs for the Violetts and Winfield Parker, and co-wrote "What Good Am I Without You," an R&B chart hit for Marvin Gaye and Kim Weston in the fall of 1964.

In all probability, the group filmed their performance of "Jump Children" for the motion picture *Go, Johnny, Go!* not in December, as often reported, but in early February, within days of the recording session that produced the version heard in the film. Introduced by teen sensation Jimmy Clanton, the six-man group strode on stage wearing jackets and ties, with Zeke Carey carrying his bass guitar and Terry Johnson sporting his electric guitar.

The dance sequence staged and performed by Wilson and Hunt, with participation from Nelson as well, is unquestionably one of the most exciting and visually dazzling vocal group performances ever captured on film. Despite energetic performances from Chuck Berry, the Cadillacs, Ritchie Valens, Eddie Cochran, and Jackie Wilson, it is the Flamingos' "Jump Children" segment that steals the show. More than 20 splits, including kneeling, sliding, up-and-down syncopated yo-yo splits, and one maneuver in which Wilson does a sliding split across the stage through Hunt's legs, highlight the three-minute clip. "My legs!" Hunt exclaimed at the memory over 40 years later. "That was the most exciting time in my life, man, because I had never done a movie. When I knew I was in a movie, I felt like I was Robert DeNiro

Left to right: Tommy, Zeke, Jake, Nate, Paul, and Terry perform "Lovers Never Say Goodbye" in an outtake from the motion picture *Go, Johnny, Go!* in 1959 (Billy Vera collection).

or somebody like that. I came out of that studio and nobody could talk to me. I said, 'I'm a movie star!' People said, 'Tommy, you just did one spot.' I said, 'Baby, that was the biggest spot in my life.' It was somewhere in New York City, a studio somewhere off of Broadway. I remember that." In 2009, Hunt added, "It was a great experience, but we never made any money out of it."

"All of the groups in those days, they all had lots of movements on stage," Hunt told interviewer McGarvey. "The Orioles, the Dominoes, you name them, the Moonglows, the Dells, all the boys. The kids today that are doing movement. They've got a little bit of movement. But, actually, a lot of what they're doing stems from what we were doing in those days."

"'Jump Children' was a thing that we used to close shows with all the time," Zeke added. "It was an old rhythm 'n' blues, a shuffle blues tune. I guess what was so unique was that it was a creation from the group itself."

Less than a week after they had recorded the songs, Goldner coupled "(They're Writing Songs of Love) But Not for Me" and "I Shed a Tear at Your Wedding" as End #1040. The rush-released disc received high marks from *Billboard* in their February 9 issue. "The group, currently scoring with 'Lovers Never Say Goodbye,' could have a big one with their smooth rock-a-ballad treatment of the Gershwin evergreen," the magazine's reviewer noted. "Solid performance is neatly backed."

Determined to finish the group's "great love songs" concept album, George Goldner recorded another 11 tunes just a week and a half later, on Tuesday and Wednesday, February 17 and 18, 1960. Kicking off the session was "Time Was," a wistful ballad composed in 1936 by Miguel Prado. Also known as "Duerme," the song's original Spanish lyrics were written by Gabriel Luna. S.K. "Bob" Russell added English lyrics, and it became a #10 pop chart hit for Jimmy Dorsey and his Orchestra with vocalists Helen O'Connell and Bob Eberly in 1941. Wilson and Johnson again delivered a stellar duet lead over tight background harmonies and discreet percussion and organ backing. "I loved 'Time Was,'" Johnson admits. "I thought that was a smash. That was a beautiful song."

Next up was "Goodnight Sweetheart," a 1931 effort from British composer and bandleader Ray Noble (1903–1978). London natives Reginald Connelly and James Campbell, who collaborated on standards including 1933's "Try a Little Tenderness," added the lyrics. Al Bowlly first sang the tune with Noble's HMV Orchestra, while Rudy Vallee popularized the song in the United States. Occasionally confused with James "Pookie" Hudson's composition, "Goodnite, Sweetheart, Goodnite," originally popularized by the Spaniels in 1954, "Goodnight Sweetheart" was a slow, dreamy ballad led by Nate Nelson over more rich harmonies and gentle piano triplets.

Terry Johnson took over the lead vocal chores next, smoothly delivering "I'm in the Mood for Love" in his natural baritone. The song was one of seven written by famed Broadway lyricist Dorothy Fields (1905–1974) and Jimmy McHugh (1893–1969) for the 1935 motion picture *Every Night at Eight*. Although Frances Langford introduced and initially recorded "I'm in the Mood for Love," bandleader Little Jack Little scored the #1 version of the song that year. Over 120 versions have been recorded through the years. Louis Armstrong, Leo Reisman, and Langford also made the national charts with it in 1935. Billy Eckstine successfully revived it in 1946, and Fats Domino offered his own unique interpretation in 1957 on the B-side of "I'm Walkin'." With Nelson singing high tenor, Johnson and the group offered a fine rendition that strayed little from the original.

At the time of George Gershwin's untimely death in July of 1937, he and his brother Ira had been working on songs for *The Goldwyn Follies*, a movie that would be released the following year. The final song the pair collaborated on was "Love Walked In." Bandleader Sammy Kaye scored a #1 hit with the tune in 1938. Jimmy Dorsey, Jan Garber, Kenny Baker, and Louis Armstrong also reached the national charts with "Love Walked In," as did the Hilltoppers, who hit #8 in 1953.

For the Flamingos' interpretation, Johnson and Wilson again sang a duet lead and shared the familiar "call and response" pattern they had used on "Lovers Never Say Goodbye." The unique whistling heard at the beginning and end of the recording was suggested and provided by session producer Goldner. "George was very creative," explains Johnson. "George would talk with me about just about everything that he wanted us to do, because he knew that I had the head for it, you know. He said, 'I want something different like 'Love Walked In' [thinking] … 'Love Walked In' … a nice thing.' And he said, 'Whistling when you walk, that's kind of nice. Play those chords!' I played the chords, and I think I recorded the intro for him. When we got into the studio, because it had to be done all at the same time, George Goldner, the president himself, did the whistling. Everybody was like, 'Wow! That's deep.' Because nobody knew he could whistle like that. He was in tune. It was really nice. I don't remember if somebody did the whistling when we went on the road and sang the song, or if we used a flute player."

In addition to the echoing falsetto tenor behind Wilson's sultry baritone, Johnson also provided the spoken "hello, darling" tag. "Paul did all of the talking things before I got into the group," Terry remembers. "Like, on 'I'll Be Home,' that recitation was Paul. But then, starting with 'Lovers Never Say Goodbye'—'so long darling,' that was me doing all the little talking things."

"Music Maestro Please," with lyrics by Academy Award winner Herb

Magidson (1906–1986) and music by Allie Wrubel (1905–1973), who co-wrote "Zip-A-Dee-Doo-Dah" for Walt Disney's *Song of the South* in 1945, was also a former #1 hit. Tommy Dorsey had scored big with "Music Maestro Please" in 1938. Bandleaders Art Kassel and Kay Kyser also cracked the top five with their own versions. The sextet's romantic interpretation effectively showcased their wide-ranging talents. "Music Maestro Please" offered listeners a pleasant, commercial lead from Tommy Hunt, expertly blended with fine minor chord harmonies from the rest of the group. "They had fantastic harmonies," agrees Hunt.

Backed nicely by some choice four- and five-part harmony patterns, Hunt also led "As Time Goes By," the song immortalized by Dooley Wilson in the 1942 Humphrey Bogart and Ingrid Bergman film *Casablanca*, and the Cole Porter chestnut, "Begin the Beguine." Written by Herman Hupfeld (1894–1951) for the 1931 Broadway musical *Everybody's Welcome*, "As Time Goes By" had been recorded successfully by Rudy Vallee and Jacques Renard and his Orchestra. At the time of the Flamingos' recording, a new version by Johnny Nash was on its way to the national pop charts. A later version, recorded by Jimmy Durante in 1963, introduced the standard to a whole new generation when it was included in the 1993 motion picture *Sleepless in Seattle*.

Porter (1891–1964) wrote "Begin the Beguine" for the 1934 Broadway musical *Jubilee*, where it was introduced by June Knight. A beguine is a vigorous popular dance of the islands of St. Lucia and Martinique resembling the rhumba. Artie Shaw and his Orchestra scored the biggest pop success with the song four years later. Johnson arranged a strong, cascading harmony figure that fit well with Tommy's warm baritone and the steady rhythm section.

For "Where or When," composed by Richard Rodgers (1902–1979) and lyricist Lorenz Hart (1895–1943), the Flamingos selected Paul Wilson to sing lead. Originally a #1 hit for bandleader Hal Kemp, "Where or When" was written for the 1937 Broadway show *Babes in Arms*, which also produced "My Funny Valentine" and "The Lady Is a Tramp."

Hunt returned to the limelight for "The Breeze and I," a Latin standard written in 1928 by Al Stillman and Ernesto Lecuona. Jimmy Dorsey, Xavier Cugat, Vic Damone, and Caterina Valenti had placed versions of the song onto the national bestseller lists between 1940 and 1955. Despite its limited commercial potential, "The Breeze and I" gave the group an opportunity to undertake a series of complex minor key changes, utilizing F sharp, C sharp, and G sharp minors, unlike any other vocal group harmony group.

Little is known about "We Were Made for Each Other" which was recorded at the tail end of the session on the 18th. Goldner never released the song, and Johnson has no memory of the tune. The eleventh and final cut of the two-day date, "Yours," a strong ballad led by Nate Nelson with Jake featured prominently in the backing harmony, brought the proceedings to a fitting end. Adapted from the 1931 Gonzalo Roig–Augustin Rodriguez Spanish language song "Quiéreme Mucho," the tune was given English lyrics by Albert Gamse and Jack Sherr. Dinah Shore, Jimmy Dorsey, Vaughn Monroe, and Benny Goodman all recorded the song during the World War II era.

Eight days later, on Thursday, February 26, the Flamingos were brought back to record one additional song, "River of Tears," which Goldner never released. That week, "Lovers Never Say Goodbye" was selected by *Billboard* as its Territorial Tip for the Philadelphia market, along with Harvey Fuqua's "I Want Somebody." The week of March 2, 1959, the record debuted on the national R&B chart. In just two weeks on the list, it peaked at #25.

There was no mistaking the fact that "Lovers" was a pop record, having earned crossover success during its 10-week stint on *Billboard*'s Hot 100. It was an achievement that opened up a whole new world for the Flamingos in terms of bookings, airplay, and sales. "I feel really honored that 'Lovers Never Say Goodbye,' which was the first song that I wrote and sang with them, crossed over from the rhythm and blues to the pop market," Johnson admits. "The white kids started singing our song, and that was an honor. I really enjoyed that. I was honored by that. You see, when I first got with the Flamingos, they were rhythm and blues only. My influences were the Four Lads, the Four Aces, and the Modernaires. That's what I brought to the table. That influence from those older groups gave us that pop sound. That's what everybody was crazy about with the Flamingos—a new sound."

All of this activity didn't go unnoticed by Leonard Chess, who combed his vaults for a pair of unreleased Flamingos recordings. In late February 1959, he issued the 1956 re-recording of "Dream of a Lifetime," pairing it with the four-year-old master, "Whispering Stars." Reviewed the week of March 2, both sides got a lukewarm reception from reviewers and record buyers. Chess also managed to beat Goldner to the punch in the LP department, issuing the group's first 12-inch disc on Checker in March.

For this, the group's lone self-titled Checker album, Chess selected 12 sides, including five previously unheard songs. The Carter–led "Stolen Love" and "Chickie Um Bah," the re-recording of "If I Can't Have You," now titled "Nobody's Love," both sides of the new single, and two Parrot masters—one of them a previously unreleased alternate take of "On My Merry Way," which was likely selected in error—were included. Although "A Kiss from Your Lips" and "The Vow" were included, Chess inexplicably did not use the group's biggest money-maker, "I'll Be Home," and didn't bother to include a photo of the Flamingos on the front cover.

On March 6, the group was back in the studio with Goldner, recording an upbeat tune geared for the teen audience, "At the Prom." Written by Johnson but credited on the label to Terry and Zeke, the song featured a duet lead sung by the tenor-guitarist and Wilson. Terry also delivered the spoken interlude while Nelson sang the prominent high falsetto tenor in the background. "Zeke had nothing to do with writing 'At the Prom,'" Johnson clarifies. "I don't know how his name got on it. Zeke was notorious for taking credit for stuff he didn't do."

Wednesday, March 25, found the Flamingos in Philadelphia, where they lip-synched "Lovers Never Say Goodbye" for *American Bandstand*'s national television audience. Immediately following their appearance, the sextet flew to Chicago, opening at the Regal Theater on the 27th with Lionel Hampton, Dee Clark, Ben Beri, and Slappy White.

With *Go, Johnny, Go!* opening in selected theaters during the month of April, George Goldner was putting the finishing touches on the 12-track

Lobby card photo of the "Jump Children" performance from the 1959 motion picture *Go, Johnny, Go!* Left to right: Zeke, Nate, Tommy, Jake, Paul, and Terry (author's collection).

For their first End album, George Goldner commissioned a color portrait of the group. Left to right: Zeke, Paul, Jake, Tommy, Terry, and (front) Nate, 1959 (courtesy Terry Johnson).

Flamingo Serenade album. Issued in true stereo, the disc featured a dozen of the great love ballads recorded between October and February. Four songs from the forthcoming album—"I Only Have Eyes for You," "I'm in the Mood for Love," "Music Maestro Please," and "Goodnight Sweetheart"—had been issued on an extended play 45 in March.

Like the two previous End LPs which Goldner had devoted entirely to one act, *Flamingo Serenade* featured an eye-catching color cover that set the mood for the contents within. From left to right, Zeke, Paul, and Jake stood smiling in their finest sky-blue stage tuxedos, right hands outstretched. In the background, Tommy struck a similar pose next to Terry, who sat on a white stool with his electric guitar in hand. In the foreground, Nate sat at a pink cloth-covered table adorned with a pair of lit candles, two champagne glasses, a bottle of bubbly sitting in a silver ice bucket, and a tiny pink flamingo. The Flamingos were riding high.

Riding High

Goldner sent the album out to disc jockeys and waited to see what cut would catch fire before beginning to push a single. "At the Prom" and "Love Walked In" was issued as End #1044 in early April, but George apparently changed his mind soon after. Initially, the group believed "Goodnight Sweetheart" would be the song End promoted. "'Goodnight Sweetheart' was going to be the [A-side of the] release, but the disc jockeys chose 'I Only Have Eyes for You,'" Johnson recalls. "They had both been on the album that came out. The disc jockeys chose that, but there were a number of beautiful songs there."

"We didn't even know which song was going to be chosen from the album to be a single," Jake admitted.

George issued "I Only Have Eyes for You" in late April, tacking "Goodnight Sweetheart" onto the flip side for good measure. Although "Eyes" only got a three-out-of-four-star rating from *Billboard* the week of May 4, it took off immediately. The week of the 25th, it was the magazine's Territorial Tip in the Philadelphia market. In its May 16 issue, *Cash Box* selected the disc a Pick of the Week, predicting the standard was "a good bet to make the chart rounds once again. This time it's dressed up with an intriguing rock-a-ballad outfit with jazz overtones supplied by the Flamingos. Lead voice softly carves out the extremely pretty set of lyrics while the rest of the crew weaves a haunting mood with their 'du-bop-shu-bop' interjections. The kids in both the R&B and pop marts are gonna hop on this one real [sic] quick."

One week later, on June 1, "I Only Have Eyes for You" entered the national pop chart. Seven days later, it was inside the Top 40. Radio stations from coast to coast, including Los Angeles powerhouse KFWB, selected the record as their "Pick of the Week." Once again, the crossover appeal of the material, and the shift in the way radio and television programs showcased African American performers and their work, brought the Flamingos in contact with a larger and more diverse audience than ever before. "By then, the recording industry was fast becoming a big business," Nate Nelson remembered. "It was pretty well known what you could do. We hoped for them to be hits during those days. It was also getting to the point where black artists' music was getting played nationwide on all the radio stations. Of course, they weren't during the Chance [and] Checker days unless it was by black dee-jays or black stations, so we were limited. [But] in the mid to late 1950s, because of more exposure of the black music artists, we did realize our chances for success were greater than ever before."

All told, "I Only Have Eyes for You" spent 13 weeks on the Hot 100 and 11 inside the Top 40, where it peaked at #11. On June 15, it reached the R&B list, peaking at #3 during a 13-week stint. The record was issued and distrib-uted worldwide, even climbing to #32 on the Australian charts. "That one, nobody could mess with," Zeke proudly recounted. "Even those who tried years later could [not] top that. We put our signature on that. It really was the Flamingos' national anthem. For a long time, we refused to tell anybody what we were singing in 'I Only Have Eyes for You.' All we're actually saying is 'doo-bop-shoo-bop.'"

"Dick Clark used to ask us that on *American Bandstand*, and we wouldn't tell him," Terry agrees. "We'd say 'You have to catch it,' and we'd sing it, you know. At the Apollo, and black theaters that we were playing, we'd say 'ham hocks,' 'collard greens,' you know, things like that. Anything dumb, because people really couldn't figure out what we were saying at first."

No fewer than four 45 RPM varia-tions of the record were issued on End in 1959. The original gray-label pressing was followed by a multicolored label on styrene plastic. Since he owned the publishing, Goldner substituted "At the Prom" for the origi-nal B-side, "Good-night Sweetheart," on the third variation of End #1046. On the final ver-sion released, "Love Walked In" was the flip side. Of the four, the initial gray-label issue with "Goodnight, Sweetheart" on the flip side typically commands the highest prices today. End also

Multicolor second pressing of the group's signature hit, 1959 (author's collection).

pressed a limited quantity of "Eyes" on 78 RPM. Today, these rarities sell in the $300 to $500 range in online auctions.

On Saturday, July 11, 1959, the Flamingos appeared live on ABC-TV's *The Dick Clark Show* in New York to perform "Lovers" and "Eyes." They were joined on the bill by Connie Francis, Anita Bryant and Dick Caruso. That month, the group performed at the Uptown Theater in Philadelphia as part of a 10-day extravaganza with Ray Peterson, the Fiestas, Dee Clark, the Drifters, Chubby Checker, Jerry Butler, and others. "The [Flamingos] were so good that you paid once through the front door, and sneaked in the back door to see it the second time," Butler told a PBS audience in 2003. "I'm telling you that these people were just absolutely wonderful. They would just dance and sing and the harmony was so marvelous. I remember at the Uptown Theater, I was standing on [the side of the] stage watching them. I said, 'I'm not going on after these guys. They're not going to leave that stage that hot for me!'"

"There was another black act on too," Hunt recalled in a 1982 interview. "Jesse Belvin. Jesse and the Flamingos were on it. We were all laid back. He used to sit and talk with me. He said, 'All this is all right, the rock 'n' roll thing, but I want a bit of class.' He was a hell of a good singer. Everybody respected Jesse as a singer. Then we found out that Jesse was going down the highway with his wife [and was killed less than seven months later] and we started getting a little bit worried. It's something strange. See, I'm one of those people who takes it to heart, and it hurts bad because friendship means a lot to me, a hell of a lot."

Following Leonard Chess's lead, Decca Records began scouring their vaults for unissued Flamingos masters in the spring of 1959 in an attempt to earn some quick cash. In May, "Ever Since I Met Lucy" and "Kiss-A-Me" became the group's fourth Decca release. "Hey Now!" and "Jerri-Lee" followed in July. Both records received a well-deserved indifferent response.

With *Go, Johnny, Go!* playing at New York's Loew's Theater, Goldner selected another pair of ballads from *Flamingo Serenade* to comprise the next End single. "Love Walked In," which had been issued twice before as a B-side, and "Yours" received excellent reviews in *Billboard* the week of August 17, 1959. On October 5, "Love Walked In" spent the first of three weeks on the national pop chart, where it peaked at #88.

That fall, the Flamingos embarked on a Southern tour, promoting their latest release and basking in the glow of their recent string of hits. September 15 found them at the Ebony Club in Houston. On September 27, they appeared at the Aristocrat Club in New Orleans with Professor Longhair. While the group still made appearances at the major urban theaters, Zeke

Carey recalled that the group's hit records put them in demand for full-scale tours and supper club dates. "Now, we talked about a different level of night club," he told interviewer McGarvey, "[and] the promoters want us for tours because of the charts. The theaters were more promotional to break the records. [In] the theaters, the disc jockey calls up, 'Can you do me a favor?' 'We did you four or five favors before!'"

In an attempt to become more self-sufficient and compete with groups like their friends, the Treniers, who were enormously successful with the supper club crowds, the Flamingos worked to make themselves self-contained. "The Treniers weren't into what the doo-wop groups were into," Hunt explained to McGarvey. "They were more or less a new version of the Mills Brothers. They were more of a class act. They worked Las Vegas, Lake Tahoe. They did the big business. They didn't have big records. No hits, but they had a big name. All the doo-wop groups that knew them wanted to be like them. A lot of the doo-wop groups came out of the church and created excitement, but some groups wanted to go class. They weren't worried about cutting rock 'n' roll records. They wanted to make the big money. I used to ask the Treniers, 'Why don't you make more records?' They'd say, 'What for? We're making more money than you are!' They had big homes, big flashy cars, money in the bank, and they worked Europe. I saw they had a reason there."

"[The Flamingos] needed a bass player, so I practiced endless hours," Zeke recalled. With Terry on guitar, Zeke on bass, Tommy playing piano and Nate sitting behind the drum kit, the Flamingos were able to work as a self-contained unit for a short period of time. "That didn't last too long," Johnson admits. "Because Nate was good, but he said, 'I can't sing and play the drums, too.' Tommy couldn't really play piano. He could, you know, tinkle, tinkle, tinkle, but he didn't know his chords. He knew what he taught himself, but he didn't know anything about piano. We were good for a while. There were certain songs that we could play."

On Tuesday, October 20, the group returned to New York for a marathon recording session at the Old Regent Sound studios, near the Carnegie Deli on 56th Street, which produced a total of seven sides, three of which were written by Terry Johnson. For the first time, Goldner brought in a full string section to back the Flamingos. "When we used strings, it was done live," Johnson explains. "Mistakes had to go. If it was a good take and there was a mistake in it, tough."

Veteran trumpeter, arranger, and producer Sammy Lowe (1918–1993) was brought in by Goldner to arrange and conduct the orchestra. A charter member of the Alabama Jazz Hall of Fame, the Birmingham-born Lowe spent 22 years arranging and composing for Erskine Hawkins's big band. He had

Promoting a self-contained lineup in 1960. Clockwise from bottom left: Zeke (bass), Tommy (piano), Paul, Jake, Terry (guitar) and Nate (drums) (Maurice Seymour photograph, courtesy Terry Johnson).

also worked with artists including Cab Calloway, Lucky Millinder, Laura "I've Got a Right to Cry" Washington, Sammy Davis, Jr., and Sy Oliver. Based in Teaneck, New Jersey, Lowe orchestrated the Platters' "My Prayer" in 1956, and arranged dozens of hits through the 1960s and early 1970s including "Sad Mood" for Sam Cooke, James Brown's "It's a Man's, Man's, Man's World," the

Tokens' "The Lion Sleeps Tonight," "You Can Have Her" for Roy Hamilton, Sylvia's "Pillow Talk," and the Moments' "Sexy Mama." Fellow trumpeter Al Hirt called Lowe "the best arranger in the business."

"I Was Such a Fool (To Fall in Love with You)," written by Michael Raymond Canosa and Danny Stradella, was the first song committed to tape. Goldner had previously recorded the song by a vocal group called the Five Budds and released it as Rama issue #1 in 1953. The song was later a pop Top 30 hit for Connie Francis in the fall of 1962. The Flamingos' rendition had hit potential, with Nelson's silky lead and the group's smooth harmony suitably augmented by the violins and fiddles. Terry Johnson wrote the raucous "Heavenly Angel," which featured Tommy Hunt and Zeke Carey singing a rare duet lead with an arrangement that would be revisited when the group tackled a Sam Cooke composition four months later. "You, Me, and the Sea," another romantic Terry Johnson ballad, was given the lush treatment by Goldner as Nelson and Hunt shared the spotlight.

The next song committed to tape was "Mio Amore." "For that song, George Goldner sat me down and said, 'I want a follow up to "I Only Have Eyes for You,"'" Johnson explains. "He trusted me. He said, 'I want you to change the chords around and do something else with it. I want a romantic thing. I want you to say something about love.' In English, it is 'My Love.' In Italian, it is 'Mio Amore.' I taught it to the guys. They loved it, and so we did it." On the same plane as "I Only Have Eyes for You," "Mio Amore" featured an expressive, soulful lead from Nelson, haunting, echoed harmonies from the group, and the familiar piano triplets. The song undeniably possessed all the hooks necessary to create a first-rate follow-up to their previous monster hit.

Although Johnson wrote the song alone, all six members of the group shared the songwriting credit on the copyright. "Now, I'm going to tell you the real deal," Johnson explains bitterly. "Zeke made me give everybody a piece of 'Mio Amore.' Now, my name was the only one on the songs when I first got with them. How come everybody's name is on 'Mio Amore'? Zeke said, 'Buzzy, you're doing too many songs. You're writing too many songs. This is a corporation. We're partners, and in our partnership, we split the money six ways. We split our cars and our clothes this way. So, from now on, anybody else that writes songs, it has to involve the whole group.' He thought I was going to get really, really rich because of what 'Eyes' had done for us. I said, 'Well, I don't care, man. It doesn't matter to me. That's cool.'" Fifty years after the fact, the composer remained angered by the deed. "I wrote 'Mio Amore.' Zeke said I had to give it to everybody. I had to share it. Isn't that unfair? And I did it like a fool."

"We always believed in organization," Zeke explained when discussing the Flamingos as a business. "We believed in parliamentary procedure, more or less a 'majority rules' type of thing. I was elected president. A lot of times, a lot of the decisions were made just because this was what the majority agreed upon. That was it."

"Dream Girl," a #2 R&B hit written and recorded by friend Jesse Belvin and his partner, Marvin Phillips, as "Jesse & Marvin" for Specialty Records in late 1952, was resurrected by the group for this date as well. Zeke and Paul delivered a duet lead that was passable, but lacked the raw charm of the original. Another 1953 R&B chart hit, the Five Royales' "Crazy Crazy Crazy," penned by the group's bass singer and principal songwriter Lowman Pauling, was given the Flamingos treatment, with Johnson and Hunt sharing the lead over a pulsing piano accompaniment.

Closing out the session was the group's first attempt at Shirley Cowell's ballad, "Never in This World," led, for the most part, by Nelson. Dissatisfied with the result, Goldner shelved the finished master and tried recording it again seven months later.

On November 20, 1959, they began a week at the Apollo in Harlem as part of disc jockey Jocko Henderson's Rocketship Revue with Little Anthony and the Imperials, the Five Satins, and the Isley Brothers. "We would do 'Eyes' and be called for an encore because 'Eyes' was so big," Terry fondly remembers. "We'd come back and do 'Jump Children' and just tear the place down. We were always next to the closing act."

Late that month, End issued "I Was Such a Fool (To Fall in Love with You)" and "Heavenly Angel," with the A-side earning a four-star review from *Billboard*'s reviewer the week of December 7, noting the record was "a pretty ballad with warmth over full string backing with a sound that can happen." On January 25, 1960, the record spent the first of six weeks on the Hot 100, where it peaked at #71.

The Flamingos, meanwhile, continued touring the country, starting the year off in the Midwest. January found them at the Copa Club in Newport, Kentucky. Curiously, Goldner released the Johnson compositions "Mio Amore" and "You, Me and the Sea" as End #1065 in January, but didn't push the disc, concentrating instead on "I Was Such a Fool," which was climbing the charts. Both sides of the new record would be reissued later in the year.

In February, the sextet returned home to New York to prepare for three days of recording at the Old Regent Sound studios. Goldner brought Sammy Lowe back to handle the orchestral arrangements for an 11-song date that took place on the 15th, 16th, and 17th. Bob Lifton served as the session engi-

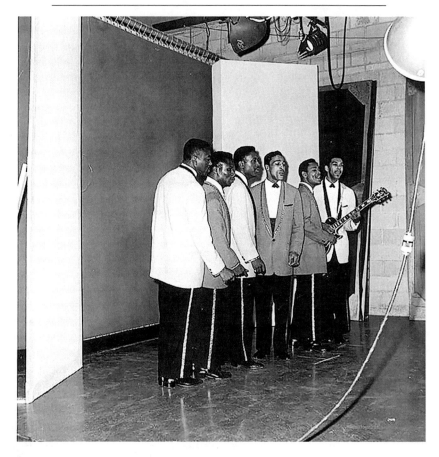

Left to right: Zeke, Jake, Nate, Tommy, Paul, and Terry in front of the lights and cameras, Phoenix, Arizona, 1960 (courtesy Terry Johnson).

neer. The first song tackled, and the one the group was most enthusiastic about, was an up-tempo tune penned by R&B/pop superstar, Sam Cooke. "'Nobody Loves Me Like You' was written for us by Sam Cooke," Nelson recalled. "It turned out to be the best thing on that particular recording session."

"Sam was our buddy," Johnson adds. "He was from Chicago, too. I met him through the guys, and we clicked instantly. I said, 'Show me how you do some of them runs, man, 'woah woah a-woah-a-wo-oh.' We just took a liking to each other. I said, 'Sam, write us one of those songs that you do, you know, like 'You Send Me.' Nate was there, too, and he said, 'Yeah, man, write us a song.' We waited and we waited, and we'd see Sam in other places, and he'd say, 'I'm writing it. Don't worry about it. I'm writing it.' Then we were at the

Regal Theater in Chicago. He said, 'Give me your guitar, Buzzy. I've got it.' He played it, and we liked it. We didn't have that many fast songs as it was. We were balladeers. It was nice and George Goldner liked it, and it was pretty big for us, too."

Produced and arranged by Jerry Leiber and Mike Stoller, the Drifters' "There Goes My Baby" may have indeed been the first R&B/rock 'n' roll hit to utilize a string section when it hit the top of the charts in the summer of 1959. By the time the Flamingos went to work on "Nobody Loves Me Like You," the Drifters had reached the Top 40 three more times with "Save The Last Dance for Me," "Dance with Me," and "True Love, True Love," all of which paired soaring strings with soulful vocals. The group's latest release, "This Magic Moment," continued the trend. Clearly in tune with what was selling, Sammy Lowe wrote a crisp string chart that sprang from the opening grooves of the record. Cooke's commercial songwriting skill and soulful attitude were imprinted all over "Nobody Loves Me Like You." Nelson delivered Sam's lyrics with confidence and style, aptly aided by Johnson's harmonic tenor and electric guitar.

"Besame Mucho," a Mexican song written by teenager Consuelo Velazquez in 1940, was inspired by an aria from a Spanish opera by Enrique Granados. English lyrics were written by Sunny Skylar, and the song became an international standard after Jimmy Dorsey scored a #1 hit with it in 1944. The Ray-O-Vacs hit the R&B chart with their version of the song in the fall of 1950. Given the big ballad treatment by Tommy Hunt, "Besame Mucho" (in translation, "Kiss Me a Lot") benefited from an exotic, Latin-flavored arrangement and towering crescendo. Eleven days after the Flamingos recorded "Besame Mucho," the Coasters recorded the song in two parts for Atco Records. Their Part 1 version cracked *Billboard*'s pop Hot 100 in May.

A beautiful ballad composed by Clifton Wayne Morris, "At Night" was given the royal treatment when the Flamingos tackled it at this session. The first song ever recorded by Sonny Til and the Orioles, "At Night" drew rave reviews despite its failure to chart when Jubilee first released it in 1950. Nelson delivered an impassioned reading, backed by stellar harmonies and simple but effective strings. "Nate was Sonny Til's cousin, but we didn't look at it that way when we recorded 'At Night,'" Johnson explains. "It was just a beautiful song."

Terry was tabbed to sing lead on "When I Fall in Love," another romantic ballad, which had been made into a top 20 hit by Doris Day in 1952. The song was a collaborative effort between Victor Young, who composed standards including "I Don't Stand a Ghost of a Chance," "My Foolish Heart," "Love Letters," and "Three Coins in the Fountain," and Edward Heyman (1907–

1981), a Songwriters Hall of Fame inductee who also penned "Body and Soul." First introduced in the film *One Minute to Zero*, the song was recorded by Nat "King" Cole in 1956 for his *Love Is the Thing* LP and became a top 10 hit for the Lettermen in 1962.

Johnson played and sang the introduction solo before the rest of the group offered up a tight, cascading harmony pattern that drew rave reviews from fellow performers and vocal group harmony fans alike. "That was just beautiful," Harptones' arranger and composer Raoul J. Cita remarked. "Their harmony on the 'forever and ever and ever' part was fantastic."

New York African American singer-songwriter Billy Myles, who wrote the Mello-Kings' "Tonite Tonite," the Dubs' "Chapel of Dreams," and his own 1957 hit, "The Joker," submitted "That's Why I Love You," which Terry arranged for Paul Wilson to lead. The baritone delivered an impassioned lead over an emotive background chant that easily fit the Flamingos' standards in terms of style and quality.

Nelson led "Bridge of Tears," a bluesy number written by singer-songwriter-producer J.W. Alexander (1916–1996), who was also Sam Cooke's business partner. Johnson recalls Alexander bringing the song to the Flamingos in the hope they would record it. Cooke himself subsequently recorded a version of the tune in 1964 for his album *Try a Little Love*. Stepping to the lead microphone next was Hunt, who complemented soaring strings and harmonies with his uninhibited performance of "In the Still of the Night." Written by Cole Porter for the 1937 MGM film *Rosalie*, the song was a top-three hit for Tommy Dorsey's Orchestra that year. Dion and the Belmonts turned it into a top 40 hit again in the summer of 1960, but their version failed to capture the full-throated magic that highlighted the Flamingos' rendition.

"Tenderly," another standard, was arranged for Wilson to lead. Written by Walter Lloyd Gross (1909–1967) and lyricist Jack Lawrence (1912–2009) in 1946, the ballad was a top 20 hit for Rosemary Clooney in 1952 and eventually became her theme song. In his 90s, Lawrence vividly recounted the song's conception. "One day in 1946, I ran into an old friend, Margaret Whiting, at a publisher's office. Maggie and I had known each other for some time; when I lived on the West Coast, I visited her home often. One Sunday, I brought a new arrival to Tinseltown along to Maggie's, Rosemary Clooney, who had just been signed by Paramount. Maggie asked me if I knew Walter Gross. I didn't know him personally but was aware of his fame as a pianist. At that time, he was working for a small record label, Musicraft. Maggie told me that Walter had written a fantastic tune that just cried out for a lyric, and that I was the one who should write it. She picked up the phone, called Walter and said she would like to bring me to his office and introduce us. I fell in love with [the melody] at once and asked Walter for a lead sheet. He scratched one out and gave it to me—I thought, reluctantly. It was almost as though he was parting with a precious part of himself. I could not get that melody out of my head and, as has happened on rare occasions, a lyric began to form itself inside me," recalled Lawrence, who also penned the lyrics for "If I Didn't Care," "All or Nothing at All," and "Beyond the Sea." "In a couple of days, I had not only come up with the title, but had finished the lyric."

After about 10 days, Lawrence phoned Gross. "Mustering great excitement in my voice, I said, 'Walter, I've got it!' He asked, 'What's the title?' 'Tenderly.' There was a protracted silence, and then Walter said, scathingly, 'That's no title! That's what you put at the top of the sheet music. Play tenderly!' Certainly, I was let down, but I asked if I could mail him the lyric for his consideration." Several months went by before Gross, who had turned down lyrics for the melody from various writers, selected Lawrence's "Tenderly." "The first vocal recording was by Sarah Vaughan and the first instrumental was by Randy Brooks," the lyricist explained. "Those were in 1946. Bit by bit, the song began to accumulate recordings, and it was establishing itself as a musician's jazz piece. 'Tenderly' was unstoppable. But it wasn't until the early '50s that it truly reached great stature when Rosie Clooney recorded it with true simplicity. No vocal tricks, just the pure melody and words."

Again, Lowe's string arrangements, the group's five-part harmonies, and Wilson's lead blended well to create a faithful interpretation of the standard. "Today there are about 150 records of this song, with new ones coming all the time," Lawrence proudly recounted in 2006. "I'm sorry to say that I have not heard the Flamingos' recording of 'Tenderly.' I gave up buying every version that was released over the years. There were just too many to keep track of."

Tommy Hunt sang lead on the next two recordings, "You'll Never Walk Alone" and "Everybody's Got a Home (But Me)." Although both were penned by Broadway legends Richard Rodgers and Oscar Hammerstein II (1895–1960), it was the powerful R&B-pop balladeer Roy Hamilton who inspired Hunt and the Flamingos to take on these two grand productions. The Georgia-born Hamilton (1929–1969) grew up in New Jersey and scored fifteen nationally charted hits between 1954 and 1961, influencing an array of artists from Elvis Presley to Jackie Wilson with his classically trained operatic baritone.

Recording for Epic Records, Hamilton burst onto the scene in early 1954 with his rendition of "You'll Never Walk Alone," which spent eight weeks at #1 on *Billboard*'s R&B chart and rose to #21 on the pop list. Originally written for the 1945 musical *Carousel*, the song gained immediate and overwhelming popularity with theatergoers who had been separated from their loved ones due to the war. Frank Sinatra scored the first charted hit with "You'll Never

Walk Alone," taking it inside the top ten that year. Although later versions by Gerry and the Pacemakers, Patti LaBelle, and Elvis Presley would make the bestseller lists around the world, it was Hamilton's powerful recording that drew Hunt to the song.

Similarly, Tommy selected "Everybody's Got a Home (But Me)," which had come from the 1955 Broadway musical *Pipe Dream*, Rodgers and Hammerstein's only financial failure. Eddie Fisher hit the pop top 20 with it in late 1955 and early '56, besting Hamilton's version, which stalled out at #42. Both songs required a powerful, affected performance, a task that Hunt pulled off well. "Tommy was doing all the big songs, like Roy Hamilton, 'You'll Never Walk Alone,' 'Everybody's Got a Home (But Me),' you know, big songs," Johnson confirms. "Tommy had a big voice."

Johnson and Wilson also sang a duet lead on "You Belong to My Heart," which featured both English and Spanish lyrics and a recitation from Tommy Hunt. Composed by Augustin Lara as "Solamente Una Vez" ("Only One Time"), the tune initially appeared in an Argentinian musical comedy film, *Melodias de America,* in 1941. In 1944, Ray Gilbert wrote new English lyrics to the melody, titled "You Belong to My Heart," and it was sung by Dora Luz in the Walt Disney film *The Three Caballeros.* Bing Crosby and the Xavier Cugat Orchestra and Charlie Spivak's Orchestra both recorded hit versions of "You Belong to My Heart" in 1945.

Eugene Roland (1921–1982), a skilled arranger, composer, and musician who spent the bulk of his career with Stan Kenton's band, wrote the dreamy "Every Time I Think of You." With Nelson leading, the song became the 12th commercial master produced in the three-day marathon session. One additional title, "Happy Birthday Elise," is listed on Goldner's surviving log. This was likely recorded as a favor for the producer and never intended for commercial release. Johnson has no memory of this "Happy Birthday" recording.

Two days after the session concluded, the Flamingos were back on stage at the Apollo, appearing for a week as part of "Dr. Jive's Rhythm and Blues Revue," along with Johnny Nash, Tiny Topsy, Nappy Brown, the Hollywood Flames, and Barrett Strong. On Friday and Saturday, March 11–12, they performed at the Lindenwood Inn in Philadelphia, plugging "Nobody Loves Me Like You," which Goldner had just coupled with "Besame Mucho." In its March 14 edition, *Billboard* wrote, "The group gives 'Besame Mucho' an infectious, stylized reading that should catch on quickly. 'Nobody Loves Me Like You' is a ballad cleffed by Sam Cooke, and this also gets a sock delivery." This time, however, it was the up-tempo side that caught on. On April 18, "Nobody" spent the first of ten weeks on the *Billboard* Hot 100.

Although some have written that the Flamingos had opted for a change of pace with the up-tempo "Nobody Loves Me Like You," Nate Nelson felt it was simply disc jockey and record buyer preference that had kept the group's previous fast songs from making the national charts. "Actually, this was nothing unusual for us," Nelson told Jones in 1979. "We always had an up-tempo and a ballad side on most of our releases. The ballads just seemed to be the ones that took off. We didn't plan it that way."

Realizing that Atco had released "Besame Mucho" by the Coasters at the same time, Goldner and Ahmet Ertegun came to an understanding, reported in the March 21 issue of *Billboard*, whereby End would change the flip side until the Coasters' hit had run its course and, in turn, Ertegun would encourage distributors to support both his own offering and the Flamingos' "Nobody Loves Me Like You."

Second and third pressings of "Nobody Loves Me Like You," which appeared later in 1960 on the white and multicolored End labels, substituted "You, Me, and the Sea" for "Besame Mucho," since Goldner owned the publishing on the Johnson original. Later, in the spring, Goldner paired the two B-sides, "Besame Mucho" and "You, Me, and the Sea."

On Monday, May 16, 1960, the group returned to the recording studio for another five-song session. Sticking with the standards, Terry Johnson and Tommy Hunt sang a duet lead on "Maria Elena," a Latin-flavored cha-cha written by Lorenzo Barcelata in the early 1930s and popularized by Jimmy Dorsey and his Orchestra in 1941. The song's English lyrics were written by S.K. "Bob" Russell, the writer who similarly translated "Time Was."

Next up was "Sweet and Lovely," originally a #1 hit for its composer, bandleader Gus Arnheim (1887–1955), who is best remembered today for launching the career of crooner Bing Crosby. Guy Lombardo, Ben Bernie, and R&B bandleader Joe Liggins also enjoyed national hits with the song in the '30s and '40s. Crosby himself charted with another version in 1941. Two years before Nino Tempo and April Stevens scored their first Hot 100 hit with the tune, the Flamingos offered their rendition. Paul Wilson provided the opening recitation and delivered the lead over a hovering flute accompaniment. "I thought Paul did a hell of a job on that," Terry opines. "He was really terrific."

Goldner kept the folks at Warner Chappell Music happy by selecting the Oscar-nominated ballad "My Foolish Heart" next, the third straight song to come from the publishing giant's catalog. The title song from a romantic 1949 film starring Dana Andrews and Susan Hayward, "My Foolish Heart" was written by 12-time Oscar-nominated lyricist Ned Washington (1901–1976) and Victor Young (1899–1956). One of America's preeminent motion picture composers, Young received 22 Academy Award nominations during a 20-

year career that saw his work showcased in over 300 films. Sadly, Young's only Oscar triumph came for *Around the World in 80 Days* in March of 1957, four months after his death from a cerebral hemorrhage.

Gordon Jenkins had the biggest pop chart success with "My Foolish Heart," taking it to #3 in 1950, 13 years before the Dimensions, a Bronx vocal group, hit #95 with a pleasant pop reading. In the hands of Nate Nelson and the Flamingos, the song was every bit as tender, the group's lush harmonies guided primarily throughout by Johnson's gentle guitar chords.

A second, successful attempt was made at "Never in This World," which had first been tried at the October 1959 date that produced "Mio Amore." The ballad featured Nelson up front, in addition to a tight, minor-chord unison lead and string accents. "Tell Me How Long," a pleasant "rock-a-ballad," featured Johnson and Wilson on a duet lead that took Terry to the upper reaches of his falsetto tenor.

The End log book lists a subsequent recording date of Sunday, May 22, 1960, but it was likely used for overdubbing or album mastering only, as the Flamingos were in the midst of a weeklong gig at the Tivoli Theater, located on Cottage Grove near 63rd Street in Chicago. From the 20th through the 26th, they performed with Sam Cooke, the Crests, Stu & Oscar, Rose Hardaway, and the Red Saunders band. Cooke and the Flamingos celebrated the success of "Nobody Loves Me Like You," which debuted on both *Billboard*'s R&B and pop Top 40 charts that week. In three weeks on the R&B list, the record peaked at #23. In the crossover market, the disc climbed to #30. On Wednesday, June 1, the Flamingos were back in Philadelphia, performing their latest hit on *American Bandstand*.

From there, the group worked their way back to New York, where they opened for a week with Dr. Jive at the Apollo Theatre in Harlem on June 24. Although some writers have previously claimed that the group shared the bill with master bluesman Sonny Boy Williamson, it was actually Apollo Amateur Night winner Sonny Boy Williams who joined them on the bill, along with Marv Johnson, the Five Satins, the Three Georgettes, the Carousels, Bertha Green, Tiny Topsy, and the Reuben Phillips band.

Later that spring, Goldner also released the group's second long-playing album, a 12-track disc titled *Flamingo Favorites*. Rather than use a picture of the group on its cover, the label owner opted for a posed photo of eight well-dressed white teenagers "enjoying" a record listening party in a suburban living room setting. "George Goldner could not get certain white stations to play *Flamingo Serenade*, so he knew he could probably get more stations to play the following albums [without a photo of the group]," Johnson explains. The LP was culled from masters recorded at the October 1959 and February and May 1960 sessions and included both "Mio Amore" and "Besame Mucho." "Maria Elena," "Dream Girl," "Sweet and Lovely," "Crazy, Crazy, Crazy," "Tell Me How Long," "That's Why I Love You," "My Foolish Heart," "Heavenly Angel," "You Belong to My Heart," and "Bridge of Tears" comprised the remainder of the tracks.

Goldner began pushing "Mio Amore" that month, pairing it with "At Night" as End #1073. On July 18, it spent the first of six weeks on the *Billboard* Hot 100, where it reached #74. On Tuesday afternoon, August 23, the sextet returned to *American Bandstand*, lip-synching the song. One week later, it debuted on the national R&B chart, peaking at #27 during a three-week stay.

On Tuesday, September 13, 1960, the group recorded a string-heavy version of "Beside You," a 1952 R&B top 10 hit for Terry's old Baltimore friends, the Swallows. Herman "Junior" Denby led the original in his cool Charles Brown–styled lead. For the Flamingos' version, Johnson stepped to the mike, delivering a smooth lead, adding a romantic recitation and soulful Sam Cooke-inspired licks. End issued the song, backed with another Johnson-led tune, "When I Fall in Love," that fall.

Five weeks later, on Thursday, October 20, Goldner produced a three-song session that gave the Flamingos the opportunity to revisit three of their earlier hits. The first, "Ko Ko Mo," featured Wilson and Nelson, who reprised the duet lead he had done with Carter six years earlier. The real gems of the date were the full orchestral arrangements of the Checker classics, "A Kiss from Your Lips" and "I'll Be Home." Both versions ran between 3:45 and 4:10, entirely too long to gain pop radio airplay at the time, but well-suited as album fillers. "They were album cuts," agrees Johnson. "Nate really just wanted them done in a lower key, because his voice cracked on the original 'I'll Be Home' cut, and he almost cracked on the original 'Kiss from Your Lips.' He wanted them done in a lower key. So I lowered the keys, and he was very comfortable with them, but they went on too long." Nevertheless, the End versions of "I'll Be Home" and "A Kiss from Your Lips," both taken at a slightly slower tempo than the originals, were every inch as beautiful as the renditions that inspired them. Inexplicably, Goldner chose to keep them on the shelf, and they remained unreleased until their inclusion in a 1992 Collectables double CD package.

With a pair of pink Flamingos gracing the cover, Goldner packaged 12 of the group's 1959–60 masters on End LP 308, *Requestfully Yours*, in October. The group's current best seller, "Nobody Loves Me Like You" was included, along with an array of standards including "In the Still of the Night," "Tenderly," and "When I Fall in Love," the Orioles and Swallows inspired "At Night" and "Beside You," Johnson's "You, Me and the Sea," and Hunt's renditions of the Roy Hamilton classics, " Everybody's Got a Home (But Me)" and "You'll Never Walk Alone."

Wednesday and Thursday, November 2–3, the Flamingos returned to the recording studio to tackle a pair of brand-new compositions from the hot songwriting team of Doc Pomus and Mort Shuman. Pomus (1925–1991) was born Jerome Felder in Brooklyn and began his career playing saxophone and shouting the blues in Greenwich Village nightclubs. After a handful of unsuccessful solo recordings on a variety of labels, Pomus switched from singer to full-time songwriter after achieving his first hit with Big Joe Turner's "Boogie Woogie Country Girl" in 1956. Over the next several years, Pomus collaborated on a number of national bestsellers, including Ray Charles's "Lonely Avenue" and "Young Blood" by the Coasters.

In 1958, Pomus formed a songwriting partnership with Shuman (1936–1991), a fellow Brooklyn native who had studied at the New York Conservatory and played piano on some of Pomus's recordings. Working a number of publishers, often Hill & Range or their subsidiaries, Pomus and Shuman plied their trade out of an office in the famed Brill Building at 1619 Broadway. In most instances, Pomus wrote the lyrics, and Shuman composed the music. Early on, the duo hit with Dion and the Belmonts' "A Teenager in Love," the Mystics' "Hushabye," and several of Fabian's pop chart hits. The week of the Flamingos' session, Pomus and Shuman held the #1 spot on *Billboard*'s R&B chart with the Drifters' "Save the Last Dance for Me," a record that had already spent three weeks atop the pop chart.

"I remember we went up to 1650 Broadway where End Records and all the real record labels were," Johnson recalls. "We went into one of the offices, and Doc and Mort were there, and they showed us the song, 'Your Other Love.' It was a good song. We were excited about it because the Drifters were hot', and they had strings and everything with 'There Goes My Baby.' I think George got in touch with them for us. Tommy sang lead on that. I had structured everybody. Nate was doing all the beautiful leads by himself, and he did [the flip side] 'Lovers Gotta Cry.'"

At the same time, the group decided to pass on another new Pomus-Shuman composition called "Kiss Me Quick." "The Flamingos had a really great hit with 'I Only Have Eyes for You,'" Shuman related to interviewer Trevor Cajiao. "We wrote ['Kiss Me Quick'] for them, but they had the good taste not to do it." Music publisher Freddy Bienstock, who often obtained material from the duo, submitted "Kiss Me Quick" and two additional Pomus-Shuman compositions, "His Latest Flame" and "Little Sister," to Elvis Presley for consideration. "We didn't have to have too many exclusive writers, and we didn't need to, as everybody wanted a record with Elvis," Bienstock recalled to a Japanese interviewer. "Pomus and Shuman were very prolific. We expected them to bring us songs every week, and they often developed a relationship with particular artists." Elvis recorded all three of the songs in June of 1961. "Kiss Me Quick" was issued on the B-side of "Suspicion," another Pomus-Shuman tune, in 1964 and subsequently reached the lower rungs of the pop Top 40. "'Kiss Me Quick' was probably the worst song I ever wrote for Elvis," Shuman candidly admitted.

Excited with his finished product, Goldner had issued "Your Other Love" and "Lovers Gotta Cry" as a single by the end of November 1960. Although none of those involved knew it at the time, the session that produced the record would be the last one to feature Tommy Hunt, Terry Johnson, and Nate Nelson as members of the Flamingos.

Crossroads

Returning to the road, the Flamingos played an extended engagement at the Town House in Pittsburgh in December of 1960 just as "Your Other Love" began its ascent onto the national charts. The disc cracked the Hot 100 on December 19 and, in five weeks on the list, peaked at #54. After completing their obligations in Pennsylvania, the group traveled to Washington, D.C., for a 10-day stint at the Howard that included New Year's Day, 1961.

A February 11, 1961, story in the *Chicago Defender* reported that the Flamingos "recently turned down some $40,000 worth of bookings because to take engagements would have interfered with the group's observance of Hebrew holidays." The Careys, the newspaper stated, called Joe Glaser at Associated Booking in New York to inform him that the group had to pass up a lucrative one-month date at the Flamingo in Las Vegas, since the final week of the engagement extended into April, coinciding with Passover. "Strongly religious in their daily lives, the Flamingos frequently retreat to a Hebrew temple at Belleville, Virginia, a short distance from Portsmouth and Norfolk," the story reported. "Current remodeling and renovation of the temple, estimated to cost upwards of $40,000, is being done with funds donated by the vocalists. Two cousins, Jake and Ezekiel Carey, are the biggest contributors to the temple building fund."

"They did that way back in the days," Fletcher Weatherspoon confirmed. "Now, a lot of entertainers do it because they're making so much money. A lot of them do it for a tax-deductible item. They did it from their heart."

Terry Johnson, however, recalls that the decision to pay for the temple with the group's money was made without the consent of the other members. "We didn't know anything about the temple front until it was already done. We received $10,000 from George Goldner which was broken down into a $1,000 per man payment. The rest went to down payments on our two cars, a green Cadillac with pink flamingos embroidered on the seats, and a green Buick station wagon for our clothes and equipment. Zeke and Jake continued to take money off the top of our gig money to pay for those cars. Whenever it was time to split the cost of something, Zeke would say we were partners and everyone should help pay. That meant that we were part owners. What we started to notice was, if we were splitting the rest of the money evenly, as we were being told, then where did Jake, and especially Zeke, get the money to buy all the suits that they were suddenly wearing? At the time, none of us could afford to buy that many suits. And where did the thousands of dollars for the temple front come from? My parents, being members of the church, told me about it and said it was done under the name of the Flamingos, but we had no clue about the temple front until it was already done. What happened to the partnership?"

One incident that garnered the Flamingos some negative publicity occurred in California as the group was preparing for concert appearances in Hawaii. "We drove to Los Angeles and headed out toward the [airport]," Hunt wrote in his memoir. "I was in the front car with Zeke, Terry, and Paul."

"Jake and Nate were in the back car, the station wagon, with all the luggage," Johnson recalled. "Paul rolled a joint, and I remember saying to him,

On stage, with Tommy Hunt singing lead, 1960. Left to right: Zeke, Jake, Paul, and Terry (courtesy Terry Johnson).

'What are you doing?', because no one had ever smoked in front of Zeke or Jake before." Nevertheless, Wilson lit the marijuana cigarette and shared it with Hunt and Johnson. "Zeke got really mad," Johnson continues. "He had the directions to the airport, but started doubting himself and decided to pull into a gas station to ask for directions. We all tried to stop him, and said, 'No, no, don't stop,' because there was smoke in the car. But Zeke didn't care and pulled into the station anyway and instead of him getting out, he rolled down the window and the gas station attendant came over to the car and saw and smelled the smoke. Paul noticed when we pulled out that the guy wrote down the license number [of our car] and saw him get on the phone."

"Ten minutes down the road, with sirens blaring and lights flashing, the police stopped us," Hunt wrote. "They came up to Zeke's window. 'All of you get out of the car,' [the officer] ordered. We got out. They searched us all, but found nothing."

"When Nate saw this, he pulled over in front of us and backed up the car and got out and ran over to see what was wrong," Johnson elaborates. "The cop asked Nate, 'Are you with them?' Nate answered, 'Yes, what's wrong?' That's when the cops decided to search the luggage which was in the car that Nate was driving." The police uncovered marijuana in Johnson, Hunt, Nelson, and Wilson's bags. "We were all carrying pot in our bags to go to Hawaii," Johnson affirms, discounting Hunt's own claims of innocence. "In those days they didn't search the bags like they do now. It probably wouldn't have been that bad, because we only had a joint or two worth of pot in the lead car, but the rest of it was in the station wagon in our bags, and that's what made the bust so bad. That's how we lost the trip to Hawaii and a few other jobs."

"We were all put under arrest and taken to the local police station," Hunt continued. "As soon as he could, Zeke got on the phone to some lawyer he knew to represent us. But we had to stay there a few hours before they let us go. We never made it to Hawaii. Instead we went back to New York by which time the incident had become national news. The scandal hit us hard."

By this point, tensions were running high within the Flamingos. "What was going on, Zeke and Jake, being that they were the bosses, they owned the name, [and] they started getting a little bit hairy," Hunt told interviewer McGarvey. "They were starting to get a little bit strong, and there was a lot of friction between Zeke, Nate, and myself."

"They would be saying, 'Where are you going?' 'Who are you going to be with?', and things like that," Terry adds.

"It was getting to the point where it was getting to be a question of power, that's all," Tommy continues. "We were at a stage in our career where things were happening very nicely, too, and that can make people change."

"It seemed to me nothing I did was right," Hunt wrote. "Nate, whose head was already on the chopping block, was also suffering the same treatment. We'd only received a thousand dollars [each] for 'I Only Have Eyes for You,' and the song had sold hundreds of thousands of copies. So where was all the money that the record must have made? We didn't understand it, and Nate and I were getting real suspicious. OK, we had new cars, new stage clothes, but never any money."

In February, Goldner issued the re-recording of "Ko Ko Mo," backed with "That's Why I Love You." "The Flamingos swing in with two strong sides," a *Billboard* reviewer wrote in their February 20 issue. "The first is the rock 'n' roll oldie that gets a high-flying reading from the group with a vocal full of showmanship. The flip is a feelingful reading of a moving rockaballad." On March 13, it entered the pop chart, stalling out at #92 after a three-week run. On April 21, the group began a week of appearances at the Regal in Chicago with the Olympics, Aretha Franklin, the Capris, the Dells, Johnny Hartman, Moms Mabley, Ernestine Anderson, Tiny Topsy, the Sarah McLawler Trio, Wade Flemons, and the Red Saunders Orchestra. Immediately after the show closed, they opened at the Uptown in Philadelphia, working with deejay Georgie Woods and Jerry Butler, the Miracles, Maxine Brown, the Vibrations, Shep and the Limelites, and Doc Bagby and his band. On May 11, they entertained students at Princeton University. A photo of the group performing Ray Charles's "What'd I Say" at the New Jersey college appeared in a May issue of *Jet* magazine.

By now, the group's troubles had come to a boil. "We were starting to more or less just do our job, sticking to the rules and regulations," Hunt told McGarvey in 1985. "But the rules and regulations became just a little bit too strong for anybody to handle. I mean, there must be an element of freedom, too. But it started being a case of 'you can't do this' and 'you can't do that'.... Soon you start taking away a person's personal life. So, I just said, 'I love you guys, and I'll always love the Flamingos.' I'll always have a deepness in my heart for them, but I figured why stay with a group you love and end up one day hating them?"

Terry Johnson recalls a strikingly different scenario that erupted when Zeke and Jake heard Tommy's solo debut, "Human," over the airwaves in June of 1961. "I didn't even hear it on the radio. I went to a meeting that Jake and Zeke had called. All of a sudden, they said, 'Everybody is meeting. This is mandatory.' I said, 'OK.' I walked in, and everybody was sitting there, and they said, 'Did you hear this?' I said, 'What?' They said, 'Tommy did a recording of a song called "Human." Have you heard it?' I said, 'No.' They said, 'They're playing it like crazy. They're playing it every five minutes.' So they turned on the radio, and it came on. I said, 'That *is* Tommy! Where *is* Tommy?' Nobody knew. So that's when it was like, 'Oh, Tommy did a dirty thing.' He should have, he could have told everybody he didn't want to be there anymore, and given us a chance to get somebody else. He should have done it right. But the way he did it, we all fell apart. And they thought that I was going to leave, too. I don't know why. But that's what caused the whole thing to really go crazy. I always said it was Zeke that caused the group to break up, but I was wrong. It was Tommy Hunt. He did one of the dirtiest things that you could do. It freaked everybody out because we had all of these big jobs in front of us. These were things we had waited for, for so long. We finally had a year or two of steady bookings with better money, and all kinds of TV things and other movies that we were supposed to do. Tommy just threw a monkey wrench into the whole thing. He didn't give a damn, and everybody freaked out over that. It wasn't right for him to do that without telling anybody. We had so much in front of us. Joe Glaser went crazy at ABC. He was like, 'What?!' Because we were a tight group, and he and Paul doing the dancing made us so different, and Nate with that velvety voice, and Paul and I with the duets. We had a different style from anybody else out there."

"Nate and I eventually had our conversation," Hunt wrote in his 2009 memoir, *Only Human*. "It was partially about me, and how I'd left without saying anything," he admitted.

"Tommy was a loner," Johnson recalls of Hunt during their days together in the Flamingos. "Tommy was a big BS'er, you know. He'd tell me to meet him. 'I've got these girls lined up, Buzz. Drop that girl you're with. She's fine, but I've got some finer ones, man, and they're twins.' I said, 'OK.' He said, 'Well, meet me down on Broad Street around 11 o'clock.' And me, like a fool, I'm driving down on Broad Street, and I'm waiting, and I'm waiting,

Tommy Hunt, solo publicity photo, 1961 (Kriegsmann photo, from the author's collection).

and I'm waiting. Twelve o'clock comes, 12:30 comes, Tommy's not there. I said 'Damn it, that Tommy Hunt!' He was known for doing that to people. He was the biggest BS artist I've ever met in my life."

After Hunt left, tensions between Johnson and the Careys ran high. "I don't know what made them think it, but they thought I was going to leave to join the Treniers," the guitarist-tenor recalls. "They would say, 'Where are you going?' 'Who are you going to be with?' 'Are you thinking about leaving the group?' They just kept bothering us. It was mainly Jake and Zeke. They kind of pushed me out. They came and said, 'I hear you're going to leave the group.' I said, 'No, why would I do that?' They said, 'We hear you're going to join the Treniers.' I said, 'Bullshit. Who ever said that?' You know, and it kept happening. So, I had my girls, and they said, 'You don't need that.' It's easy to be influenced. Maybe a week or two after Tommy left, I did, too. I left because they were just badgering me so much." Immediately, Johnson left New York and headed for Philadelphia, where he organized a competing group, the Modern Flamingos.

Although the Flamingos had been scheduled to perform at Robert's Show Club in Chicago from June 14 through July 2, it's likely that the gig was canceled, prompting rumors that the act had broken up for good. The story of Hunt and Johnson's departure soon made the papers in the group's hometown. "The Flamingos in Personnel Change" read the headline in the June 24, 1961, edition of the *Chicago Defender*. The newspaper reported that Jake Carey, "business manager and spokesman for the Flamingos, is angry over rumors that the popular singing aggregation is breaking up. 'The Flamingos are definitely not breaking up or splitting up. We just had to release two members for personal reasons we thought might prove detrimental to the group in a long run. I won't elaborate on the actual reasons right now, because we're still on good, friendly terms, and we wouldn't want to injure their chances to work with other groups or by themselves.' No longer with the group are Tommy Hunt and Terry 'Buzzy' Johnson. But Tommy lost no time in getting himself started as a single. His first single releases of 'Human' and 'Parade of Broken Hearts' on Scepter Records were out within a week after he left the Flamingos."

Things went from bad to worse for the Careys when Nate Nelson walked away a month or two after Tommy and Terry. "He tried to stay with them, but they had just become overbearing," Johnson states. "Nate was mad. He couldn't believe that they let me go. Nate said, 'How the hell could you guys just let Buzzy just walk away. That was the damn head of the whole thing. You knew what it was like before we got him, and we got all these hits and everything after he joined. How could you just let him walk away?' Nate said they should have offered me more money, or offered me something, you know. They just said, 'Shut up, Lips.' They always called him 'Lips' because he had kind of big lips, you know. They argued, and Nate just argued, and they weren't happy with each other anymore. So, Nate said, 'Man, f--- you guys. I'm going to join Buzzy.'"

Before heading to the Modern Flamingos, Nelson recorded one ultra-rare single for the Prigan label, owned by Lloyd Price and his manager and business partner, Harold Logan, in New York City in July of 1961. One of seven imprints the duo used in the late 1950s and early to mid–1960s, Prigan also issued a single by Chris Kenner, "Don't Make No Noise," in 1961. Monte Bruce, who first recorded the Harptones with his partners Morty Craft and Leo Rogers for his eponymous Bruce label in 1953, served as Prigan's

Nate Nelson promotional photo, summer of 1961 (courtesy Colton Thomas).

general manager. Nelson did his best Jackie Wilson imitation on the up-tempo, string-heavy "Tell Me Why," but really shined on the ballad side, "Once Again," which he co-wrote with Billy Wheeler. Nate also wrote or co-wrote several songs, including "Rubber Leg Twist," which was recorded by the Isley brothers on their Wand debut LP, *Twist & Shout*, in 1962. In 1965, Nelson produced and co-wrote both sides of Lee Jackson's soulful Atlantic single, "Ad for Love" and "Keep Your Mouth Shut."

Reorganization

With their principal arranger, their recognizable lead voice, and half of their charismatic dance team all gone, the Flamingos reluctantly canceled $10,000 worth of bookings and scheduled open auditions to find two suitable replacement vocalists. Goldner, meanwhile, kept the group's name in the record stores, issuing "Time Was"/"Dream Girl" in June. The A-side cracked *Billboard*'s pop chart on July 3, 1961. In eight weeks on the list, it peaked at #45. In the midst of the first rock 'n' roll revival, a reissue of "Golden Teardrops" on Vee Jay Records hit #108 on the pop list the week of August 21.

"Nobody [was] left but me, Jake, and Paul, so we had to seriously restructure," Zeke admitted. "[We] did some auditions, [and] got Billy Clarke, formerly with a group called the Strangers. He played drums and sang." William J. Clarke, born in Brooklyn, New York on July 6, 1936, grew up in the Putnam-Tompkins Avenue area of Brooklyn's Bedford-Stuyvesant neighborhood. In 1952, at the age of 16, he formed a quintet called the Strangers. In addition to his role as the group's second tenor and alternate lead, Clarke also handled the Strangers' business dealings.

In 1954, Clarke contacted Henry Glover, who signed the Strangers to King Records, for whom they recorded in 1954–55. Clarke sang lead on eight of their 12 King sides: "I've Got Eyes," "Beg and Steal," "Just Don't Care," "Drop Down to My Place," "Get It One More Time," "How Long Must I Wait," "Without a Friend," and "Think Again." Clarke also sang second tenor on the Strangers' R&B group harmony classics "My Friends," "Hoping You'll Understand" and "Blue Flowers" behind lead Pringle Sims (1935–2005).

"We also got a lyric tenor named Eddie Williams, a guitar player named Joe McCoy, and a saxophone player named Julien Vaught," Zeke explained. Born in Wilmington, North Carolina, in 1940, Julien Westley Vaught, who also doubled on flute, was living in Brooklyn when he was discovered by the group while gigging in a local night club at age 21. "I got the agent, Joe Glaser, and he found out-of-the-way clubs where we could develop the act, and it got tight," Zeke added.

In the August 10, 1961, issue of *Jet* magazine, Jake Carey confirmed the group had "added three new vocalists, a guitarist, and a saxophonist to enlarge and give the ensemble a new look." The reorganized quintet first recorded for Goldner in New York City on Thursday, September 7, 1961. Coming on the heels of three consecutive nationally charted records, the results could

The Flamingos in 1961. Top row, left to right: Eddie Williams, Jake Carey, Paul Wilson. Middle, left to right: Zeke Carey, Billy Clarke; Bottom, left to right: Joe McCoy, Julien Vaught (Maurice Seymour photo, courtesy Colton Thomas).

only be described as utter failure. The decision to turn the Harptones' 1954 R.J. Cita classic, "My Memories of You," from wistful lament to twisting rocker was deplorable. Fans could only be left to ponder what a Johnson-arranged and Nelson-led ballad version would have sounded like.

Clarke took a brief solo on the unison-led remake of "I Want to Love You," written by Nelson and first recorded for Checker in 1955. Like "My Memories of You," the bluesy piano triplet–driven version of "I Want to Love You" was an inferior remake that crystallized the group's shortcomings.

Hunt, meanwhile, was screaming up the charts. "Human" debuted on the R&B list on September 25 and rose to #5 during an 11-week stint. In 10 weeks on the pop chart, the Scepter disc peaked at #48. "I went on to do a solo career. I signed on with Scepter and Wand. I didn't leave the Flamingos because of any animosity," Hunt told Boone in 2001. "I left the Flamingos because I feel that every man has a destiny. Who knows what's around the corner for any man? We don't know what's going to happen tomorrow. It was like something came over me to try a solo career. I was walking down Broadway the very next day after I left the Flamingos and I was walking down near a place called the Brass Rail. I went into the Brass Rail and was sitting at the bar, and a voice came behind me and said, 'Are you Tommy Hunt?' I said, 'Yes, I am.' I turned around and it was a guy named Luther Dixon [1931–2009]. Luther said, 'I heard you left the Flamingos.' I told him yeah, and he said, 'How would you like a recording contract with Scepter/Wand?'

"At the time [they] had the Shirelles, Chuck Jackson, and Maxine Brown," Hunt continues. "So I went there scared to death because after working with a group so long on stage and having the support of five other guys on the stage, you know, which gave you Dutch courage, I thought, 'Well, can I do it by myself?' I told Luther, 'I'm a little bit nervous.' He said, 'Look, Tommy, you sang "Everybody's Got a Home (But Me)." If you can sing that on the stage.... You didn't see the Flamingos when you were singing it. You were singing it from your heart, and you were singing it to the audience. That's the same way as you sing a single of your own.' He came to me and said, 'I have a song for you.' I said, 'What's it called?' He said '"Human,"' and I said, 'Oh.' So, when I heard it, I knew right away that it was my kind of song. But he wasn't going with that for the A-side. He was going with 'Parade of Broken Hearts.' I told him, 'Luther, I'm not trying to tell you your business, but 'Parade of Broken Hearts' is not me.' He said, 'No, Tommy, it's commercial, more commercial than 'Human.' And the record company is always right. So, I didn't know, because the man had made hit records for the Shirelles, and Chuck Jackson and everyone else. I'm not going to argue with him. I'm just going to do the song. So, I did the song and Jocko and Tommy Smalls were playing 'Parade of Broken Hearts' and they weren't getting any reaction to it. One day, a guy in New Jersey said, 'Ladies and Gentlemen, here's Tommy Hunt, formerly with the Flamingos, with a new song, 'Parade of Broken Hearts.' He had accidentally turned it over and 'Human' started playing by mistake, and the phones started ringing off the hook.

"I was on Scepter a week after I left [the Flamingos], and had a hit four weeks after I left them," Hunt encapsulated to McGarvey. "I was amazed, and so were they!" On October 9, 1961, "Lovers Never Say Goodbye" returned to the charts, hitting #117 on *Billboard*'s "Bubbling Under the Hot 100" list.

The revamped Flamingos in late 1961. Julien Vaught (top) and Eddie Williams (below). Middle row, left to right: Jake Carey, Paul Wilson, and Billy Clarke. Front row, left to right: Zeke Carey and Al Fontaine (author's collection).

Tommy Hunt, meanwhile, starred in a weeklong stage show at the Regal Theater with Jerry Butler and Maxine Brown.

The Flamingos returned to Bell Sound in New York City for their next recording session in mid–November of 1961. Before their own two-song session on the 17th, Zeke and Jake participated in a Ral Donner recording date that Goldner produced on the 14th and 16th. Eight songs were recorded by Donner, four of which found their way onto Gone label 45s: "To Love Someone," "Loveless Life," "She's Everything," and "Will You Love Me in Heaven." Two others, "Silver and Gold" and "Half Heaven, Half Heartache," were released on LP and CD reissue1 packages decades later. Two more, "Tender Years" and "Castle in the Sky," were lost or unfinished. Although Zeke recalled that the Careys backed Donner on at least one song, aural evidence has failed to identify the specific track.

At their own session, the Flamingos returned to their most recognizable remaining voice, Paul Wilson, who sang a duet lead with Williams and a solo segment on the 1934 standard, "For All We Know." With lyrics by Sam M. Lewis (1885–1959) and music by J. Fred Coots (1897–1985), who wrote "Santa Claus is Coming to Town" in 1934, "For All We Know" was first popularized by bandleader Hal Kemp and, later, Isham Jones and Nat "King" Cole. Sonny Til's Orioles also recorded the earthy ballad for Vee Jay in late 1956, but the Flamingos' version was done in their own inimitable style. It was an artistic triumph, considering the changes the group had undergone.

The other song attempted was "Lover Come Back to Me," a 1928 collaboration between Oscar Hammerstein II and Sigmund Romberg that was first introduced in the stage operetta *The New Moon*. Two years later, the song was featured in the motion picture of the same name, and went on to become a standard, with dozens of recorded versions by the likes of Paul Whiteman's Orchestra, Jeanette MacDonald, Nelson Eddy, Billie Holiday, Al Hibbler, and Nat "King" Cole. Goldner apparently had an affinity for the tune. He had issued a version of the song as "Lover Come Back" by the Velours on End in April of 1961. Unhappy with the Flamingos' rendition, Goldner kept it in the can and recorded a new version with the Cleftones, which they took into the *Billboard* Hot 100 in late 1962.

As the Flamingos returned to more high-profile gigs, it was inevitable that Hunt and his former group would cross paths again. On February 9, 1962, they were booked into the Apollo for a week of appearances, along with the Vibrations, the Ronettes, the Capris, and Bobby Lewis. "The next legitimate job we took was the Apollo Theatre [with] headliner Tommy Hunt. They wanted us to open," Zeke admitted. "I just said, 'No.' So, they made us the second act, and I settled for that."

The Flamingos rose to the occasion and, in Zeke's words, "went on and stopped the show. What we stopped the show with was our rendition of 'Ol' Man River.'"

"I was topping the bill at the Apollo, and the Flamingos were on the show with me," agrees Hunt. "I was so nervous that time because when I saw the fellows on stage, I knew what they could do, but I didn't know what I could do by myself. I just stood in the wings, waiting."

"I had mixed emotions," Hunt later wrote. "I [was] glad to see Paul again, but Zeke and Jake could go to hell. The whole week at the Apollo I got the cold shoulder from those two, and Paul only spoke briefly in passing. When I heard the Flamingos singing 'A Kiss from Your Lips,' they sounded real good. I was still proud to know I'd once been with them. I thought what a shame it was we hadn't stuck together."

After the Flamingos' dynamic presentation, nerves momentarily got the better of Hunt. "After they came off, everyone was applauding and shouting, and the emcee said, 'Now, ladies and gentlemen, former Flamingo, and now a star in his own right, Tommy Hunt,'" the singer recalls. "When I walked out, they were all waiting. They knew who I was, thinking, 'Come on, Tommy, let's see what you can do by yourself.' And what did I do? I forgot my words! But it came [out] all right."

Two new tunes were brought to the group's March 8, 1962, session at Bell Sound. Ronnie Lewis and John Pearson brought in "It Must Be Love." Pearson had sung baritone in the Velours from 1956 to 1961 and became the Flamingos' road manager shortly thereafter. He would occasionally write for the group into the late 1960s. The late New York singer-songwriter Dorian Burton, who had penned "A Tear Fell" for Ivory Joe Hunter, and the Four Dots' "Rita," composed "I'm No Fool Anymore" with Joe Simmons. A second attempt was also made at "For All We Know," but Goldner opted to keep the November 1961 version as his finished master. One month after the session, he paired the two new songs as End #1111. In May, *Cash Box* declared "I'm No Fool Anymore" was "a captivating cha cha weeper that the group waxes with loads of feeling."

In early May, the Flamingos appeared at the Vogue Terrace dinner theater in Pittsburgh. On May 11, still in the Steel City, they performed before 13,000 fans in a Porky Chedwick–produced event that grossed $35,000. Sharing the stage with the Flamingos were Jackie Wilson, Jerry Butler, Bo Diddley, the Drifters, the Coasters, the Castells, the Angels, the Blue Belles, the Skyliners, the Marvelettes, the Jive Five, the Carousels, Bobby Vinton, Gene Pitney, Ketty Lester, and Big Maybelle.

Back in New York, the group cut yet another oldie, "Near You," on July

3. Francis Craig, one of the song's writers, enjoyed a #1 hit for 17 weeks with the tune in 1947. The Cardinals had also cut the song in their last session for Atlantic in December of 1956. Goldner released "For All We Know" and "Near You" as a single in September and was disappointed to see it sink without a trace.

The failure of his most recent Flamingos discs was the least of Goldner's worries at the time. Gambling losses had forced the producer to sell his Rama-Gee empire to Morris Levy and Phil Kahl in March of 1957. Now, five years later, he was in the same precarious position with his Gone-End holdings. After reportedly having borrowed from Levy to cover his significant gambling debts, George was unable to repay the loan, and Goldner's entire catalog was purchased by Levy's Roulette Records firm in June of 1962.

The group toured endlessly through the summer and fall, returning to the Beachcomber Club in Wildwood, New Jersey, for a week, beginning July 20. From there, they jetted their way to Chicago, sharing the Regal stage through August 3 with Sam Cooke, the Upsetters, the Falcons, Ketty Lester, Chuck Jackson, and comedian George Kirby. On August 10, they were back in New Jersey for a week of shows at Atlantic City's Hieleah Club. On the 18th, they hit Carr's Beach in Annapolis, Maryland.

On August 24, they began another week at the Beachcomber. From August 31 through September 6, the Flamingos performed in Washington with Brook Benton at the Howard. Heading north, Benton and the Flamingos opened at the Apollo on September 14, where they were joined for the week by Ruth Brown and Patti LaBelle and the Blue Belles. October 15–27 found them at the Peppermint Lounge West in Pittsburgh. On November 21, Porky Chedwick booked them back into Pittsburgh for a show at the Syria Mosque, which also starred Hank Ballard and the Midnighters, the Coasters, the Olympics, Maxine Brown, Lou Christie, Jerry Butler, the Isley Brothers, the Clovers, the Majors, Huey "Piano" Smith and the Clowns, Shep & the Limelites, the Drifters, Little Esther, and Bo Diddley.

Although the group was working steadily, they had yet to produce a hit record in the two years since Nelson, Hunt, and Johnson left. In the spring of 1963, the Flamingos were brought into the studio to record a dozen tracks with respected producer-arranger-songwriter Henry Glover. Born in Hot Springs, Arkansas, Glover (1921–1991), joined Buddy Johnson's band as a trumpeter in 1944 and soon found himself playing and arranging with Lucky Millinder's Orchestra at King Records. King president Syd Nathan hired him as the label's Artists and Repertoire Director and was rewarded with a dizzy-ing string of hits that ran the gamut from blues to country and western. Glover wrote or co-wrote hundreds of songs, including "Blues Stay Away from Me," "Annie Had a Baby," "Drown in My Own Tears," "Boogie at Midnight," and "I'll Sail My Ship Alone."

Federal-King artists from Moon Mullican and Little Willie John to Hank Ballard and the Midnighters and James Brown worked with Glover, who, as the head of the firm's New York office, was one of the first successful black producers and record executives in America.

In September of 1959, Glover parted ways with Nathan to join Hy Weiss's Old Town label. The pair launched a short-lived Glover subsidiary, but soon the veteran producer found himself working for Morris Levy's Roulette enterprise, where he would be offered the opportunity to produce a variety of jazz, R&B, and rock 'n' roll artists. Sarah Vaughan, Dinah Washington, Ronnie Hawkins and the Hawks, and Louisiana Red all benefited from Glover's many talents. Levy was undoubtedly pleased when the future Country Music Hall of Fame and Rock and Roll Hall of Fame inductee co-wrote and produced a #1 record for the company in Joey Dee and the Starliters' "The Peppermint Twist" in late 1961.

By this point, the Flamingos had replaced Joe McCoy with New York guitarist Alan Fontaine, who would later gain fame in the original Broadway production of *Hair*. Three of the dozen songs selected for recording at the session, likely held in March of 1963, were written by Eugene Roland, the Stan Kenton band arranger who wrote "Every Time I Think of You," which the group had recorded for the *Requestfully Yours* album in 1960. Seven of the titles, according to saxophonist Julien Vaught, were led by Williams, while Clarke fronted three, and Wilson handled a pair.

"Blessed with perfect pitch, he could, and did, write without the aid of a piano whenever the mood struck him, on and off the [tour] bus," Kenton historian Noel Wedder wrote in his online biography of Roland, *A Composer/Arranger for All the Right Reasons and Seasons*. "Completely and totally irresponsible, he constantly lived on the edge, and was forever being chastised for leaving his instrument behind on the stand, never having any money, sneaking women aboard the bus, and fueling his system with a smorgasbord of pharmaceuticals. Roland lived for jazz. It was his passion. It was the guiding force which kept him going. Unquestionably a genius, he had a difficult time handling such mundane things as tying his shoelaces, feeding himself, balancing his checkbook, paying his bills. Yet, it was his over-the-top lifestyle which enabled him to write with such broad strokes and flowing colors. He long labored under the delusion that everyone was capable of doing what he did."

With Eddie Williams delivering a vibrato-filled tenor lead and Fontaine providing a Hawaiian-flavored guitar accompaniment, Roland's "I'm Coming

Home" was the first song committed to tape. Next, the group tackled "The Sinner," originally composed by the Mexican-born violinist Ruben Fuentes. Best known for his contributions to mariachi music, Fuentes, born in 1926, wrote the tune as "El Pecador." Hall of Fame lyricist Mitchell Parish (1900–1993) added the English verses. One of the most potent of the post–Nelson group's recordings, "The Sinner" featured a magical blend of echoing and full-throated, pleading tenor harmonies with Billy Clarke in the forefront as lead. The arrangement was stellar, the performance superb. Inexplicably, when it was released, the composers were listed as Parish and Roth.

Returning to the Gene Roland songbook, Williams led the group on a lush arrangement of "My Lovely One" and the Bill Nash–penned "I Know Better" before their attention turned to the traditional "Danny Boy." The melody was first collected by Jane Ross of Londonderry, and published by the Society for the Preservation and Publication of the Melodies of Ireland in 1855 as "anonymous air." It was first called "Londonderry Air" in 1894 when Katherine Tynan Hinkson paired her "Irish Love Song" lyrics to the melody.

English attorney Frederick Weatherly wrote the enduring lyrics, titled "Danny Boy," in 1910, and set them to the air three years later. Ernestine Schumann-Heink made the first known recording in 1915. A worldwide standard, the song has been recorded by literally hundreds of artists, including Judy Garland in 1955. During the pop-rock era, three versions, a rockabilly sendup by Conway Twitty and a tenor sax instrumental by Sil Austin, both from 1959, and Andy Williams's 1961 rendition, reached the *Billboard* pop charts before the Flamingos put their stamp on it.

Alto saxophonist Julien Vaught, obviously influenced by Austin, delivered a golden-toned instrumental lead for the majority of the song, backed by strings, unobtrusive background harmonies, and, nearing the climax, a falsetto tenor sung by Williams.

Next, the group recorded their version of "Ol' Man River," the song that had stopped the show during the Flamingos' 1961 appearance at the Apollo with solo star Tommy Hunt. Zeke Carey reported to interviewer McGarvey that he had tried unsuccessfully to interest Hunt in singing the song while he was a member of the group. With music by Jerome Kern (1885–1945) and lyrics by Oscar Hammerstein II, the song was written for the 1927 musical *Show Boat*. Vividly depicting the struggles of African Americans in the South, it was sung by Paul Robeson in the 1936 motion picture adaptation of *Show Boat*, and later popularized by artists ranging from Frank Sinatra to the Ravens. At a running time of 5:15, the song was too long for a single release, but ideal for the burgeoning rock 'n' roll album market.

Watching the Flamingos perform the song live inspired the Temptations to adopt it for their stage repertoire as well. "One of the good things about playing rooms like the Copa was that we got to work more standards into our act, which we loved. Probably the most difficult of all the songs in our repertoire is 'Ol' Man River,'" group founder Otis Williams wrote in his 1988 autobiography, *Temptations*, with Patricia Romanowski. "We started doing [it] in 1964 after seeing the Flamingos do it at the Uptown in Philadelphia. We changed it around a little, but Melvin [Franklin] sings lead, as the Flamingos' bass singer, Jacob Carey did." For their recording, however, it was Eddie Williams, according to Vaught, who sang lead.

Next, Paul Wilson led "You're Mine," a ballad written and recorded by former Checker labelmate Danny Overbea in July of 1954. A unison-led version of the Orioles' 1948 classic, "It's Too Soon to Know" followed, with Clarke smoothly handling the crescendo. End erroneously titled the song "Too Soon to Know" when they released the recording, crediting Don Gibson instead of the actual composer, Deborah Chessler.

"[When You're Young and] Only Seventeen" featured lush orchestrations and a broad baritone lead from Paul Wilson. The song was written by lyricist Mann Curtis (1911–1984), who penned the English lyrics to the French tune, "Je t'appartiens," creating "Let It Be Me," and Arthur Kent (1920–2009) whose composing credits included Etta Jones's "Don't Go to Strangers" and the Skeeter Davis hit, "The End of the World." Kenton arranger Gene Roland also wrote "Flame of Love," another ballad led by Williams. Billy Clarke returned to the lead mike for "Without His Love," a rare spiritual effort penned by Lawrence Smith. Closing the session was the standard "Moonlight in Vermont," written and published by John Blackburn and Karl Suessdorf in 1943. Pop songstress Margaret Whiting scored a hit with the tune in 1944, and later versions by jazz guitarist Johnny Smith with tenor sax ace Stan Getz, Frank Sinatra, and, into the late 1970s, Willie Nelson, continued to keep the song in the public's ear. The Flamingos' version of "Moonlight in Vermont" is a harmonic delight, with both Zeke and Jake Carey featuring prominently in the mix, along with Fontaine's plaintive guitar chords and Williams' lead tenor.

"The 'Ol' Man River' group, '61, '62, was unique," Zeke recalled to McGarvey. "Seven of us, with a horn player. The horn player [Vaught] played drums when the drummer [Clarke] came up to sing. The guitar player [Fontaine] was a very funky rhythm and blues player, but he could sing a certain kind of song with a lot of excitement which we performed some great routines behind. Paul Wilson was still there, with his great choreography and great charisma, and ability to make things happen. He created routines that were just fantastic."

"I Know Better" was paired with "Flame of Love" and released as a single in April of 1963. Although it fared better than the group's two previous efforts, "I Know Better" only reached #107 on *Billboard's* Bubbling Under the Hot 100 list during a four-week chart run beginning May 4. The dozen tracks recorded at the spring session were culled for the group's fourth End long-player, *The Sound of the Flamingos*, issued at the same time as the single. Production credit was shared by Henry Glover and George Goldner. While the LP did include the names of all of the group's current members, no photo of the Flamingos was used on either side of the jacket.

"The failure of 'I Know Better' to make it onto the Hot 100 does not reflect the song's impact on the public," historian and author Pruter asserts. "The song did appreciably better in some regional R&B markets, notably Chicago. While the Windy City fans apparently responded to the number's proto-soul styling, East Coast fans apparently felt it was too great of a departure from the sound that the Flamingos had established on End. In subsequent years, East Coast record collectors would routinely value the flip, 'Flame of Love,' while sniffing at 'I Know Better.' In Chicago, on the other hand, 'I Know Better' only grew in reputation, so that eventually it became the most commonly played Flamingos 'dusty' on African American oldie shows, notably Herb Kent's *Love Dusties* show every Sunday morning."

Glover and the Flamingos returned to the studio on Tuesday, June 18, 1963. The first of three songs attempted, "Shout It Out," was never released. "Come On to My Party" was written by Earl Jackson and Gregory Carroll, the former Four Buddies' second tenor who had co-written the current smash, "Just One Look," with singer Doris Troy. "(Talk About) True Love" was composed by the Cashmeres' lead, Windsor Jackson King, who briefly worked for Roulette-End as a staff writer before moving over to Sue Records. The latter two songs were coupled as End #1124 in July but died a quick death. The final master number assigned to the date, #942, went unused. Another catalog number, End LP #317, was assigned to an album titled *The Spiritual and Folk Song Moods of the Flamingos*. Apparently, the album never went further than the planning stages, as no further recording sessions took place.

In September of 1963, the group's recording of "Ol' Man River" was pulled from the *Sound of the Flamingos* album and released as both sides of a single on the parent Roulette imprint. "[Goldner] was a bad businessman," Zeke opined. "Not so much on the royalties side, but the record business. I tried to tell him, 'This is becoming an album business.' We did 'Ol' Man River,' over five minutes long, and when they put the record out, they split it up. People don't listen, and this was George Goldner's problem. He destroyed himself by seeing today, not tomorrow."

In any case, the fact remained that the Flamingos, after placing nine records on the national pop charts in a span of two and a half years, had gone two years without returning to the Hot 100. With their focus on jazz, twist, and mainstream rock 'n' roll, vocal groups like the Flamingos became less and less of a priority for Roulette after Goldner gave way to Levy. In early 1964, as Beatlemania swept over the United States, the Flamingos were dropped from the label.

"I have to give Zeke credit," Terry Johnson states. "He tried. He really tried. But the hits stopped. George Goldner lost interest in Zeke, and they had to let him go."

The Modern Flamingos
and Starglows

Upon leaving the Flamingos in June of 1961, Terry Johnson left New York and headed for Philadelphia where he organized the Modern Flamingos. "I was so pissed off with them because they drove me out. I didn't want to stay in New York anymore. When I left the Flamingos, I told them, 'I'm going to put another group together that will sound exactly as we sound.' I knew some people in Philadelphia. I had friends there. I told a friend I had left the Flamingos, and I wanted to put a group together, and he said, 'Oh, man, I know a group.'"

Initially, the Modern Flamingos consisted of Johnson singing lead, playing guitar, and serving as the musical and vocal arranger, drummer Duke Johnson, bassist Eddie Thomas, first and second tenor Sonny Ross, and former Del-Knights members first tenor Warren Sherrill, bass Jerry Abel, and baritone Eddie Edgehill, who was also an original member of the Valentines. "I put that group together and just taught them all of our stuff, and they were doing the dancing like Tommy and Paul, so they fit perfectly for what I needed." Johnson recalls. "Not as smooth, but it got over. It was almost the same type of thing. That was the first Modern Flamingos."

Their lineup was soon enhanced by the addition of Nate Nelson in late 1962 or early 1963. "Nate had joined me, and so we were Terry Johnson and the Modern Flamingos featuring Nate Nelson," he explains. "We started working, and we had one of the best combinations that you could have. I sang 'I Only Have Eyes for You' and all the other leads until Nate joined. Then he sang his songs, and he and I sang the duets together as Paul and I had done. We were booked all over the place." The week of March 1, 1963, the Modern Flamingos performed at Harlem's Apollo Theater.

Soon after, during an appearance in Pittsburgh, Johnson and Nelson were approached by Joe Rock, the longtime manager and songwriter for the Skyliners. "We went to Pittsburgh and Joe Rock came to see us, and he approached me and Nate. He said, 'Oh, man, you guys are fabulous. I've got the main voices in the Flamingos right here. Would you guys like to record?' We said, 'Hell, yeah. What have you got in mind?' He said, 'I've got "Walk Softly Away." We'll just do a single shot right now. Terry, can you come up with a song—write something for us?' I said, 'Yeah, come on, Nate.' We went back to the hotel room that night, and sat down. I started playing some chords, and Nate said, 'I like that. I like that,' and we made up 'Let's Be Lovers' that night. That's how fast it comes when it's flowing."

Previously Johnson's Modern Flamingos had done some independent recordings that Terry produced and tried to shop to various labels. However, none of their efforts saw the light of day. "We did a few songs. We did 'If I Didn't Care,' 'Love at First Sight,' 'My Seventh Heartache,' but these weren't ever released. I was traveling so much that I didn't have a chance to really shop them."

On June 10, 1963, Rock recorded two masters by the Modern Flamingos: the Nelson-Johnson ballad "Let's Be Lovers," and "Walk Softly Away," which had been written by the team of Bruce Belland and Glen Larson. Original members of the Four Preps, Belland and Larson had previously penned the group's 1958 #2 pop chart hit, "26 Miles (Santa Catalina)."

Nelson sang lead and duetted with Johnson on the pleasant rock-a-ballad, "Walk Softly Away." "The other members of the group were Joe Johnson, he played organ, Hardy Hall, who played saxophone, Larry Jones was singing second tenor in the background, and a guy we called Shug. I cannot remember Shug's last name. I can't even remember his real name. But he was the drummer. We didn't have a bass player, so Joe Johnson was playing the bass on the organ with his foot. They were my Modern Flamingos, and they were the Starglows. Hardy Hall sang bass on 'Walk Softly Away.' He was a saxophone player, but he had a good bass voice." Hall (1935–2009) had previously sung bass with the Belltones, who recorded "Estelle" for Grand Records in 1953.

"Let's Be Lovers" was a splendid follow-up to "Lovers Never Say Goodbye," opening with the same recognizable guitar chords from Johnson and featuring a romantic duet lead from Nate and Terry that even included the title of their former hit in the lyrics. Although Peter Grendysa, in his notes for the Rhino double CD set *All Night Boogie—The Great Atlantic Vocal Groups, Volume 2*, tabs journeyman vocalist Ray Brewster, formerly of the Cadillacs, the Penguins, and the Hollywood Flames as playing a role in this session, Johnson dismisses the notion.

Rock apparently made a deal with Atlantic Records to release both the Modern Flamingos sides and a new recording of the Buddy and Ella Johnson standard "Since I Fell for You" by his primary clients, the Skyliners, in June of 1963. Both records appeared on the firm's Atco subsidiary. Not wanting to incur the wrath of Levy and Goldner, Ahmet Ertegun, Jerry Wexler, and the powers at Atco/Atlantic credited the Modern Flamingos sides to the Starglows.

Despite the name change, the imprint of the Flamingos was all over the record, through the sound and style of two of their most creative former members. When the Careys, who had been struggling to break "I Know Better" into the Hot 100, heard "Let's Be Lovers," they were less than pleased. "When they heard it, Jake and Zeke shit," Johnson admits with a laugh. "It

Terry Johnson (holding the group's End albums) with a Modern Flamingos lineup, ca. 1963. Top row, left to right: Bill Hawks (organ), Carl Chambers (drums). Middle row, left to right: Eddie Thomas (bass guitar), Kent Peeler (tenor vocals), Troy Anthony (tenor vocals) and Tony Drake (baritone vocals) (courtesy Colton Thomas).

sounded too much like the Flamingos with Nate and I singing the lead like Paul and I did on 'Lovers Never Say Goodbye.' They cried to George Goldner, and Goldner probably had someone go over to Ertegun. You know, like 'I'll pay whatever it is, but you can't let these guys go out, because you're hurting me, now.'" Goldner and Levy, according to Johnson, had their Starglows record killed, effectively ending the group's hopes to make it to the national charts on their own. "Zeke was so stubborn, you know," Johnson confides. "We should have gotten back together. As soon as we broke up, and we saw that it wasn't happening, we should have gotten back together. We should have said, 'Let's let bygones be bygones, and let's get back together and make the money.'"

Not long after the Starglows record, Johnson organized a new lineup. "I hired a group called the Modern Ink Spots," Johnson explains. "I put a lot of groups together and called them the Modern Flamingos." The Modern Ink Spots, North Philadelphia natives who had first recorded in 1958 as the Equadors for RCA Victor, consisted of first tenor Oscar Drummond, second tenor Rilly Foreman, bass Reginald Grant, baritone Gary Evans, lead Al Turner, and drummer Claude Higgs. They recorded one single, "Spotlight Dance," for Rust Records in 1962, and waxed "Why Don't You Write Me" as the Cardinals for the Rose label in 1963.

Born and raised in North Philadelphia, Grammy® Award winner Billy Paul (1934–2016) performed with Johnson's Flamingos long before topping the charts with "Me and Mrs. Jones" in 1972. I

Terry Johnson &

THE FANTASTIC FLAMINGOS

JOLLY JOYCE AGENCY
2028 Chestnut St.
Phila., Pa. 19103
Booking Direction
Norman M. Joyce

A mid–1960s lineup featuring Terry Johnson (Michael Denning photo, courtesy Colton Thomas).

was one of the Blue Notes at one time," Paul told interviewer Lee Tyler in 2009. "I didn't want to dance, so Harold Melvin fired me, [and] I had a six-month stay with the Flamingos. I was with the Flamingos for a while."

A later Modern Flamingos lineup found Johnson singing lead, arranging, and playing guitar with Kent Peeler, a tenor who recorded with the Dreamers vocal group on Rollin' and Grand, baritone Tony Drake, and tenor Troy Anthony. Filling out the rhythm section were Eddie Thomas on bass, Bill Hawks on organ, and drummer Carl Chambers.

Born Samuel Garner, Tony Drake (1945–2017) was a big fan of the Flamingos. He had seen them perform at Philadelphia's Uptown Theater, met them on one occasion, and, recognizing Johnson in Philadelphia, approached him about a job. Johnson asked Drake if he was a singer. Desperately wanting to join him, Drake lied and said he was singing with a local group. As he auditioned for his idols Terry Johnson and Nate Nelson, Drake's nerves got the best of him. "I was so nervous, I couldn't sing," Tony admitted to researcher Marv Goldberg. Nelson dismissed Drake outright, but several months later, Johnson gave him another opportunity, and this time, he was

The Modern Flamingos in 1967. Front, left to right: Sonny Ross and Jerry Abel. Top row, left to right: Duke Johnson, Warren Sherrill, Eddie Edgehill, Terry Johnson and Eddie Thomas (courtesy Terry Johnson).

ready. Drake would perform with the Modern Flamingos, singing lead on the songs that Hunt had popularized with the group. After about a year, Drake left, and was replaced by Nelson Dupree. As a soloist, Tony Drake enjoyed some success in the soul era, cutting solo sides for Musicor and Brunswick in 1969–70 and writing the Chi-Lites' "Living in the Footsteps of Another Man."

While Johnson wanted to focus on recording, Nelson's sights were set on the income associated with personal appearances, and eventually the pair went their separate ways when Nate was offered a spot in the Platters. "I stayed in Philadelphia, and just kept working," Terry explains. "I said, 'Let's keep recording,' but Nate said, 'I have a family. I've got to work.' He had a wife and a child. So Nate went with the Platters, and I said, 'OK, man. God bless you.'"

Still, Johnson's Modern Flamingos found work in resorts and nightclubs around the country into 1967. "We were working constantly because the Flamingos' name was big." As with the 21st-century group, Johnson organized the Modern Flamingos throughout their career. He selected the material and the harmonies, developed the stage presentation, chose their material, and rehearsed the music with his band and vocalists.

Starting Over—Flamingos and Platters

Teaming up with songwriter John Pearson, Zeke Carey co-produced an independent session for the Flamingos in the spring of 1964 that yielded two new masters. The first, "Lover Come Back to Me," was first recorded by the group in November of 1961, but Goldner, who was unhappy with the finished product, never released it. The B-side, "Your Little Guy," was credited to Ronnie Lewis and John Pearson and copyrighted on January 13, 1964. The group released the songs on their tiny Bellville Record Company in May. The plain white label with black print erroneously credited the producers with having written the A-side, a 35-year-old Oscar Hammerstein II and Sigmund Romberg collaboration. In his search for a bigger label to reissue and distribute the single, Carey settled on his old friend, Leonard Chess, who gave the group a one-shot deal on Checker. While some sources have listed the songs as having been recorded on June 15, 1964, this is apparently the date that Chess purchased or leased the masters from Carey, as the Checker release was out within days of this date, and therefore does not take the Bellville release into account.

The record did sell well enough to go into a second pressing on the new powder-blue Checker label, complete with the black and red checker pawn logo, and a follow-up session was scheduled. On August 7, 1964, the group recorded Al Collier's "Does It Really Matter" and a new version of "Goodnight Sweetheart," which were released on Checker in September. On Monday, September 28, 1964, the Flamingos appeared at the Graystone Ballroom in Detroit, along with Big John and his Caravan, and organist Milt Buckner and his band. Tickets could be had for only a dollar.

By this point, turmoil had again enveloped the group. "Towards the end of the 'Ol' Man River' group, I hired a guy named Doug McClure," Zeke recounted to McGarvey. "Just as he got pretty good, Eddie Williams and Billy Clarke left within the same week. No warning, less than a week before an engagement. So I took over as emcee, and Doug McClure was forced into doing lead."

Douglas Paul McClure was a second-generation R&B singer born in New Haven, Connecticut, on March 18, 1940. His father Sam (1921–1965), a baritone, toured with Andy Kirk's band as part of the Jubalaires in 1946. Between 1949 and 1954, he recorded and performed with the Shadows, one of New Haven's first R&B vocal groups. Recording three singles each for Lee, Sittin' In With, and Decca, McClure sang lead on three sides, "Jitterbug Special," "Beans," and "Big Mouth Mama." "My father Sam McClure was in the business with the Shadows, and I grew up in music," McClure explained to interviewer Richard Phillips in 2006. "That is the stuff I grew up with, real tight harmony. My dad just loved music. He played the guitar, and he would teach my sisters and I harmony. I used to sit around with the Shadows in their rehearsals. I did a lot of singing in church, and as soon as I found a way, I started singing rock and roll. I never did any [voice] training. Mom could sing, too. She sang in the church. It was just a natural gift. It was in my blood."

Doug McClure began singing as a teenager, harmonizing with New Haven groups including the Chestnuts and the Pyramids. He was with the latter group when they backed up Ruby Whittaker on her Mark-X release, "I Don't Want to Set The World on Fire," in 1957. "I used to sing with the Five Satins and the Chestnuts and the Pyramids," McClure clarified. "I did some tenor with the Five Satins, but I was still in school and they were older than me. I was a young singer. We used to sit around on the stoop and sing. We had a lot of good groups out of New Haven." After graduating from Hillhouse High School in the city in 1958, he served in the United States Army.

McClure recalled traveling to New York with a singing buddy who was going to audition for the Flamingos in 1964. "At the time, I was singing gospel with a friend's group out of New Haven called the Goldenaires. The Flamingos needed another voice, and I went down with this friend who was going to audition. I actually had no intention of auditioning. When we did get there, it didn't work out for my friend. So they asked me to try it, and I gave it a shot and the next thing I knew, I was hooked up. We started recording right away."

A powerful tenor with a clear, impassioned delivery, Doug McClure would serve as the group's primary lead for the next dozen years. "Basically, I did the lead vocals," he stated. "I listened to a lot of gospel, Claude Jeter of the Swan Silvertones, the Soul Stirrers with Sam Cooke, and they influenced my singing. Bill Kenny of the Ink Spots had a style all of his own. Actually, I was influenced by his style, you know, taking my time as a balladeer. There's taking your time and there's taking your *sweet* time. When I sang the lyrics, I took my sweet time and pronounced the lyrics so the people could understand what the song was all about. When I sang, there was no doubt what I was singing about."

The group soon lost another member when Paul Wilson was released in late 1964. Although Zeke stated that Wilson had "retired," Johnson admits that alcohol dependence got the 12-year veteran fired. "Paul and I used to drink vodka and Coca-Cola or vodka and ginger ale or vodka and orange juice," Terry recalls of their days together. "He kind of influenced me. He'd say, 'Come on, Buzzy, let's get a drink.' I was the youngest one in the group, so I was a follower. I would get a little drink. But Paul always managed to drink more than me. So once Tommy left, and then I left, and then Nate left, Paul was there with Jake and Zeke. There was nobody for him to dance with, nobody for him to be pals with. There was nobody for him to have fun and to drink with, I guess, so Paul kind of lost it. He drank a lot, and Jake and Zeke fired Paul."

Around the same time, Nate Nelson and Terry Johnson parted company as well. "I stayed in Philadelphia and just kept working with my group," Terry states. "Nate and I had to split, because he wanted to keep working [on the road], and I wanted to record. I was more into recording, and Nate wanted to just work. Nate had a shot to go with Herbie Reed and the Platters, and I said, 'Well, OK, man, hey, God bless you. Let's stay in touch with each other. If you get in a better spot than me, let me know. Help me out. If I get in a better spot, I'll let you know. I'll help you out. That's the way that ended."

In the twilight of a splendid 11-year association with Mercury Records, the Platters, in late 1964, consisted of Sonny Turner, who had replaced original lead Tony Williams in 1960; original recording members David Lynch, Paul Robi, and Herb Reed; and Barbara Randolph, who had recently taken over for fellow original Zola Taylor. Nelson was invited to take Robi's position. The circumstances surrounding Nelson's opportunity to join the group were detailed in Southern California District Court Judge Judith N. Keep's background briefing in the case *Robi vs. Reed*, which was heard in the United States 9th Circuit Court of Appeals in 1989. "Paul Robi severed his relationship with the group in 1965, when he was arrested and convicted of felony narcotics possession charges; he did not leave Reed's group for the purpose of starting a new group, nor did Robi return to the Platters ... after his release from prison."

By 1965, Nelson had replaced Robi, assuming the role of tenor and second lead. Betty Jackson took over for Randolph, but was soon replaced with Sandra Dawn, who had sung lead with the Chantels in 1963–64. Longtime manager Buck Ram brought the group to Musicor Records in early 1966. Their initial recording for the label, Luther Dixon and Charlie Foxx's "I Love You 1000 Times," reached #31 on the Hot 100 and #6 on *Billboard*'s R&B chart that spring.

BREAKING OUT BIG FROM THEIR HIT ALBUM
"I LOVE YOU 1000 TIMES"
"I'LL BE HOME"
THE PLATTERS
FLIP SIDE "THE MAGIC TOUCH" MUSICOR 1211

Musicor Records advertisement, 1966. Left to right: Herb Reed, David Lynch, Sonny Turner, Sandra Dawn, and Nate Nelson (author's collection).

With the Platters, Nelson had the opportunity to perform nightly, write new songs, and record regularly. Nate and Herb Reed collaborated on "Don't Hear, Speak, See No Evil," the soulful up-tempo flip of "I Love You 1000 Times." For their third release, issued in November of 1966, just in time for the Holidays, Nelson was brought to the forefront to lead a revival of his Flamingos classic, "I'll Be Home." Opening with a trumpet playing "Taps" and military-styled drums throughout, the recording was unquestionably aimed at record buyers whose loved ones were serving in the war in Vietnam. Reed delivered an updated version of Wilson's original recitation, and Nelson was in fine voice throughout. The disc spent two weeks on the pop chart in December, peaking at a disappointing #97.

That same year, Nelson got his old friend Paul Wilson, who had been fired from the Flamingos, an opportunity to sing with the Platters. The gig could have been a perfect fit for the charismatic baritone's many talents, but Wilson's dependence on alcohol caused him to be terminated quickly by Reed, who never tolerated such behavior. "Nate got Paul with Herbie Reed's Platters," Terry Johnson confirms. "But Paul was drinking so heavy. One time he was so drunk he just fell off the stage, and they had to let him go."

In the early spring of 1967, "With This Ring," featuring a powerful performance from Turner, took the Platters to #12 on the R&B list and #14 on the pop chart, their final Top 40 hit. Two additional charters, "Washed Ashore (On a Lonely Island in the Sea)," and "Sweet, Sweet Lovin'" came in the summer and fall of '67, ensuring the group a long life on the concert stage.

In 1969, Herb Reed, the last of the original members remaining with Ram's group, left the fold and began his own group, which he continued to front until his death in 2012 at age 83. By 1972, they consisted of Reed, Nelson, Liz Davis and Ron Austin, all former Ram employees, and Duke Daniels. Herb Reed's Platters eventually established their home base in Massachusetts, where Nate Nelson and his wife, Angel, also settled. In concert, Nate led the majority of the group's songs. All told, he would spend 18 years with the Platters, more than double his seven-year stint with the Flamingos.

While the Platters were back on the charts in the mid–1960s with Nate Nelson in the lineup, the reorganized Flamingos were poised to make their own run at success with a new, revitalized sound and a new label.

"The Boogaloo Party"

In December of 1964, Slim Rose's Times Square label released a 45 RPM of "A Lovely Way to Spend an Evening" and "Walking My Baby Back Home," which it attributed to the Flamingos. According to researcher Marv Goldberg, the company pushed the record in publications like the New York–based *Keep the Big Beat Alive* as a couple of early Flamingos recordings or rehearsals. In fact, the record had nothing at all to do with the legendary act. "They were probably white a cappella groups," Goldberg sums, "[and] I say groups because it doesn't even sound like both sides are by the same people. These were some horrendous masters that Slim Rose obtained and decided to put out under the Flamingos name. I can't image how he got away with this, since the Flamingos were still performing."

After their brief return to Checker, the real Flamingos signed on with Philips Records, a division of Mercury, during the summer of 1965. Founded by the Dutch electronics firm of the same name in 1950, Philips served as the United Kingdom's distributor for recordings that initially appeared on Columbia Records in the United States. In 1961, Philips signed an exchange agreement with Mercury. Subsequently, the company purchased Mercury and its various subsidiaries, and merged its record business with Deutsche Grammophon in 1962. "We were with End from '58 to '64, then we went to Philips," Zeke summed to McGarvey, omitting their two-disc deal with Checker. "Roulette took the whole End catalog over."

"End of '65, I added a good strong drummer," Zeke continued. "So, it was Doug [McClure], me and Jake, the saxophone player [Julien Vaught], the guitar player, named Al Fontaine, and the drummer, Reggie. We kept it to six, an exciting group, high energy all the time."

"Alan Fontaine, oh, could that guy play the guitar!" McClure agreed. "He was beautiful. When we were doing our shows, he had a part where he would actually bite the guitar strings with his teeth and play it. Boy, he was good. Zeke Carey played the bass, and there was me and Jake Carey, and Julian Vaught, who was a horn player. As the Flamingos, we were self-contained. We sang and we played."

For the group's first recording session, held on Sunday, April 18, 1965, they were paired with Luchi DeJesus (1923–1984), a veteran songwriter, arranger, and conductor who worked with artists including Art Blakey and Chet Baker, and at one time served as the vice president for Mercury Records' Latin music division. DeJesus had worked with Dinah Washington and Brook Benton on "A Rockin' Good Way," and shared a songwriting credit on the 1960 hit. Later, he composed the music for the 1973 motion picture *Detroit 9000* with Lamont Dozier.

Selected for recording was "Temptation," originally written by Broadway and motion picture composer Nacio Herb Brown (1896–1964) and lyricist Arthur Freed (1894–1973). The team, best remembered for their classic "Sin-

Left to right: Jake Carey, Julien Vaught (saxophone), Zeke Carey (bass guitar), Doug McClure, Reggie (drummer) and Al Fontaine (guitar) performing for dancers, ca. 1965–66 (courtesy Joe Mirrione).

gin' in the Rain," penned the tune for the 1933 movie *Going Hollywood*. Bing
Crosby had a #3 chart hit with the song in 1934. The Everly Brothers resurrected it in 1961 with a rocking rendition that climbed into the pop Top 30.

"We would do standards, [and] the guy would say, 'Hey, man, this doesn't
go too well because the melody doesn't go there,'" Jake recalled to interviewer
Tancredi. "But we would compromise. We would try it, but we had big fights.
The arranger would say, 'Hey, man, I didn't write it this way.' But this is the
way we feel it. You must project your feeling. That's the only way people can
relate to you. You find people walking to the counters and saying, hey, man,
I want this particular tune, because they can relate to a certain feeling. That's
what people buy. This is their appreciation for what you've done. They understand what they want, and that's what the artist is supposed to put into music.
That's how you become an artist. He can put into music what the people have
in their minds. Many times, this is how we had to do these things and to
compromise. But at no time did we ever make such a big compromise that
we would harm the effectiveness of the Flamingos. Because everybody there,
you know, every time the clock rolled around, you were spending money, so
the arguments were never long."

The Flamingos' funky doo-wop version featured Doug McClure singing
lead, accompanied by strong harmonies and a heavy bass guitar line throughout. "We really had the Flamingos sound on that," McClure opined. "It was
arranged and done nicely." McClure also fronted "Call Her on the Phone," a
Curtis Mayfield composition that carried a similar groove. The songs were
issued on July 2, 1965. *Billboard* selected "Call Her on the Phone" as a spotlight
pick on July 24, proclaiming, "The popular group is back and Philips has
them. A powerhouse rhythm ballad cleverly delivered has hit written all over
it. Great sound." Despite the hype, the single failed to click.

To regain their hit-making status, the Flamingos needed to try something new, and they knew it. It came together in a session held in New York
on Thursday, December 16, 1965. "In '65, there was another change in the
group," Zeke explained. "Dance crazes were becoming predominant. That's
when we came up with 'Boogaloo Party.' That came from the routines of the
Flamingos."

"The action was in the head and not in the hips," Jake asserted.

"We used to close the show saying, 'Dance hearty, stay with your party,
and don't bother nobody,'" Zeke remembered. "So we wrote the song and
recorded it. Philips wouldn't even let me record it the way I wanted to." "The
Boogaloo Party," a very danceable R&B tune with a strong back beat, was
credited to Zeke Carey, lead singer Doug McClure, and former Flamingo
Billy Clarke, and arranged for the group by Bob Halley, who had previously

worked at Philips with Dusty Springfield. An award-winning songwriter and arranger, Halley (1938–2017) co-wrote Nat "King" Cole's 1962 hit "Dear Lonely Hearts," and later arranged and conducted "Lovin' You," a top 40 hit for Bobby Darin in 1966. "We called it 'Dance Hearty' when we first did it," Zeke added. "Then we decided to call it 'Dance Hearty, Boogaloo Party.' It was a long time before the Boogaloo caught on. It was the first real big up-tempo song we had after 'Nobody Loves Me Like You Do.'"

"The first Boogaloo song was the one that I penned," McClure asserted to interviewer Richard Phillips 40 years after the fact. "We had a language within the group we used to call incoherency. Bill Cosby had a record out at the time [that featured a comic routine] called 'Incoherency.' We would talk to each other without words—just [gibberish], incoherency. If anyone was listening, it wouldn't make sense to them, but we understood what we were talking about. So we were doing this show one time, and they asked me what dance I was doing. I caught myself doing the Philadelphia Dog. I loved to dance, but I really wasn't a dancer. And the kids would ask you questions (on the show). They said what's the name of the dance that the tall guy was doing? I said the Boogaloo. And that's how that name came about. I just made it up. You slide two on your left foot, and you glide two on your right. You shook your head along with your hips, and you sort of had that rhythm thing. We used to have a lot of fun with that dance."

McClure also led the group's elegant interpretation of Academy Award–winning composer Hoagy Carmichael (1899–1981) and twelve-time Oscar-nominated lyricist Ned Washington's (1901–1976) 1937 love ballad, "The Nearness of You." "When I hear that song, I'm reminiscing to when I first met my wife, Francine," McClure wistfully recalled. "It just stirs up my heart—the smile that she had when I first met her. It constantly reminds me of it when I hear that song." Although the tune has mistakenly been attributed to Gladys Swarthout in the 1938 Paramount film *Romance in the Dark*, it was never even scheduled to appear in the motion picture.

JazzStandards.com musicologist K.J. McElrath writes that, "according to Richard Sudhalter's Hoagy Carmichael biography *Stardust Melody: The Life and Music of Hoagy Carmichael*, 'The Nearness of You' was a melody that Carmichael dashed off for a screen adaptation of Shakespeare's *A Midsummer Night's Dream*, featuring fifteen-year-old Mickey Rooney. With Washington's lyric, it became 'The Nearness of You,' scheduled for inclusion in the feature *Romance in the Rough*. The film was never produced, and the song had to wait for republication in 1940 to win its place as a standard. Probably as a result of the similar titles, *Romance in the Rough* versus *Romance in the Dark*, the introduction of 'The Nearness of You' is mistakenly credited to Ms. Swarthout in

Romance in the Dark in at least one reference book, numerous sheet music books, and, consequently, the error appears on hundreds of websites."

In 1940, the Glenn Miller Orchestra with vocalist Ray Eberle recorded the song for Bluebird Records, earning a top five chart hit. Bob Manning with the Monty Kelly Orchestra took "The Nearness of You" back into the

THE FLAMINGOS
The Originators of the Boogaloo

Clockwise from top left: Zeke Carey, Doug McClure, Al Fontaine, Jake Carey, and Julien Vaught, 1966 (Billy Vera collection).

Top 20 in 1953. Faron Young, Brook Benton, and Lou Donaldson also recorded it between 1958 and 1960.

The songs were released by Philips on December 29, 1965, and began selling well across the country. On March 19, 1966, "The Boogaloo Party" spent the first of two weeks on *Billboard*'s pop chart, where it peaked at #93. On the 26th, it hit the R&B list, reaching #22 during a three-week stay. It was the group's first charted hit in nearly six years. "When we got to the Apollo Theater, James Brown was on the show, and I actually showed James Brown how to do the Boogaloo on the Apollo stage," McClure remembered. "He took it up to another level. He was a great entertainer."

Bookings increased, and the Flamingos became regulars on the college and university touring circuit, which included acts like the Drifters and Shirelles. In September, they held court at the new Downbeat Room in the Maryland Hotel. In December, they were back at the Apollo for a dazzling two-week stand with Billy Stewart, Aaron Neville, Jimmy Castor, Tommy Hunt, Inez and Charlie Foxx, the Manhattans, the Falcons, and Sad Sam.

The group's next recording session took place on Monday, March 28, 1966. The Flamingos were teamed with producer Ted Cooper and veteran arranger and conductor Leroy "Roy" Glover. A child prodigy educated at the Juilliard School of Music, Cooper (1938–1975) had joined Shapiro-Bernstein music publishing in 1965 as a "general professional manager," working with the Drifters, Dobie Gray, and Leslie Uggams. Born in New York City, Glover (1933–1995) was an accomplished musician, having studied piano, organ, trumpet, clarinet, alto sax, vibraphone and bass, and held a bachelor of music degree. Early in his career, Roy worked with Cootie Williams's band and studied with prolific arranger Maury Deutsch. Eventually, Glover developed into an in-demand session arranger and musical director, working with artists including Connie Francis, Bobby Vinton, Maxine Brown, Ben E. King, the Impressions, the Platters, the Drifters, and Ruby and the Romantics, whose hit "Our Day Will Come" featured an organ solo played by Roy himself.

Zeke Carey, Doug McClure, producer Ted Cooper, and former Velours baritone singer John Pearson, who had previously co-written "It Must Be Love" and "Your Little Guy" for the group, were credited with writing "Brooklyn Boogaloo," the logical follow-up to their recent hit. Borrowing the horn riff from Larry Williams's 1957 hit, "Bony Maronie," the song was another funky McClure-led rave-up with a strong dance beat. "Dance crazes were going on, that's what it was back then," McClure told Phillips. "You had all kinds of dances, the Monkey and the Stroll and so many little dances that they were all doing, and the Boogaloo just came along with the rest of them. We just had fun with it, and then came out with the 'Brooklyn Boogaloo.'"

"The Flamingos will have tons of kids dancing to this groovy sound that is made to order for the most recent steps," *Cash Box* wrote in its July 16 review. "Loads of potential here for vast exposure."

Zeke Carey wrote the unison-led B-side, "Since My Baby Put Me Down," and published the song in the group's own BMI registered Belleville Music firm, named for the small Virginia town where their Jewish temple was located. Released on June 29, 1966, the disc failed to match the interest generated by "The Boogaloo Party."

Color image taken for the 1966 Philips album. Top row, left to right: Jake Carey and Julien Vaught. Bottom row, left to right: Zeke Carey, Doug McClure, and Al Fontaine (author's collection).

Both sides of the group's two Philips singles were included in a 12-track album, *The Flamingos—Their Hits Then and Now*, which became their first LP in three years when it was released that April. Issued in both mono and stereo, the album had a cover that featured a full-color photo of the Careys, McClure, Vaught, and Fontaine, smiling broadly in matching plaid suits. Two additional new recordings—a version of the traditional folk song "The Yellow Rose of Texas," which Zeke took sole songwriting credit for, and "I'm Not Tired Yet," credited to both Zeke and Doug—opened and closed side two. "That's one of the songs that I wrote," McClure clarified. "I've been loving you, baby, for a long time, but 'I'm Not Tired Yet.' I was just in love with love. I was really in love with my wife, Francine, just going from day to day."

Sandwiched in between the new songs were six re-recordings of the group's best-known Checker and End hits. All of the additional songs were recorded at the March 28 studio session. Entertaining the ill-conceived notion of re-recording their classic sides may have seemed a good idea to the group and the label. In hindsight, however, trying to recreate the magic of the original "Lovers Never Say Goodbye" and "I Only Have Eyes for You" was an artistic failure. Some record buyers may have been enticed to purchase the album based on the familiar song titles, but had to have been disappointed with what lay within the grooves. To his credit, McClure was competent and pleasing in the lead vocalist role, Glover provided good arrangements, but it just wasn't possible to improve on, or even equal, the originals.

"I don't know why those tunes [specifically] were chosen," McClure confessed. "I just felt confident that I could do them, and I just hoped that people liked my versions. I always took my sweet time and enunciated and sang and people enjoyed it. Everything was live, so we had to get it right all the way through. We kept going until we got it right. Every time you start and make a mistake, you start all over again at square one. You psyched yourself up if you had to do fifty takes. It didn't matter. You had to go from A to Z like a good actor. When you're singing your song, you just have to put your mind right and blank out everything and go."

"Eyes," which immediately followed "The Boogaloo Party" on side one, was passable, and "A Kiss from Your Lips," featuring a melodic alto sax accompaniment from Vaught, was excellent as a stand-alone recording. A funky version of "Nobody Loves Me Like You" and a competent reading of "I'll Be Home," with Glover playing organ in the background, appeared on side two. The exotic arrangement of "The Yellow Rose of Texas," with Vaught on flute and unison vocal harmonies, was entertaining; but the Latin-tinged "I'm Not Tired Yet" and the re-recording of "Your Other Love" missed the mark. Worst of all, however, was "Lovers Never Say Goodbye." Aside from Vaught's capable horn playing, the entire production was just plain amateurish. The duet lead, likely sung by McClure and Zeke Carey, was especially dismal—weak and devoid of soul.

Although the LP failed to make *Billboard's* national album chart, it did sell reasonably well. In its April 30 review, *Cash Box* called it "all up to date danceable music built on a firm R&B foundation." Original copies were only fetching $15 to $25 among collectors when the unauthorized *The Flamingos—The Complete Philips Recordings* appeared on CD in the early 2000s. If it was completed, one Philips-era master which has yet to surface is "I Done Fell in Love." The song was copyrighted by Zeke Carey on November 9, 1965, and assigned to Belleville Music listing him as the composer.

In 1966, baritone and alternate lead Sidney Hall was recruited into the act. Hall began singing as a teenager in Washington, D.C., first recording as a member of the Enjoyables on Capitol in 1964. After their lone release for the firm, "Push a Little Harder" and "We'll Make a Way," failed to catch on, the group signed with the local Shrine label, waxing "Shame" and "I'll Take You Back." Hall also recorded a solo disc for Shrine, "The Weekend" and "I'm a Lover," before joining the Flamingos in mid–1966.

THE FLAMINGOS
The Originators of the Boogaloo

The sextet in late 1966. Top row, left to right: Julien Vaught, Sid Hall, Doug McClure, Jake Carey. Bottom row, left to right: Zeke Carey and Al Fontaine (Billy Vera collection).

Billy Carl, Joe Venneri, and Richard Grasso wrote the group's next single, the mid-tempo Motown-inspired "She Shook My World," with Sidney Hall leading, which was paired with "Itty Bitty Baby." Both were recorded on October 5, 1966, and issued by Philips on November 15. Carl and Venneri, who produced the Lollypops on Smash that same year, produced the single, which featured arrangements by old friend Sammy Lowe. On December 3, *Cash Box* tabbed "She Shook My World" as a Best Bet, opining that the "strong, thumping ditty could be a big one for the Flamingos." On March 29, 1967, the group taped a television appearance on disc jockey Clay Cole's Diskotek show, which was broadcast over WPIX in New York.

Another two-song session held on March 7, 1967, produced the group's fifth Philips single, which was issued on April 12. Zeke Carey and Doug McClure shared co-authorship on "It Keeps the Doctor Away" and the Hall-led "(You Gotta Be) Koo Koo," another "Boogaloo" follow-up. "The idea sort of just hit me, I guess," McClure told interviewer Richard Phillips in 2006. "I got the idea from an older couple that had been married for like 60 years, and they were actually holding hands. I said to myself, 'Wow, that's love.' And I actually asked them, and they said love kept them going. The love that they had for each other just kept them going, and then the idea hit me. A little loving every day keeps the doctor away. I never really finished the song. There was a part in that song where it didn't have any words at all. I tried to think of what to say and absolutely nothing came. So, I just went with a la-la-la-la-la … Oh I know they didn't know, so I told them so. It keeps the doctor away. A little love keeps the doctor away.' And I started laughing, and we had to do it again and again and again because it was funny. But it worked out all right."

Zeke Carey earned a label production credit on the group's final Philips single, the danceable Ronnie Lewis–penned "Do It, To It," and "Oh Mary Don't You Worry," which was credited to Carey and McClure. The songs were recorded at the group's final session for the company in early October. "Zeke was really good in the studio," Hall recalled in 2015. "He knew his way around and what he wanted." Sammy Lowe did the arrangements once again, and the record was released on October 23, 1967. On November 4, *Cash Box* tabbed "Oh Mary Don't You Worry" a "poignant R&B ballad [that] could take flight." The following week, *Billboard* selected the record as a spotlight pick to hit the top 10, lauding "two equally commercial and powerful sides that should bring the Flamingos back to the top of the charts in short order." They didn't, and when the disc failed to click, Philips Records and the Flamingos parted company.

Motown and
Terry Johnson

Terry Johnson's reorganized Modern Flamingos continued performing out of the Philadelphia area into 1967, but the artist's interests were rooted in writing, producing, and arranging. After a meeting with William "Smokey" Robinson of the Miracles, Terry was offered a job at Motown Records as a songwriter, producer, and artist. "What had happened was, Smokey Robinson came to Philadelphia at the Uptown Theater, and I went down and I saw him. I said, 'Man, can you help me at Motown?' I didn't know Smokey was important there. I thought he was just an artist there. He said, 'Why? What do you do?' I said, 'I've got some songs that I wrote. I've got a partner, a girl named Terry.' We were called T&T. It was on the order of Marvin [Gaye] and Tammi [Terrell]. He said, 'Let me hear it, Buzz.' I said, 'I can't lug this big tape recorder in here.' He said, 'Well, bring it over to the Marriott Hotel.' He said, 'I'll be glad to listen to it out there, because I don't want to listen to it in the theater.' I said, 'Cool.'"

The next night, Johnson drove his '66 Cadillac Fleetwood over to the Marriott to meet Robinson. "I played him my songs, and he said, 'Damn, man, this is good. Yeah, Buzz. I can definitely get you into Motown. I can guarantee you I can get you into Motown. Man, do you write more stuff like this?' I said, 'Yeah, Smokey, this is what I do.' He said, 'Beautiful. When do you want to come?' I said, 'As soon as possible.' So I left everything in Philadelphia. I just took my clothes and my jewelry and my guitars and went to Detroit. I was going to come back to Philadelphia, but everything was so new and nice in Detroit, I just stayed in Detroit. I had the rest of my stuff, my furniture and all, shipped to me."

In the late 1960s and early 1970s, Johnson worked at Motown as a staff writer and producer, working with artists including the Four Tops, Martha and the Vandellas, the Supremes, the Temptations, the Miracles, Edwin Starr, David Ruffin, Mickey Denton, and the Spinners, among others. Johnson shared songwriting credits with Robinson and Al Cleveland (1930–1996) on

A 1960s studio portrait of Terry Johnson (courtesy Colton Thomas).

the Miracles' 1969 hits, "Baby, Baby Don't Cry" and "Here I Go Again," and "Malinda," a top 20 R&B hit for Bobby Taylor and the Vancouvers in 1968.

Robinson had met songwriter Al Cleveland, formerly a vocalist with the Halos, at the Apollo and struck up a friendship. "Al Cleveland met Smokey after [our group] the Gees sang at the Apollo," Al Springer recalled. "He told him he was a writer and producer, and Smokey got him an audition with Berry Gordy. Al's wife, Lorraine, and Smokey's wife were friends, too. Then he told Smokey he had an idea for a song called 'I Second That Emotion.'"

A collaboration with Robinson, "I Second That Emotion" became a #1 hit for the Miracles in 1967. Earlier that year, Cleveland had penned "Everybody Loves a Winner," a national pop hit for Memphis R&B singer William Bell. Riding the success of "I Second That Emotion," Al Cleveland was offered a job as a songwriter with Motown. Cleveland and Robinson became the best of friends. Eventually, Cleveland brought his former singing and songwriting partner, Arthur Crier, into the Motown family.

Much to his chagrin, Terry was utilized primarily for his talents away from the microphone during his days at Motown. "I can hear a hit," he states. "When I was at Motown, Smokey and the others used me a lot to do that. Although Billie Jean Brown, that was her job in quality control, I could hear a hit. I knew what songs were going to make noise."

He even managed to make an occasional gig with the Modern Flamingos whenever the opportunity to perform arose, keeping the name active. In late 1969, the first of Terry's three solo discs, "My Springtime" and "Suzie," was released on the Gordy subsidiary. Although it did little at the time, "My Springtime" is now a popular Northern Soul record which has been reissued on CD and gained popularity in the United Kingdom. "I'd love to go over there and do that song that I did at Motown called 'My Springtime,'" Johnson confesses. "I don't know why I sang it so high, but I laugh when I listen to it."

For his second release, "What'cha Gonna Do," the label again used "Suzie" for the B-side. "'What'cha Gonna Do' was a nice song," Terry opines. "I wish I had let Marvin Gaye do it, though. Smokey tried to get me to do that. He said, 'Let Marvin sing it, man. Let somebody with a big name do it, because you don't have a name yet, Buzz. But if you write a song for somebody, and it's a smash, Marvin could eat it up...' I said, 'Well, damn, I really like this song, Smokey. I can write another one for Marvin.' I should have let Marvin Gaye sing that song because it's a good song, and he would have probably killed it. But I kept it, and it's gathering dust!"

Johnson's third and final Gordy single, issued under the name "Buzzie," was "Stone Soul Booster" and "Sandy," issued in early 1970. None of the discs garnered much attention at the time. The next Gordy release after "Stone Soul Booster" was Edwin Starr's "War," a #1 record. Whether he knew it or not, Terry's days as a solo artist at Motown were over. "I wish they had recorded me more," he laments. "Smokey didn't want me to come to Motown as an artist. He wanted me to come there as a producer and a songwriter with him. Everything had to go through him. Smokey was going to be executive producer over everything, and I didn't realize that. I should have let Marvin Gaye sing 'What'cha Gonna Do.' But would have, should have, could have, doesn't mean anything today."

In December of 2018, 88 unreleased tracks from the Motown archives were released on a pair of digital albums, *Motown Unreleased 1968 Parts 1 and 2.* Alongside recordings by the Four Tops, the Temptations, and Gladys Knight and the Pips were five polished, soulful, and commercial Marvin and Tammi–influenced duets recorded by Terry Johnson and Theresa Botial under the name T&T. Instrumental tracks for three songs written by Terry, "The One Who Loves You," "What Happened to Love," and "Terrie," and one credited to Terry Botial, "What Do You Know About Love," were recorded on January 12, 1968, with the lead vocals committed to tape on January 19. An additional master, the funky Johnson composition "Psychologically," was initially tracked on February 6 and completed on March 1, 1968. Smokey Robinson and Al Cleveland produced the songs, which inexplicably languished unheard for 50 years. The basic track of "Terrie" was subsequently repurposed and overdubbed by Terry Johnson for the aforementioned 1970 solo release, "Sandy."

Johnson remained part of the Motown family for a total of ten years, staying until 1977. "After about eight years, they moved out to California," Johnson explains. "At that time, I had gotten into astrology like a nut, because I had so much time on my hands. When I first got there, I was traveling with Smokey everywhere he went. I was with the Miracles. Everywhere they'd go, Smokey had me with him. He said I was his partner. We would be writing and producing while he was on the road. After that, I told Smokey he was going to leave the Miracles. He said, 'No way, Buzzy.' After a year, he came to my house and said, 'Buzz, I don't believe this. How the hell did you know when I was going to leave the Miracles?' I said, 'That's what your charts showed, Smokey.' He said, 'How the hell did you know to the day? I just left the group.' I said, 'You're kidding me.' I don't read charts anymore. But I did then."

"When they moved out to California, everybody's charts were saying that all the planets were going to line up in a perfect symmetrical formation. That would mean possibly a drastic thing was going to happen to the earth. That's when they were saying there could be an earthquake so bad that L.A. would break off and fall into the ocean. I believed this stuff because everything I was telling people was really coming to pass. I said, 'I'm not going out there.' So, everybody else moved out there, and I didn't. I stayed in Detroit.

"I did some more recordings, but not as many. I stayed there a couple more years, and Smokey came back home to Detroit, and he wanted to take me out. He said, 'Come on, let's go down and see Harold Melvin.' I said, 'Harold Melvin? That's my buddy. I haven't seen him in years.' We went down to Harold Melvin's birthday party in this club, and when Harold saw me, he ran over to me and grabbed me and said, 'I've been looking for you for years.

Damn, Buzzy, how have you been, man? I've got my own record company, Million Dollar Records. I'm the president, and I've been looking for you. You're the vice-president.' I was like, 'Huh?'

"So that's when I left Detroit, because Smokey was out in California, and I didn't have any real writing partners in Detroit, and it was getting stale. So I went back to Philadelphia with Harold Melvin and did a few things with him. Then I found out he was into cocaine and drinking and smoking pot and being crazy. He was ruining his life, and I had to get away from him.

Clockwise from top left: Theresa Trigg, Terry Johnson, Jerry Abel, and Eugene Rice, early 1977 (courtesy Terry Johnson).

That's when I got another group together. I started my group, Terry Johnson's Flamingos, again." In 1977, they consisted of Terry Johnson, Theresa Trigg, Eugene Rice, and Jerry Abel, who had been in the first Modern Flamingos lineup in 1961.

During the 1960s and 1970s, Johnson never crossed paths with the Careys. "Once I left, I closed the door. I didn't care about them anymore, because they had treated me very mean. They had accused me of things I didn't do, and they were very nasty to me. They were trying to tell me who I could be with and who I couldn't be with and what I had to do with my life. Almost, like, what time I had to go to bed. It was like, 'Come on, I'm a man. I don't need this kind of stuff from you guys. Where are you coming from all of a sudden?' But Tommy just threw everybody for a loop when he did what he did, and he made everybody suspicious of everybody else."

Ronze Records

While many of the stars of the 1950s found renewed success in the latest revival craze, which was jump-started by Richard Nader's first Madison Square Garden concert in 1969, Zeke Carey and the Flamingos refused to allow themselves to become exclusively an oldies act. After leaving Philips at the end of 1967, they decided to form their own enterprise. The Careys, who had previously formed their own Belleville Music publishing firm, called the company Ronze, with the last two letters coming from the president's first name. It was headquartered at 1234 Fulton Street in Brooklyn, between Bedford and Nostrand Avenues.

"We handled our own business because we knew that it had to be done," Vice-President Jake Carey told an interviewer in the early 1970s. "We had to turn around and handle the building of the group. When the records were put out, we had to learn to promote them. Any record we ever did, really, we produced it. This goes on back to being unaware. But still, this all goes into the management of yourself. So, you paid the dues, but you still learned how to do it, and this made us able to survive today. This taught us how to say 'This is a good deal,' or 'This is a bad deal,' or 'This doesn't relate to us,' or 'This isn't good for us.' Having that basic training from the [start], a dedicated guy [like Ralph Leon] saying, 'Man, I want you guys to learn how to take care of yourselves whether I'm around or not.' Now that we are aware, what do we do? We paid the price. We paid a lot of dues. That's the reason we have our own club. Picture being part of a club. You're paying dues, and they never let you become a member. Now that ain't too hip, is it? That's what life is. So, when you pay your dues, you automatically become a member of the club. This is the plane we have launched on now. We look at it in a broader scope. We found out what the business is about. We've sang, we've recorded, we've been on the stage. We've met the audience and signed autographs, and now we come back into the mechanics of it. That's how this thing is done. Then the guys that were with the same company [as we were] started saying, 'Why wasn't I given any statements monthly?' That's how you find out what all these things are about."

Tenor Keith Williams became a key member of the organization during this next phase in the Flamingos' career. Born in the Bronx on April 15, 1942, the fellow Brooklyn resident had begun his career with the Velours, replacing Troy Keys for their February 1959 Cub label session. Williams was featured on "Blue Velvet," "I Promise," "Little Sweetheart," and "Sweet Sixteen" into 1961 before the Velours went their separate ways. Williams was likely brought into the group by another former Velours member, baritone John Pearson, who had become the Flamingos' road manager in the early 1960s. Another Carey joined the Flamingos in 1969 when Jacob Charles "J.C." Carey, Jake's 23-year-old son, was recruited to sing second tenor and baritone. "I learned from schooling, and I learned from my father," J.C., born November 17, 1946, told interviewer Charlene Arsenault in 2007. "I always listened to their records. I listened to them constantly. When I became grown and the offer was made to me to join, it was very easy for me because I used to sing the songs all the time. I loved it because of the uniqueness. I wanted to pattern myself after it. I had other groups I was in, but I wanted to pattern myself after The Flamingos. I loved them."

The first recording the group came up with was "Dealin' (Groovin' with Feelin')," a funky dance tune that fit in perfectly with what was happening at the time. It was written, produced, and led by Zeke Carey.

Veteran mastering engineer Phil Austin, who worked with the group throughout the Ronze era, initially at the Mercury Sound Studio at 110 West 57th Street in New York City, remembers "Dealin'" as the start of his relationship with the Careys and the beginning of Ronze as well. "I met the Flamingos through a custom pressing thing we had at Mercury," Austin recalls. "This was back in 1969. At the time, we had a custom division at Mercury where people could come in off the streets with a tape, and they could get so many copies made, and they could have a record made. So I got this thing in from Ronze Records, and it was a 15 ips [inches per second] tape, and it was called 'Dealin (Groovin' with Feelin')' by the Flamingos. I looked at it, and I said, 'Oh, the Flamingos. I'm familiar with them.' I put the tape on, and I heard the funkiest track you ever wanted to hear in your life. Even if you couldn't dance, you'd want to try to, because it was a great-sounding tune. There was a little distortion on the vocals, but it had soul. It had quality to it. So I mastered it and everything, and about a week later, in comes Zeke and Jake Carey. They wanted to meet the engineer who had done their record. They said they'd never had a record mastered that hot before. They thought it was great, and they wanted to meet me. So, we struck up a relationship back in '69. That record, 'Dealin (Groovin' with Feelin')' went on to sell 20,000 copies."

Austin, who had been with the Mercury Custom Division for a little under two years, would work with Zeke Carey, mastering the Flamingos' session tapes all through the 1970s. "I had started at Mercury Studios about November of '67," Austin recalls. "I was looking for television work, and I had to go through this agency that dealt in radio and TV people. The last studio they sent me to on a Friday was Mercury Sound. This was when they used to be on 5th Avenue. I saw a guy there, Doug Hawkins, the chief engineer, was an ex-WOR engineer. He used to be in charge of all the transcription recording at WOR radio. They were planning on moving over to West 57th Street. I was the last interview of the day. He looked at my resume and said to me, 'Do you want to cut records?' I said, 'You bet I do!' He said, 'OK, you report to work on Monday, and bring your work clothes because we're moving into new studios.' So that was my start. In those days you could just literally walk in the door and they would throw you into mastering because they needed people. Today you need credentials behind you for them to even look at you. But it was great. It was the start of my career, and it was fun. I was with Mercury for seven years, and I had a ball there. It was a great learning place, too. So I got my learning skills at Mercury, but I wasn't coming in just cold. I knew something about it. This was where I met the Flamingos and had a great relationship."

Although Austin specifically remembers the song coming to him through Ronze, the group apparently licensed the master for release to Julmar Records, located at 1674 Broadway in New York City. The company, which also owned the Fun City subsidiary, was co-owned by R&B-soul songstress Marva Josie, hence the last three letters of the Julmar name. Four of the label's nine releases featured Josie, who later recorded with bandleader Earl "Fatha" Hines. Julmar's deal with the Flamingos was noted in the July 31, 1969, issue of *Jet* magazine.

"Dealin'" was released as Julmar #506 in June of 1969. Carey also penned the instrumental flip, "Dealin' All the Way," essentially a wordless rewrite of the A-side. "Dealin'" caught on with disc jockeys and record buyers and cracked the national R&B chart on September 27. In two weeks on the list, it peaked at #48, becoming, by far, the label's biggest success.

That summer, the group was making noise overseas as well, as "The Boogaloo Party" became the first Flamingos record ever to make the British charts. Three and a half years after its initial release, the song made it to #26 in the United Kingdom in June.

With interest in the group building once again, Zeke signed a licensing agreement for the Flamingos with Polydor Records in late 1969, which was likely arranged through New York producers Bob Feldman and Wes Farrell.

Originally an offshoot of the Deutsche Grammophon Gesellschaft, Polydor was introduced as an export label in 1924 and began releasing pop records in 1946. Popular German entertainers had recorded for the label for decades.

For their initial recording, Carey teamed up with producer Ted Cooper, who had worked with the group at Philips. Since their previous association, Cooper had produced a string of hits for Walter Jackson at Okeh Records and served as Epic's Artists and Repertoire Director in the pop field. Guitarist Al Fontaine wrote the arrangement on what would become the centerpiece of the Flamingos' latter-day output, "Buffalo Soldier." "We knew that we would be faced with the challenge of change again," Zeke stated. "[We] reached way back into military history and [brought] worldwide attention to some seemingly forgotten American heroes commissioned as the Ninth and Tenth Cavalry soldiers in the United States Army. They were most popularly known as the Buffalo Soldiers."

Comprised of former slaves, freemen, and black Civil War soldiers, the Buffalo Soldiers were the first African Americans to serve in the United States Army during peacetime. Two of the six all-black peacetime regiments created by Congress after the Civil War ended in 1865, the Ninth and Tenth Regiments fought American Indian tribes from Montana to Arizona and were responsible for escorting railroad workers, pioneers, and cattle herds across the Wild West. Will Crowdy, who established the Church of God and Saints of Christ, and whose congregation included the Careys, was a Buffalo Soldier with the Fifth Cavalry, serving as a quartermaster sergeant until his discharge in 1872.

According to the website "Buffalo Soldiers," "throughout the era of the Indian Wars, approximately twenty percent of the U.S. Cavalry troopers were Black, and they fought over 177 engagements. The combat prowess, bravery, tenaciousness, and looks on the battlefield, inspired the Indians to call them 'Buffalo Soldiers.' Many Indians believe the name symbolized the Native American's respect for the Buffalo Soldiers' bravery and valor. Buffalo Soldiers, down through the years, have worn the name with pride." At least 18 Buffalo Soldiers were Medal of Honor recipients.

The song "Buffalo Soldier" was written by David Barnes, Margaret Ann Lewis, and Mira Ann Smith. From the mid–1950s until the early 1960s, Mira Smith ran a recording studio and owned the Ram and Clif labels in Shreveport, Louisiana, recording local artists including teenage guitarist James Burton, Joe Osborne, and Tarheel Slim. After the label went out of business, Smith joined forces with fellow songwriter Lewis, a swamp-rockabilly performer who had previously recorded for Ram. After relocating to Nashville, the duo wrote hit records for Margaret Whiting, Connie Francis, Peggy Scott and Jo Jo Benson, and country and western singer Jeannie C. Riley.

The long version of "Buffalo Soldier," at seven minutes and forty seconds, was backed with a shorter version for radio, which was only three minutes and forty-five seconds in length. The soulful Keith Williams–led song struck a nerve with record buyers, and the Flamingos soon had another national hit, their third charted record, including the UK appearance of "Boogaloo Party," in three years on three different labels. "'Buffalo Soldier' was the first soul hit Polydor had in this country," Zeke proudly told McGarvey during a 1991 visit to Great Britain. "It crashed through a highly competitive market soaring high on the national charts. Critics noticed that this one record contained velvet harmonies ... that infectious rhythmic groove, yet a contemporary message."

One thing Carey was not happy with, according to engineer Phil Austin, was the final mix. "On 'Buffalo Soldier,' the guy that produced it wanted to remix it. He wanted to put in a trumpet section that wasn't on the original mix, and they didn't like it. Bob Feldman was the producer. He was known for 'Hang On Sloopy' by the McCoys. That was his big claim to fame. He got a hold of them, and he said, 'I'm going to produce "Buffalo Soldier," and I'm going to add the horn section to it,' and blah blah blah. I never really liked the mix, and they didn't either. They said it sounded stupid, and it didn't do anything for the record, but this guy wanted it in there. The producer had the final say, and Zeke didn't have a choice. In those days, the labels had their guys produce because they wanted control over it. Today, it's a different story. So, we had to cut it with the stupid horn segment in it. I forget how many records it sold. It sold a number of records on Polydor, but it wasn't a smash like their other ones were. In those days when I was working at Mercury, you could master for another label. I used to master for Paramount, too."

Polydor released "Buffalo Soldier" on January 30, 1970. *Cash Box*'s February 14 review of the disc declared that the Flamingos "perform possibly their first out-of-stage character side. Based on the historical black soldiers of the western frontier, the material could become a blues market breakaway." Radio airplay followed, with urban markets including Cleveland supporting the record. On March 21, 1970, "Buffalo Soldier" hit the national R&B charts, peaking at #28 during a five-week stint. On April 4, the song spent the first of two weeks on *Billboard*'s Hot 100, where it climbed to #86. In June, Polydor issued "Buffalo Soldier" in the United Kingdom, backing it with the Al Fontaine creation, "Fontaineous Combustion." All told, "Buffalo Soldier" was the group's biggest pop chart hit in nine years. Seemingly against all odds, the Flamingos had managed to put a record on the national bestseller lists in three consecutive decades, a feat rarely duplicated by even the brightest of pop stars. Although new recordings would appear over the next half-dozen years, primarily issued on their own label, the group would never appear on the *Billboard* charts again. Chart success notwithstanding, the Flamingos would rarely be without work for the remainder of the century.

For a follow-up, the group chose to revisit the 1928 Hammerstein-Romberg standard, "Lover Come Back to Me." The Flamingos had unsuccessfully tried to record the song for George Goldner in late 1961; a later version was issued on Checker in 1964. Al Fontaine arranged a funky, hard-core soul version with strings added by Herb Bernstein, a producer-arranger-songwriter who had worked with artists including the Four Seasons and Connie Francis. The flip side, a nondescript soul ballad called "Straighten It Up (Get It Together)," was penned by Keith Williams and Zeke Carey. Zeke and Ted Cooper produced the recordings, which were recorded and issued on Polydor on September 11, 1970. Hammerstein connoisseurs considered the new version of "Lover Come Back to Me" to be sacrilege; soul devotees ignored it altogether. Most likely introduced through their mutual producer Cooper, McClure teamed with soul-funk keyboardist Edwin Birdsong (1941–2019) to co-write several songs that appeared on Birdsong's 1971 Polydor album, *What Is It.* Cooper formed his own independent production company, Fiddler Ted, in 1973, but didn't live to work with the Flamingos again. He succumbed to a fatal heart attack on August 24, 1975, at the age of 37.

Zeke Carey's contacts and experiences in the music business, and his ability to produce nationally charted records like "Dealin'" and "Buffalo Soldier," did not go unnoticed at Mercury, where the Flamingos utilized the Custom Division for recording and mastering. Shortly after beginning his association with Austin, the engineer remembers that Mercury executives tabbed Carey for a high-level position at their Blue Rock soul subsidiary.

Between 1964 and 1969, Blue Rock Records released nearly 100 singles by a myriad of artists including Dee Dee Warwick, the Chi-Lites, Sir Mack Rice, Otis Leavill, the Shirelles, Junior Parker, and Junior Wells. It was, according to reviewer Joann D. Ball, "a determined effort by Mercury to enhance its roster beyond pop-slanted acts like Dinah Washington, Brook Benton and Clyde McPhatter. Unfortunately, Blue Rock was less coordinated than Motown and less recognizable than Stax. Unlike those two legendary homes of soul music, Blue Rock Records lacked a geographical urban identity. Blue Rock operated out of New York and Chicago, and signed talent from across the country without the benefit of a signature house band."

"Zeke told me that he had a deal with Mercury," Austin explains. "Mercury was [reorganizing] their label called Blue Rock. They wanted him to head the label. Oh man, when he heard that, he thought it was great. He was finally going to be in charge of a label and was going to get the acts on the label that he wanted. But the guy that was at Mercury pulled a few strings politically, and he wound up screwing Zeke out of the job. Zeke never forgave the guy. I forget the guy's name. I knew him, too. Zeke never forgave him and was very bitter about it. Blue Rock only lasted [another] year because they really didn't have that much on the label. They didn't have anything that was really that good, so it folded. If Zeke had had the job, I think maybe the label would have survived because he knew what he was doing. He had more knowledge of the producing end of it."

Color Them Beautiful, the Flamingos' first Ronze LP, was released in 1971. Jake designed the cover featuring a multicolored cartoon drawing of a giant pink flamingo for the 10-track disc, which failed to include a photo of the Flamingos and did not mention any of the members by name except for Zeke and Jake. Produced by Zeke, the album was engineered by Chuck Irwin and mastered by Phil Austin at Mercury Sound Studio on West 57th Street. "They were getting a new sound," Austin explains. "They wanted to get out of the doo-wop and into the modern sound. From that point, they did some albums. I think we did maybe four albums over the years. Zeke used to call me up and tell me maybe a week ahead of time that he was going to go into the studio, and he'd be coming out in about another week with some tapes. He used another engineer who was a good friend of mine, Chuck Irwin. He was the recording engineer, so he did all the stuff for him. He'd let me know about a week ahead of time so I could get ready and book some time for him. We did all of the albums that way. He was always happy with what we did. *Color Them Beautiful* was outstanding. We did that at the Mercury studio."

Opening with "She's Gone," a bass-heavy R&B number credited to Zeke and Doug, the disc continued its soul theme with "Gotta Have All Your Lovin,'" which was penned by Ronnie Lewis and John Pearson, the Velours' former baritone and Flamingos road manager who had composed for the group on End and Philips. Singer-songwriter Al Collier's "Does It Really Matter," originally waxed for Checker in 1964, offered the group a comfortable vehicle to shine, with '50s-styled unison harmony leads and a strong, if a bit obtrusive, saxophone blowing throughout. Doug McClure added a falsetto-tinged lead to Ivory Joe Hunter's "I Need You So," and shared the lead with Zeke on a misguided remake of "Goodnight Sweetheart," which the group had first waxed in 1959 minus the 1970s dance beat. "Suddenly We're Strangers," an obscure Doc Pomus and Mort Shuman song originally recorded by Marci and the Mates for Big Top Records in 1962, featured a nice falsetto from Zeke and a pleasant organ and/or Theremin accompaniment.

The group delved into the Robert Mellin songbook and pulled out a winner in "You You You," a 1953 Ames Brothers hit. With a polished lead from McClure, Fontaine's ringing guitar, and falsetto flourishes reminiscent of Johnny Carter, the song remains fresh and vibrant today. A #1 pop hit for Nat "King" Cole in 1951, "Too Young," which featured a swinging sax section and a strong lead vocal, was composed by Sid Lippman and Sylvia Dee. When the LP was pressed and printed, the order of these two songs was mistakenly reversed on the jacket. Both sides of the Julmar single, "Dealin,'" and its instrumental flip were included on the album as well.

The gem of the LP, however, was "Welcome Home," a pleasant, contemporary ballad. With a stellar lead from McClure, the song reprised the "I don't want another love" background chant that the Flamingos had initially utilized in their Philips recording of "Temptation." "I wrote 'Welcome Home' coming home from the Army," McClure explained to Phillips. "I hadn't seen my girlfriend in so long. I always wrote songs that related to my progress in life as I was growing. That way, especially when you're singing them, you're actually living the song so you don't have to do a lot of convincing. People hear that, and they say, 'yeah,' they can hear the truth coming out in the song itself."

Roulette Records, which owned Goldner's back catalog, countered by reissuing two of the group's original End albums, *Requestfully Yours* and *Flamingo Serenade*, along with LPs by Frankie Lymon and the Teenagers, Little Anthony and the Imperials, and the Chantels, in the fall of 1971.

Ronze also issued a white-label promo 45 of "Welcome Home" to disc jockeys with a mono version on one side and a stereo mix on the other. Inexplicably, the tune was credited to Fontaine as the sole composer instead of McClure. For the regular release, "Gotta Have All Your Lovin,'" published through the Careys' Belleville Music, was selected for the B-side. "'Welcome Home' does have a really crisp sound," Austin agrees. "With the equipment we had at Mercury, I made things work. I mean, it was a little outdated stuff, but at least I had gotten together a few different equalizers, and I got the kind of sound they wanted. All we had was shelving equalizers. We didn't really have any of the things they have today like Sontechs. But, by just getting together some shelving equalizers, I used that for different things, and got a good sound. The way that Mercury had it set up, basically, they just went from a work tape that was fully EQ'd. You didn't touch it. It was like assembly line mastering, which I didn't really go for. So, with the Custom Division, you had a little more freedom to do what you want with the client."

Distribution was a problem for the start-up company, and consequently few record buyers even knew of the album's existence. Undeterred, the Careys addressed all of the shortcomings of their initial effort with their second album, *Flamingos Today*, in 1972. At this point, the group consisted of lead and harmony singer and sometime percussionist Doug McClure, Zeke Carey singing second tenor and falsetto, Jake Carey on bass, Al Fontaine playing guitar, arranging and writing, baritone-tenor J.C. Carey, tenor Clarence Bassett, and a returning Billy Clarke. "William Clarke sang and was the drummer," agreed McClure. "Billy was a great entertainer."

Born in Jamaica, Queens, New York, on March 13, 1936, Clarence Henry Bassett, Jr., was a veteran vocal group harmony ace who was utilized as a first tenor and alternate lead. Bassett had been the first tenor in the Five Sharps, the obscure Queens group that recorded a haunting version of "Stormy Weather" for Jubilee Records in the fall of 1952 that would become the most widely sought-after rhythm and blues vocal group record of all time. After the Five Sharps' lead singer Ronald Cussey (1936–1960) completed his military service, he formed a new group called the Videos with Bassett, second tenor Charles Baskerville (1936–1995), baritone Johnny Jackson and bass Ron Woodhall. After finishing second in an Apollo amateur night program singing the Orioles' "At Night," the group was awarded a contract with Casino Records in Philadelphia and recorded the oldies radio staple, "Trickle Trickle," in 1958.

Soon after, Cussey and Woodhall both died, and Bassett and Baskerville teamed up with old neighborhood friend James "Shep" Sheppard, the famed lead of the Heartbeats, to form Shep and the Limelites. Recording for Apt and Hull Records from 1960 to 1965, the group recorded some of the finest examples of vocal group harmony with just three voices, including the top five pop and R&B hit, "Daddy's Home" in 1961, and "Our Anniversary," a top 10 R&B charter from the winter of 1962. Sheppard's ego ultimately led to the group's demise in the late 1960s. Shortly after reforming the group with new members, he was found robbed and murdered in January of 1970. Baskerville joined the Drifters for a few months in mid to late 1967 before joining the Players. Bassett was more than happy to join forces with the Flamingos.

Returning member Billy Clarke had sung lead and played drums with the Flamingos from 1961 to 1964 and again for a short spell in the late '60s. During his hiatus from the group, the Brooklyn singer spent some time playing drums behind Pookie Hudson and the Spaniels. Back with the Flamingos, Clarke would again fill the drum chair and handled a significant portion of the leads. "It was hard times, and we had a lot of transitions within the group," J.C. Carey told interviewer Geoffrey Hines in 2001. "But my father and his cousin were determined to keep the group alive, and I think they did a good job of doing so."

"Most of our appearances [are] college dates or private affairs," Zeke told Gossert in 1971.

In the spring of 1972, they appeared at the Boston Music Hall for a show with Jackie Wilson, Del Shannon, the Cleftones, Earl Lewis and the Channels, Arlene Smith's Chantels, and Johnny Maestro and the Crests. "By that time, they'd turned into a vocal/instrumental group, pretty much," recalls musician Billy Vera, who occasionally worked the same gigs with the Flamingos. "When Clarence was with them, they were doing a combination of oldies shows, oldies nightclubs and other nightclubs. They were still attempting to get a hit record, without success. Their set list is a dim memory. They did their End hits, plus 'I'll Be Home' and had started doing 'Golden Teardrops' again, due to requests arising from airplay on New York oldies radio. When Billy Clarke of the Strangers was playing drums and singing with the group, he would do a little stand-up comedy, telling a few off-color jokes. These later groups never had a great lead singer, in the mold of the earlier guys." Several soundboard recordings of Flamingos concerts from this era are known to exist. Two cuts, an extended version of "Nobody Loves Me Like You," featuring Zeke on lead, and a McClure-led rendition of "I Only Have Eyes for You,"

The Flamingos on stage at the Music Hall in Boston, spring 1972. Left to right: Jake Carey, Clarence Bassett, J.C. Carey, Zeke Carey, Doug McClure, and Al Fontaine (Joe McDermott photo, from the Paul Power collection).

The Flamingos on stage at the Music Hall in Boston, spring 1972. Left to right: Jake Carey, Clarence Bassett, J.C. Carey, Zeke Carey, Doug McClure, and Al Fontaine (Joe McDermott photo, from the Paul Power collection).

reportedly recorded in New England, were issued on an unauthorized various artists' concert CD in the 1990s.

The seven songs that comprised *Flamingos Today* were recorded at the Mercury Sound Studio in 1972 with Chuck Irwin serving as the recording engineer. Zeke supervised and produced the session while guitarist Al Fontaine wrote the arrangements. The opening cut, a fine reworking of "Golden Teardrops," employed a multitude of effects which aptly set the mood for the track. Backed by the sounds of rustling winds, chirping crickets, gentle rainfall, and Fontaine's docile playing, Zeke delivered a dramatic recitation that captured the spirit of the original author, Bunky Redding.

"For over 20 years, super talent has emerged from the dark, dismal depths of the big city ghettos, only to be struck down by the mighty horse … better known as dope," Carey stated. "This song was composed by such a talent. With his face saddened by the perils of an ever-losing battle for mere survival, I heard him say that the one thing he hated most about being an addict was his inability to love or care about anybody or anything that in some way didn't relate to the source of his next fix—for this had caused him to burn every bridge that linked him to all the beautiful things in life. But there was one thought, one memory, still lingering vividly in his mind. It was about his one true love. You know, that girl he felt loved him for what he was and not who he was. But he knew he had hurt her. And feeling that he had not apologized enough, he wrote this particular song about the many tears he saw her shed for him, and begged it be recorded, so someday, someway, she might hear it. He called the song 'Golden Teardrops.'"

Over organ accompaniment, the sound of rain falling, and a strong falsetto from Zeke, Billy Clarke delivered an impassioned lead that rivaled the emotion McElroy had poured into the original a generation earlier. "That was a great, great track," Austin agrees. "Oh man, I'll tell you, that was a remarkable track. Zeke did a good job on that. I mean, the guy was creative. He came up with a lot of good things, and he had a good head on his shoulders. He knew what he was doing. He didn't just haphazardly say at the last minute, 'Oh, we're going to do this,' or 'I'm going to put this in it.' He'd think things out. He knew what he wanted in the beginning. That's what made everything so great. I've worked with some producers who didn't know what planet they were on. That was the music business back then. But when you work with professionals like Zeke Carey, when you work with a producer who knows what he's doing, it makes your job even easier."

Clarke was equally effective on "As Time Goes By," one of four songs the group originally recorded during their heyday and resurrected for the *Flamingos Today* LP. "Virgo, Virgin Lady," a contemporary bit of R&B that opened with a monologue from Zeke on the subject of astrological signs, was written by Doug McClure and Carl "Let the Little Girl Dance" Spencer. Even by today's standards, the lyrics remain a bit too suggestive to be associated with the Flamingos. Clarke joined forces with McClure or Bassett for a strong duet lead on "Time Was," which closed out the first side. Another published tune credited to McClure and Spencer, "Do the Reggae," if recorded, remains unreleased.

The second side opened with "Let It Be Me," originally a French song composed by Gilbert Becaud and Pierre Delanoe with English lyrics by Mann Curtis. Introduced by Jill Corey in 1957, the song reached the national charts four times during the 1960s, with the Everly Brothers, Betty Everett and Jerry Butler, the Sweet Inspirations, and Glen Campbell and Bobbie Gentry all putting their stamp on it. The Flamingos performed a slow, unison-led version, complete with falling rain accompaniment.

Revisiting their 1960 chart hit, "At Night," the lead vocal chores were turned over to Clarence Bassett, who had sung the song on Amateur Night at the Apollo with the Videos in 1958. Bassett's heartfelt lead was complemented admirably by the group's strong backing harmony. Closing the 30-minute disc was "Why Can't Susie Go to School with Lucy," a Zeke Carey–Al Fontaine creation that delivered a tale of racial segregation over a funk beat.

When it was released in May 1972, *Flamingos Today* was issued with a gatefold cover featuring black and white photos and brief bios of each of the group's seven members, including their astrological signs. The graphics were designed and printed by the New York–based Lee Myles Associates under Jake's supervision. The album soon appeared in record stores and oldies specialty shops around the country and became the best-selling and most widely recognized of the group's Ronze discs. Spotlighting the album as a pop Best Bet pick in its May 13, 1972, issue, *Cash Box* remarked that "their biggest hit, 'I Only Have Eyes for You,' is currently enjoying new popularity via the Jerry Butler version. What more opportune time then for these master balladeers to make a fresh new stand for musical acceptance on a large scale? For the oldie freaks, there is a new version of their legendary 'Golden Teardrops.' At the opposite end of the continuum, a lyrically strong integration and pro-busing song, 'Why Can't Susie Go to School with Lucy.' Probably more successfully than most, this seven-man group has managed to retain their old sound while seeing groups like the Stylistics and the Chi-Lites looming large in the scheme of things."

By year's end, however, the group's personnel had changed yet again. Clarence Bassett departed to form Creative Funk, a New York–based act that wrote and performed their own material and released it on their own self-titled label in the mid–1970s. Billy Clarke also left, leaving the Careys and McClure in need of another voice.

Open auditions were held in Brooklyn to find a new vocalist. The cousins ultimately selected Frank "Mingo" Ayers, a 35-year-old Brooklyn resident who had already spent a dozen years in the public's eye. Born March 14, 1937, Ayers was a childhood friend of Del Vikings founder, bass singer, and principal songwriter Clarence E. Quick (1937–1983). In late 1958, Quick, having received his discharge from the United States Air Force, left the Del Vikings to join the Eastmen, another act that was signed to Mercury Records.

Consisting of Watsie Lumbard, brothers Jethro and Russell Worthy, Harold Allen, and Quick, the Eastmen recorded one single for the label before Jethro left the group in the spring of 1959. Seeking a replacement, Quick brought in Ayers, who was capable of singing lead, first tenor, and second tenor. This lineup of the Eastmen remained intact for over a year, until Quick and Russell Worthy left. Ayers, Lumbard, Allen, and new members LaVangelis Hicks and Ivan "Lincoln Fig" Figueroa, of Lincoln Fig and the Dates, recorded "Passion" and "Hum Diddy Doo Wah" for Glow Records in late 1960.

After "Come Go With Me" lead singer Norman Wright was discharged from the service in January of 1960, he and Quick formed a new Del Vikings unit with Ayers and Clarence's cousin, William Blakely, who had initially joined the Mercury lineup in 1957. According to Wright, the quartet performed sporadically in the 1960s as the Del Vikings while "Whispering Bells" lead Kripp Johnson fronted his own Del Vikings group and recorded for ABC-Paramount.

From 1970 to 1972, Johnson, Quick, Wright and Ritzy Lee reorganized the group for concert appearances. Ayers returned to the Del Vikings briefly in 1972 when Johnson left. The group, without Ayers, recorded a new version of "Come Go With Me" for Florence Greenberg's Scepter Records in November of 1972. It reached #112 on *Billboard*'s Bubbling Under the Hot 100 chart in January of 1973.

Ayers remembered in a 1996 interview that he had already left to join the Flamingos by the time the Scepter disc was issued. "My father got into the Flamingos through an audition that Zeke and Jake had to fill the spot," Ayers's son Tyrone Ismael recalls. Impressed with his vocal ability and experience, the Careys hired him as their new lead singer.

"My father and mother were never married, even though Frank asked her to marry him on several occasions," Ismael explains. "My grandmother in Virginia would not allow it. My mother tells me that even then, all that my father wanted to do was sing, and my grandmother wanted someone for her daughter that had a stable ambition. I was raised in Virginia, but I would go to New York almost every summer to visit my father. During one visit, I was sitting on the bed looking through his photo album of all the groups he had been with while he was getting dressed to do a show. I asked him, 'Hey Pops, what group are you with now?' I could see him watching me through the mirror with this smile on his face, and he said, 'I'm with the Flamingos.' Hell, I had no idea who in the heck the Flamingos were, but I saw the look on his face like I was supposed to know who they were. So, I acted like I knew them and said, 'Oh man, that's neat!'"

That evening, Ismael accompanied his father to a Flamingos concert in New Jersey. "That night I found out who the Flamingos were," he recounts with a smile. "There were all these women running up to me asking me if I could get an autograph from the Flamingos. They were asking me stuff like, 'Who are you?' I said, 'Frank, the lead, is my father.' They said, 'Can we get your autograph too?' Needless to say, I was blown away. So, I go down to the dressing room with this shocked, stupid look on my face, and tell the Flamingos that a bunch of women want their autographs. They looked at me and all busted out laughing. I think Pops told them that I had no idea who they really were, and when they saw that stupid look on my face, they all knew that I had just found out who the Flamingos were!"

The Flamingos' next recording project paired the group with soul singer-songwriter J.J. Jackson and New York producer Johnny Worlds. A native of Brooklyn, Jerome Louis Jackson scored a trio of R&B crossover hits in 1966–67, including the danceable "But It's Alright," which had been recorded in London. Before moving to the United Kingdom in 1969, the gritty 300-pound singer had worked as an arranger for Jack McDuff and Jimmy Witherspoon and developed a songwriting style that reflected a keen social awareness. Jackson and Ruby Dean (Jenkins) Coates wrote "Think About Me," a catchy, romantic soul groove, which the Flamingos recorded in 1974. With a capable lead from Zeke Carey, contemporary, soul-influenced background harmonies, and a first-rate arrangement from Jackson, the song was mastered by Austin. "I believe I worked on that with them," he recalls. "I remember the title, but that's about it. After Mercury Sound closed their doors in 1973, I started working for Trutone in New Jersey. Of course, I told Chuck to tell Zeke that I was at a new location. So he started coming in at Trutone to do work like we did at Mercury. And, of course, we had a little better equipment, more updated equipment there, a lot better mastering system. So we did the rest of the albums there."

"Think About Me" was produced by Johnny Worlds and released in December of 1974 on his own Worlds label, which was headquartered in New York City and distributed by Big Apple Record Distributors. Worlds came to New York from Baltimore in 1964, where his hometown friend, Sonny Til, introduced him to Clyde McPhatter, who helped Worlds begin his career. Beginning in marketing and promotion at Forest Green Records, Worlds worked with a variety of artists, including King Curtis, Baby Washington, and Lester Chambers. "Four decades in the industry, and nobody owes me five cents," Worlds proudly recounted in a 2002 interview. "None of my acts ever got screwed, either."

With Ayers getting involved in the production end of things with Zeke, the group cut six additional masters at C.I. Studios for a new album, *In Touch with You*, which was released in 1974. "After Mercury Sound was sold in 1973, they sold the recording studio upstairs and Chuck Irwin and the other engineer that was working with him, they took over the studio, and they called it C.I. Recording," Austin explains. "It was still the same Mercury Studio, but they called it C.I., and it was run independently by Chuck and the other engineer. The only reason that the studio failed was that they couldn't get a good maintenance engineer to help with the breakdowns. They used to have breakdowns in the middle of a session and everything. They couldn't find a good, reliable maintenance engineer to take care of the maintenance on it. So finally the whole studio folded."

Leading off the album was a re-recording of Zeke's composition "Since My Baby Put Me Down," which was initially waxed as the B-side of "The Boogaloo Party" in 1966. Featuring a full horn section and an infectious, danceable rhythm track, the Carey-led song was a vibrant, contemporary opener. "(Ain't Nothin' Better Than) Making Love," written, led, and co-produced by Zeke Carey, with production assistance from Billy Nichols and arranged by Patrick Adams, featured female voices in place of the familiar Flamingos harmonies.

Country-rock artist Kip Carmen wrote "Spring of My Life," an uninspired ballad that suffered from a sub-par double-tracked lead from Zeke and a mediocre production effort. Closing side one, however, was "Heavy Hips," a funky R&B tune written and fronted by Zeke, who explained to listeners, "My daddy told me a long time ago that behind every beautiful woman, there's a beautiful behind." Veteran bandleader and guitarist Leroy Kirkland arranged the song, which featured Jake and the backing voices prominently in the mix. Today, the song remains a favorite among 1970s soul and Northern Soul devotees. "Oh, I know why, too," offers mastering engineer Phil Austin. "It was a great mix, and oh, I just couldn't stop listening to it myself. It was great. I enjoyed mastering that one."

Side two opened with the Worlds label single "Think About Me," and closed with the Clarke-led "Golden Teardrops" that kicked off *Flamingos Today*. Frankie Ayers was given the chance to exercise his strong tenor lead on the 1926 Gershwin brothers chestnut, "Someone to Watch Over Me," which the group had never attempted before. First appearing in the musical *Oh, Kay!*, the song had been recorded by dozens of performers including Frank Sinatra, Ella Fitzgerald and Rosemary Clooney. Despite his role in the group's personal appearances, "Someone to Watch Over Me" was unfortunately the only opportunity Ayers was given to sing lead on a Flamingos studio recording. The remaining track, "Bump Your Buns Off," was a Kool and the Gang rip-off written by Zeke that unequivocally rates among the group's worst recordings.

Zeke paired "Heavy Hips" and "Someone to Watch Over Me" on a red-label Ronze single in 1975, but failed to attract the necessary airplay to gain another hit. A new version of McClure's "Love Keeps the Doctor Away," originally recorded as "It Keeps the Doctor Away" for Philips in 1967, featured another opening monologue from lead singer Carey and became the group's next single in 1976. The green-label Ronze disc, again produced by Zeke, engineered by Irwin at C.I. Studios and mastered by Austin at Trutone, featured a shorter version of the song on the flip side, in an unsuccessful attempt to snare some disc jockey support. "Love Keeps the Doctor Away" earned the distinction of being the last 45 RPM disc of new music the Flamingos ever released.

"Zeke would bring the tape in, and I would just put it up and listen to it," Austin recalls of his mastering work for the Flamingos. "Basically, they didn't have to tell me a thing. I knew what they wanted, because I just used the first record, 'Dealin', as an example, as a guide as to what they were looking for. They wanted it hard, tight, really up-front with a lot of punch, and I gave it to them that way." In the same way that George Goldner supervised and controlled every aspect of the group's End recordings, Zeke Carey handled every facet of their later efforts. "I always dealt with him exclusively," Austin adds. "He was the man to see. Sometimes, Jake would come in, you know, and every time he would come in, he would come in with a different pipe. He had this collection of beautiful hand-carved pipes, and he'd come in with

Dressed for the stage, 1973–1976. Left to right: Frankie Ayers, Jake and Zeke Carey, Doug McClure (courtesy Tyrone Ismael).

a different one every time. They were remarkable. I remember that Zeke liked good clothes, too. I always looked forward to when they came in because you knew you were going to get something great. That was something I looked forward to. The memories that you've gathered over the years doing this stuff, they can't take that away from you. They can take everything else away from you. But they can't take away the memories, and that's what counts. I'm glad that I have my memories of my 30 years, and if I had to do it over again, I wouldn't change a thing."

"I Only Have Eyes for You" was introduced to a whole new audience when it was included in the soundtrack of the 1973 blockbuster motion picture, *American Graffiti*. In 1975, the group also guested on an album by Shirelles lead Shirley Alston, titled *With a Little Help from My Friends*. Issued by Prodigal records, the album featured Shirley's version of classic oldies, backed by the original artists associated with the songs. The Drifters backed her on "Save the Last Dance for Me." The Five Satins sang "In the Still of the Night," and the Flamingos, naturally, offered their doo-bop-shoo-bops on "I Only Have Eyes for You." Despite good reviews from music critics, the album failed to sell.

"We took it seriously, as a business," Zeke told *Goldmine* interviewer Jeff Tamarkin in 1981. "I expected to last a long time, but I didn't know whether it would be 30 years or what it would be. Some of the groups got into it so they could get next to the girls, or be seen in the bright lights. We took it very seriously. I knew [the style of music] would change. I didn't think it would stay the same as it was. We came along during a period of change, and we knew that in time there would be changes. [But] we worked all through the Beatles era, all through the '60s and '70s. I don't think you can compare then with today. Everything was just beginning then. There was no electronics to deal with, and you really had to know what you were singing. You had to really know how to sing. You had to have naked ability."

The group performed faithfully through the remainder of the decade, but more and more of their gigs began to revolve around the oldies, as fans clamored for their classic 1950s material. Ayers's son, Tyrone Ismael, recounts a 1976 performance in Virginia attended by his mother. "Pops was down there doing a show with the Flamingos, and while singing 'I Only Have Eyes for You,' he was calling her to the stage. She said how totally embarrassed she was that Pops was doing this in front of all those people, but she loved it!" Fellow historian and writer Marv Goldberg recalled the group performing "Buffalo Soldier" for an oldies audience in the New York area in the late 1970s with disastrous results.

In June of 1975, the group joined Fats Domino, the Persuasions, the Five Sharps and the Five Satins at a Gus Gossert–hosted show at New York's Academy of Music. *New York Times* reviewer John Rockwell wrote of their performance, "The Flamingos act and move with a zombielike stiffness, but remain capable of some eerie close harmonies, especially in the introduction to their 'Golden Teardrops,' a hit from 1953."

In June of 1977, the Careys drew a mention in *Billboard* following their complaints to the American Federation of Musicians that they were being "unfairly impersonated by at least two other groups operating out of Philadelphia." While the "other groups" are not mentioned by name, there can be little doubt that Terry Johnson, who was working with his Flamingos in upscale rooms like Shepherd's, located in the stately Drake Hotel at Park Avenue and 56th Street in New York City, was an intended target. Soon after, the Careys filed paperwork to obtain a federal trademark for the Flamingos name.

Around this time, Zeke Carey moved from Brooklyn to the Portsmouth area of Virginia, close to the headquarters of the Church of God and Saints of Christ, where he would remain for the final 25 years of his life. Zeke and Jake Carey and Frankie Ayers would stay together through the rest of the 1970s. McClure remained with the Flamingos for several more years before he left and was replaced by Jerome Wilson. "I think the last time I sang with them was around the Bicentennial, 1976," McClure recalled to interviewer Phillips.

Accepting a major concert gig in New York City for producer-promoter Tony DeLauro in May of 1981, Zeke reached out to an old friend. In his groundbreaking tome *They All Sang on the Corner*, author Phil Groia set the scene. "The Flamingos made what seemed to be a routine appearance at a Royal New York 'Doo-Wop' concert in the Beacon Theatre. On an especially electric evening, a hush fell over the audience as a puff of smoke emanated from stage right. From behind the curtain came, 'My love must be a kind of blind love.' The 'voice of champagne,' for the first time in approximately twenty years, was making an appearance with the great Flamingos. The famous green suits were gone. The exciting dance steps of Paul Wilson were absent. But there on stage, just as cool and stately as ever, was Sonny Til's cousin from Chicago, the incomparable Nate Nelson."

Nelson's appearance, however, was a one-shot deal. Following his triumphant return to the group, Nelson resumed his worldwide touring schedule with Herb Reed's Platters, never again to return to the group with whom he had first tasted success. "He did the show with them because they paid him a good amount of money," Terry Johnson recalls of Nelson's 1981 cameo. "They really came to him like they needed his help. They had this shot at being at the Beacon Theatre. They really needed him. He did it, but he told me they were nothing like what we were. He said it was pitiful."

Nonetheless, the group's schedule remained full and diverse. On July 29, 1981, the Flamingos headlined at the Bottom Line on West 4th Street in New York, sharing the stage with Frankie Lymon's Teenagers and Fourteen Karat Soul. Their touring schedule also included venues like Durdy Annie's in San Antonio, Texas, in early 1983, and Ricochet, located in Fort Worth's Americana Hotel, in January of 1984.

After 11 years with the Flamingos, Frankie Ayers left in 1983 to return to the Del Vikings, right around the time that the group's founder, Frank's childhood friend Clarence Quick, passed away. Frank remained the group's principal lead singer and mainstay for the next 14 years, and sang lead on their 1991 single "Do You Remember," issued on the BVM label.

"Once I went down there to visit him and my vocals had got pretty nice, and Pops heard me sing," Ismael recalls. "He asked me if I wanted to sing for a living and I said, 'Heck yeah.' I'm about 17 at the time, so he took me and a singing partner I knew way over to Queens somewhere, far as hell from where we were living. He took us to the home of a friend of his, and told us that three times a week he wanted us to take the subway all the way to Queens to this guy's home and have rehearsals. Needless to say, after about two rehearsals we stopped going. Hell, at 17 years old, I had those fine New York girls on my mind. But what I see now is that Pops wanted to see if I really wanted it. That's why he made the rehearsal so far away."

On June 25, 1997, Frank Ayers died of kidney failure in Brooklyn at the age of 60.

Voices Stilled

After 18 years on the road with the Platters, Nate Nelson's health began to deteriorate in 1982. Although the singer was only 50, heart disease had begun to rob him of energy and stamina. He had suffered a series of heart attacks and was now in heart failure. On Thursday, May 31, 1984, most of the Boston-area television stations' news broadcasts included film of an emotional press conference called by Nelson's wife, Angel, who hoped to find a suitable heart donor for her husband, who lay seriously ill in Brigham and Women's Hospital, one of the city's largest institutions. "I'm appealing to people all across the country who love Nate and his music," she said. "Through your generosity and loving, you can give the most precious gift—life." Nelson's name had been on a waiting list for a heart transplant for several days, but no donor was found. On Friday, June 1, 1984, Nate Nelson, the "Voice of Champagne," died at the age of 52.

His obituary, as reported by United Press International, erroneously reported that Nelson had sung with the Platters on "Only You," "The Great Pretender," and "Twilight Time," while summing his career with the Flamingos in one brief sentence. The singer was laid to rest in Southborough Rural Cemetery in Southborough, Massachusetts, between Worcester and Boston. His military-issued grave marker simply stated Nathaniel J. Nelson, Seaman Apprentice, U.S. Navy, Korea, and listed his dates of birth and death. Unsuspecting visitors would have no notion that the grave marked the final resting place of one of the most revered R&B vocal group harmony lead singers of all time.

"I saw Nate a few times over the years," Terry Johnson states. "Nate was great. He was one of the main ones who got me into the Flamingos. When I met them in Baltimore at the Royal Theater, Nate was the one who was really pushing for me. They needed another voice, because Johnny was gone, and they needed an instrument. They were looking for a guitar player or a piano player, somebody, and I just happened to be the one. Nate fought for me, because I don't think Jake wanted me in the group. He was very cold. But then Nate fought for me. Nate wasn't that close to me throughout my time

Herb Reed's Platters in the 1970s. Left to right: Reed, Nate Nelson, Regina Koco, Charles Johnson, and Duke Daniels (author's collection).

with the Flamingos, but once I left the Flamingos, Nate called me and joined forces with me for the Starglows and we did 'Let's Be Lovers.' Nate was really my friend."

Paul Wilson's later years were clouded by alcoholism. On May 6, 1988, the 53-year-old suffered a heart attack. He was taken to St. Bernard Hospital on West 64th Street in Chicago, where he was pronounced dead. After funeral services at an East 79th Street funeral home, Wilson was buried on May 11 in Mount Glenwood Cemetery, the first black cemetery in Illinois, in the southern Chicago suburb of Willow Springs. Also interred at Mount Glenwood is blues pioneer Hudson "Tampa Red" Whittaker. Wilson was survived by his wife, Georgia "Peaches" Wilson, a son, Ron, and a brother, Joseph Dennis.

"Paul was my best friend," Terry wistfully recalls. "That's why I gave him half of 'Lovers Never Say Goodbye.' When I got with the Flamingos, I was from Baltimore and I was green. I was square. I was wearing high-water pants and boots. I thought I was so hip. But when I got to New York, I was looking around at all the tall buildings and Paul took me around. He said, 'Come on, Buzzy!' 'Come on, Buzzy!' He figured he had to school me. He even taught me how to talk smooth on the phone, like with the operator. He would say, how do you say 'T'? 'T like in terrific,' and make a blush-type thing. Paul was really my close friend. He taught me so much."

In later years, Johnson returned to perform in Chicago, and tried unsuccessfully to coax Wilson back into the spotlight. "I went to Chicago with my group, Terry Johnson's Modern Flamingos, and Paul and his wife, Peaches, came to see the show. I said, 'Paul, I've been looking for you. Let's join forces. Nate was with me. I can get Nate back.' I know that if Nate knew Paul was with me, he would probably come back, and help to clean Paul up. But Paul said, 'No, no, man, I'm through with show business. I don't think I can do it. I'm through with it, Buzzy. You've got it.' I said, 'Come on, man,' but he said no. That was the last I saw of him. He was only 53 when he died. It was a shame. But he drank a lot. As a matter of fact, he wound up being a night watchman there, and he would be drunk. It was a drag."

In 1984, the Careys added Archie Satterfield and Bennie Cherry to the lineup, creating a new Flamingos quartet which would stay together for the better part of seven years. "We try to keep stability," Zeke told McGarvey in 1991. "I try to find reasons to keep things together, rather than reasons to make them fall apart." Still in demand for live performances, the Flamingos joined the Moonglows, Little Anthony, Arlene Smith and the Chantels, and others for Doo-Wopp at the Garden VII at New York's Madison Square Gar-

The Flamingos' 1984–1991 touring lineup, pictured in 1987. Left to right: Bennie Cherry, Zeke and Jake Carey, Archie Satterfield (author's collection).

den's Felt Forum on March 23, 1984. On April 18, 1986, they co-headlined the Royal New York Doo-Wopp Show at Radio City with the Moonglows. In October of 1987, the group appeared at Boston's Symphony Hall, along with Little Anthony, Jimmy Beaumont and the Skyliners, and Rudy West and his Keys. Taking the stage with "Besame Mucho," the group weaved their way through "Lovers Never Say Goodbye," "Nobody Loves Me Like You," "Golden Teardrops," "I Only Have Eyes for You," "I Heard It Through the Grapevine," and "I'll Be Home."

Fans who saw the group during this era were often treated to a diverse collection of material ranging from Flamingos favorites including "Your Other Love" and "Mio Amore" to covers of popular 1950s and '60s hits. A version of "Blueberry Hill" with Jake singing lead, Sam and Dave's "Soul Man," the Temptations' "My Girl," Otis Redding's "The Dock of the Bay," and a medley of Chuck Berry and Little Richard hits were all regular inclusions in the set list. Always sharply dressed, the group favored white dress suits and, amidst the glitz and glitter of the casinos, brightly colored sequins. On stage, Zeke was the primary lead vocalist and spokesman, exuding an air of confidence and a witty sense of humor, winning over new fans and pleasing longtime followers.

"I have a little grandson who came to see the Flamingos for the first time," Zeke related with a laugh in 1989. "He's about eight years old. We did the show, and we did the number, 'Soul Man,' and he saw me doing all the dancing. After the show was over, he said, 'Granddaddy, you all were good. I especially like that song where you did all that old rubber leg stuff, and you all were dancing.' I said, 'Yeah?' He said, 'Yeah. You know the one where you said, 'I'm an *old* man!' I said, 'I'm an old man? No, it's I'm a *soul* man!'"

Carey relished the role of elder statesman with sincerity, eagerly meeting with fans, greeting fellow artists, signing autographs, posing for photos, and giving interviews. The common thread that friends and acquaintances identify when remembering their friendships with Zeke Carey today is loyalty. "You talk about loyalty in this business?" asks engineer Phil Austin. "Usually in this business, there's no loyalty. I mean, a producer will love you until he finds another place that the price is cheaper for mastering, and then he'll go there. But these guys, they were pros. They had been around the block more than once. They knew what they were doing, and if they liked you, they stuck with you. They were honest, and I had a great 20-year relationship with these guys."

Through the years, the Careys also kept up with Fletcher Weatherspoon, occasionally performing for him in Chicago at a discounted rate. "Yes, every two or three years we'd work together," Weatherspoon recalled. One such event took place on April 5, 1987, at the Grand Ballroom on South Cottage Grove. "The money they were making, I could never pay," the group's original manager confessed. "They would never charge me that kind of money, but I would never ask them to do it [for less]. Most of the time, they would be like in St. Louis for a show. They would call me and tell me they were going to be in St. Louis for a big show on a Saturday, and if I wanted to do something that Sunday, they'd give me a deal. Or if they were up in Milwaukee and they had to pass through here going home, they would call."

Zeke even hired Fletcher's son, El Warren Weatherspoon, to play drums in the Flamingos' road band. "Zeke knew my son ever since he was born," Fletcher stated. "He knew he wanted to play drums. I didn't have to say too much. He called me and asked me for Zeke's number. I gave it to him, and he called Zeke himself. The next thing I knew, he was playing with the Flamingos. He stayed with them for five years. The only reason he left them was because he had an opportunity to be sponsored by the Maplewood Drum Company. Later he was the drummer for the band Heat Wave that had the record 'Always and Forever.'" Today, El Warren Weatherspoon, his three brothers, and their family oversee Dove Productions LLC, an entertainment and promotions firm established by their father in 1973.

As part of a special 1950s tribute honoring the 30th anniversary of the Grammy Awards, the Flamingos were invited to perform on the live television broadcast from New York's Radio City Music Hall on March 2, 1988. Host Billy Crystal introduced legendary disc jockey Jocko Henderson, who rapped his way through a charming segment featuring the Cadillacs, the Flamingos, the Regents, the Angels, and Dion and friends. Zeke led the quartet through an abbreviated version of "Eyes," beginning with the "I don't know if we're in a garden" lyric line.

In the spring of 1991, the Flamingos made their United Kingdom debut, appearing at the Wembley Rock and Roll stage show with the Cleftones, Jive Five, and Jimmy Jones, among others. Promoter Tom Ingram arranged an hour-long television production of the show's highlights, titled *The 1991 London Rock 'n' Roll Show*. Unfortunately, the Flamingos were now only a trio, consisting of the Careys and Archie Satterfield. Clips of "I Only Have Eyes for You," "Nobody Loves Me Like You," and "I'll Be Home" gave television viewers their first look at the Flamingos in many years. Dressed in white leisure suits, the trio, led by Zeke, who now wore glasses and a hairpiece, were vocally strong, but unable to duplicate the group's classic four- and five-part harmonies with only three voices. On June 1, 1991, the Flamingos headlined "The Classic New York Doo-Wopp Show" at the Universal Ampitheatre in Los Angeles, sharing the bill with the Spaniels, the Capris, the Dixie Cups, and the Calvanes.

Carey brought Ron "Meatball" Reace into the group to replace Cherry, and the lineup soon grew to five with the addition of guitarist Keni Michael Davis in 1991. Born in Washington, D.C., in 1963, Keni Michael Davis and his friends discovered music at a very young age. "We used to perform Chuck Berry songs in front of our parents," Keni recalls. "My father was convinced I had a real desire to perform and play music, so he bought my first guitar and set me up with lessons when I was seven."

In addition to his work with the Flamingos, Davis also performed worldwide with the Clovers, Percy Sledge, and the Davis/Pinckney Project. "I was introduced to Zeke and Jacob by Ron Reace," Davis recalls. "My first gig with the group was in Reno, Nevada, at John Ascuaga's Nugget Casino. Then, we went to the Trump Plaza Casino in Atlantic City, New Jersey, and then came to Las Vegas at the legendary Sands Casino. I would play guitar, bass, and sing background vocals on live performances. I was a part of the Flamingos from 1991 to 1995. Performing with the Flamingos was priceless and memorable."

In 1993, the group, now based out of Springfield, Virginia, where Zeke resided, returned to the recording studio. They reworked "Welcome Home," cut a new Zeke Carey song, "If the Bed Breaks Down Baby," and also recorded new versions of Holland-Dozier-Holland's "Where Did Our Love Go," and an a cappella "I'll Be Home." Reace and Carey shared production credits on several of the masters, including a re-recording of "Time Was."

The first Ronze CD, *Welcome Home (My Love)*, a ten-track disc, featuring the new recordings and remastered versions of several of their earlier Ronze titles, was issued in 1993. "I just did the vinyl," explains Austin, who received a mastering credit in the CD notes. "Apparently on the CD, it was done by another company. They took the tracks and had a compilation made at another studio. Chuck [Irwin] happened to be in Nashville at the time, and so he booked the studio down there to record some of these things. After he left C.I., he worked freelance." The only photos included with the disc were portraits of the Careys. "I sang background vocals and played guitar on the *Welcome Home* CD," Keni Michael Davis recalls.

In 1996, another CD, *Unspoken Emotions*, was issued. The opening track, "Ain't Nothin' But a Party," was nothing more than a remixed version of their 1966 hit, "The Boogaloo Party." Again lacking a photo of the group on the cover, the nine-track disc included one new song, a cover of Jerry Lee Lewis's "Great Balls of Fire." The remainder of the songs were recycled from the *Welcome Home (My Love)* CD and the 1974 *In Touch with You* LP.

After leaving the Flamingos for the final time in the mid–1970s, Billy Clarke continued to dabble in music, playing drums with Ron Anderson and the Versatiles in New York City. In 1991, he and original member Pringle Sims reformed the Strangers for a one-time United in Group Harmony Association collector's concert. In his final years, Clarke worked as a director for the Brooklyn Parks Department. On July 26, 1996, three weeks after celebrating his 70th birthday, Billy Clarke died in Brooklyn.

In the early 1990s, Clarence Bassett reunited with Charles Baskerville and new member Al Handfield in Shep's Limelites. He died from emphysema at his home in Richmond, Virginia, on January 25, 2005, at age 68. Keith Williams moved to Pasadena, California, after his stint with the Flamingos. In May of 2007, he reunited with his old friends from the Velours, John Pearson, Jerome Ramos, John Cheatdom, and Donald Haywoode, and performed for producer T.J. Lubinsky's PBS-TV concert event, *My Music: Doo Wop Love Songs*. In his later years, Williams toured with a California-based stage production honoring the father of black gospel music, Thomas A. Dorsey. Diagnosed with cancer, Williams died on August 2, 2016, at his home in Pasadena shortly after having one of his lungs removed. He was 74.

Julien Vaught remained with the Flamingos until 1970. Later, he toured internationally with artists including Ray Charles, Dizzy Gillespie, and Bobby "Blue" Bland, and recorded extensively with artists including Sarah Vaughn, B.B. King, and Wilbert Harrison. He teamed with soul singer Ella Pennewell, and they released a CD, *That's the Way It Is*, in 2006. Today, he resides in Oakland, California.

Sollie McElroy

After leaving the Flamingos, Sollie McElroy joined the Moroccos in late 1954. McElroy, baritone George Prayer, tenors Ralph Vernon and Melvin Morrow, and bass Fred Martin recorded their first session together for United Records in 1955. Their initial release, "Pardon My Tears" and "Chicken," got the group some attention around the Windy City. McElroy's fine rendition of "Somewhere Over the Rainbow," backed with the Vernon-led "Red Hots and Chili Mac," was recorded in May and gained sporadic airplay and sales in various regions of the country, including Chicago, where both songs clicked. "I put some soul in it," McElroy proudly recounted upon hearing "Somewhere Over the Rainbow" decades later. "That's my version. I had an open voice. Most guys used a falsetto, but I just sang right up there. I stretched out more with the Moroccos than I did with the Flamingos, and we specialized in high voices."

That spring, the Moroccos beat out several other local groups to earn a spot in Larry Steele's Harlem Blackbirds show, along with Mabel Scott and Pigmeat Markham, touring Australia for eight weeks without Vernon, whose mother would not allow him to leave school to make the trip. The group flew from Chicago to Honolulu and landed in Sydney on June 4, 1955. "Larry Steele was from Chicago, and he produced a lot of shows," Sollie stated to interviewer Rallo. "He knew me, and knew that I was capable of doing what he wanted me to do. We hadn't been together even a year."

"We did a variety of songs," McElroy recounted to interviewer Pruter in his book, *Doowop: The Chicago Scene*. "I remember doing 'Money Honey,' also 'Unchained Melody,' which was done in such a way that we had a standing ovation. We did it practically a cappella. We had a 26-piece band backing us, but we didn't use all the instruments on this song. We did another song, a spiritual called 'Go Down Moses.'"

The Moroccos did none of their recordings, nor any of the sides McElroy had recorded with the Flamingos. "The reasons we didn't do too many R&B numbers was because Australia was way behind the United States," McElroy explained. "If we did any numbers that were current or popular in the United

MOROCCOS   UNITED RECORDING ARTIST

The Moroccos. Left to right: Ralph Vernon, Fred Martin, Sollie McElroy, Melvin Morrow, and George Prayer, 1955 (Fairbanks photo, from the Billy Vera collection).

States, they would have no idea what we were singing. So, we would do mainly things like what Nat 'King' Cole would do."

Returning home in February of 1956, the quintet backed Lillian Brooks on a four-song deal for King Records before returning to United for one final session in July with Calvin Baron replacing George Prayer, who had joined the Marines. "What Is a Teenager's Prayer?" and "Bang Goes My Heart," issued in September, and "Sad Sad Hours," featuring McElroy and Vernon singing lead, backed with "The Hex," failed to ignite much interest. "They were scared to invest, or didn't have the money. I don't know, and we began to decline," McElroy recounted. "We were going back to making 25 to 30 dollars each." One final single, "Believe in Tomorrow," which, according to McElroy, was recorded at the Briggs session for King, was issued on Salem Records in 1957 as by the Moroccans.

Vernon and Martin followed Prayer's lead by joining the Marine Corps, after which Morrow decided to join the U.S. Army Special Services, bringing the Moroccos to an end. Periodically, McElroy would dabble in music on and off for the remainder of his life. "I could have gotten back into singing many

The Moroccos, 1957. Top, left to right: Ralph Vernon, Sollie McElroy. Front, left to right: Fred Martin, George Prayer, and Melvin Morrow (Billy Vera collection).

times, but I wanted that paycheck every day," he confessed. "I went out on too many gigs when the man said, 'We didn't have enough crowd,' or 'The guy ran away with the money.'"

In 1961, he joined the Chaunteurs, which consisted of first tenor Eugene "Gino" Record (1940–2005), second tenor Robert "Squirrel" Lester, baritone Clarence Johnson, and bass Eddie Reed. In 1959, this group had recorded a couple of singles for the tiny Renee label. With McElroy in the lineup, the Chaunteurs recorded one rare single for the LaSalle imprint in 1961 backed by King Kolax and his band, "New Rockin' Baby" and "Wishin' Well," with Sollie and Eugene trading off the leads. At least one additional side, "I'll Do What You Want Me to Do," was never issued. While some historians have claimed that this group was also the Chaunteurs who recorded single discs for Vee Jay and Bolo in 1963, the personnel on those records is unknown. "I recorded at least six songs with them as the Chaunteurs," McElroy recalled.

What is known, however, is that shortly after their LaSalle session, Record, Lester, and Johnson teamed with Marshall Thompson and Creadel Jones to form the Hi-Lites, who became the Chi-Lites in 1964. Over a career that spanned five decades, the Chi-Lites recorded over 40 nationally charted hits, including a pair of #1 R&B records. "Me and Gene had a conflict about who was going to sing lead, and I said, 'You take it, Gene,'" Sollie stated.

McElroy joined the Nobles in late 1961 and sang lead on both sides of their Stacy label single, the soulful "Serenade," and "You Ain't Right." "Noble was the name of one of the five guys in the group, and he named us. They were from 43rd and Indiana Avenue." Issued in November of 1961, the disc credited the Nobles featuring Sollie McElroy. In 1966, McElroy recorded a solo single, "Angel Girl" and "Party Time," backed by a soulful but uncredited female group for James Shelton's new Ja-Wes label.

Sollie performed occasionally at local clubs into the early 1980s, when he decided to form a new Moroccos group with original bass Fred Martin. Recruiting Larry "Hi-C" Johnson (1936–1999), who had been a member of the Moroccos prior to their recording days, and original El Dorados bass Richard Nickens (1936–1991), the quartet took to the stage whenever the opportunity to sing came up, but gigs were scare and paid lightly. When Martin died in 1986, the Moroccos disbanded. Eventually, both Johnson and Nickens would join Pirkle Lee Moses, Jr., in a revamped El Dorados lineup, remaining active until their deaths.

In late April of 1992, McElroy traveled to New York City, representing

The Chaunteurs, 1961. Left to right: Clarence Johnson, Robert Lester, Eddie Reed, Sollie McElroy and Eugene Record (author's collection).

the original Flamingos at their induction into the United in Group Harmony Association (UGHA) Hall of Fame at their second annual awards ceremony. "It was magnificent," he related. "I went up there with no idea of what was going down, and when I got there, how the people treated me and received me, it was just like boom—a big explosion. They told me things and showed me things that I didn't know about. It's hard to explain. I had no idea that I would get such recognition. I sing. I enjoy it. But I don't see it as that important. It wasn't my priority in life. I never got that [ego] thing. Having a buck in my pocket was important. I never got that, 'Hey, I'm Sollie McElroy,' giving autographs and stuff like that. I felt embarrassed to sign an autograph. I was very humble. I always had a low profile. I never wanted to be up front. I let everybody else do the talking."

Through the years, McElroy and the Careys remained on cordial terms. "It was no personal thing," Sollie explained. "There was no animosity at all between us. Whenever I saw them, we greeted each other, hugged each other. They didn't smoke or drink, but I liked my nip. I never embarrassed the group. I never missed a gig or anything. They tried to convert me, but I did my thing, and they did theirs. I didn't have anything against [their religion], but I couldn't relate because I'm a Baptist. When we went out and Passover and the other holidays came, I went my separate way. I didn't do the fasting and all. We had a lot of good days, though. You know, when you stay with a group for a long time, you become brothers. You watch my back. I watch your back. Don't think there were no flare-ups, though. Brothers can fall out, but we would overcome that. The show must go on, no matter what you felt. You could be tearing up the dressing room, but when the show was on, we were professionals. I think the only time I had a hundred dollars in my pocket from singing was one Christmas. I was at the

Original Flamingos lead singer Sollie McElroy visiting the United in Group Harmony Association in New Jersey, 1992 (from the collection of Richard and Eunice Tulimieri).

Regal Theater with Duke Ellington, and that's the highest I had ever been paid for singing. I never got a dime from royalties."

On November 14, 1992, Sollie returned to the UGHA stage, backed by the Ecstasies for a special "Collector's Concert." With his hearing compromised and his voice weakened by years of cigarette smoking, McElroy admittedly could not perform "Pardon My Heart," "Sad, Sad Hours," "Golden Teardrops," "Dream of a Lifetime," and "Jump Children" the way he had four decades earlier, but his audience didn't seem to care. His many fans in attendance stood and applauded his efforts, but, in essence, were expressing their appreciation for the man himself, and what his pioneering work had meant to them through the years.

In later years, Sollie and his wife, Cathy, shared their life together in a home on South Aberdeen Street on the South Side of Chicago. In 1994, he was stricken with cancer. United in Group Harmony Association members and Flamingos fans sent cards, letters, and donations to help defray the costs associated with his medical expenses. As long as he was able, Sollie hand-wrote thank-you cards to all of his well-wishers. On January 15, 1995, Sollie McElroy died in Chicago at the age of 61. His body was returned to his birthplace of Gulfport, Mississippi, and buried in Evergreen Gardens Cemetery.

Rhythm & Blues Foundation Pioneer Award

On February 29, 1996, at the Hollywood Palladium in Los Angeles, the Washington, D.C.–based Rhythm & Blues Foundation paid tribute to the Flamingos, honoring all of the group's hit makers with its Pioneer Award and a $25,000 cash payment to be divided among its members. Formed in 1988, the Foundation, an independent nonprofit service organization solely dedicated to the historical and cultural preservation of R&B music, provided financial support, medical assistance, and educational outreach through various grants and programs to support pioneering R&B artists.

Also honored at the seventh annual awards night were Dave Bartholomew, the Cadillacs, the Chantels, Betty Everett, Eddie Floyd, the Isley Brothers, Jay McShann, Johnny Taylor, Doris Troy, Johnny "Guitar" Watson, Bobby Womack, and Bo Diddley, who received the Foundation's Lifetime Achievement Award.

A photo of the reunited Flamingos appeared in several industry trade papers. "We all went there, and everybody said, 'Are you guys going to sing?' 'Are you guys going to sing?'" Johnson recalls. "I said, 'I don't know, man.' I had taken my track to 'I Only Have Eyes for You,' the way I do it with my group. I had heard Zeke sing it, and Zeke murdered it. He was not a lead singer. I'm not that great of a lead singer myself, especially on 'I Only Have Eyes for You.' That was Nate's baby. I do a decent job with it, but Zeke was horrible. So, Jerry Butler said, 'Well, if you guys are going to sing, all of you have to go on stage together. It can't be just one or two guys. It's got to be everybody.' So, we said, 'Well, you guys want to sing the song?' They said, 'OK, I guess so.'"

As they had done countless times in the late 1950s and early 1960s, the surviving Flamingos gathered in Terry Johnson's hotel room to work out an arrangement. "I had my guitar, and so I said, 'Let me get it straight with everybody first of all. Zeke, I don't mean any harm to you, but you've been singing this song for all these years. I have been doing it all these years also. I think it's only fair that I should be able to sing it this one time since we're joined together now. I feel I do a better job than you. I don't mean any harm,

The surviving Flamingos reunited at the Rhythm & Blues Foundation Pioneer Award ceremony, 1996. Left to right: Terry Johnson, Ezekiel Carey, Johnny Carter, Tommy Hunt and Jacob Carey (Cohen photo, courtesy Terry Johnson).

but to your face, I'm telling you that I would like to sing the song.' Zeke said, 'I don't agree with that.' Johnny Carter said, 'Let Buzzy try it, man. I think Buzzy's got a good voice.' Tommy said, 'Well, whatever.' Tommy had always been riding the fence. But when Jake said, 'Zeke, Buzzy sounds good. Let Buzzy do it,' Zeke was so pissed off. He was mad with Jake for that."

Soon, the room was filled with the familiar strains of the Flamingos' five-part harmonies. "We rehearsed it, and I structured the harmony the same way I did with the original Flamingos. I had Tommy doing more under the second tenor. I had Zeke doing the second tenor. Johnny Carter did the baritone, and Jake did the bass. I did the lead. Zeke was so pissed off. He said, 'Look, they want it in the original key.' I said, 'I can't really sing it in the original key and do justice to it.' I had to drop it at least a half-step down. Zeke said, 'Well, I sing it in the original key, so let me sing the part, "I only have eyes for you," and that's when you can do your [floating] tenor.' I said, 'All right. I'll try that.' So, I structured the harmony, we rehearsed it, and it sounded just like the Flamingos. We went on stage. Little Richard was there, the Isley Brothers, Claudette Robinson, Bo Diddley, all of the superstars that were being honored."

"The honorees offered thanks; they reminisced, and they raised their voices in fondly remembered songs," Jon Pareles wrote in the *New York Times*. "As the band played the blues, Johnny 'Guitar' Watson sang to accept his Pioneer Award. 'I have been nominated for a few Grammys,' he intoned above a rolling vamp. 'But the R&B award is the real deal.' Bobby Womack, accepting his, was even more to the point. 'Where's the check?' he asked, and was handed one. The Flamingos sang tremulous harmonies on 'I Only Have Eyes for You'.... Most of the songs pledged their faith in the power of love, with a fervor that transcended the pitfalls of the music business. While the Grammys celebrate the recording business and promote the latest best sellers, the foundation's Pioneer awards provide a corrective view. They honor music that was perfected on the road as much as it was in the recording studio, and that survived long after the Top 40 had moved on to other things."

Of their assessment of the Foundation and its mission, Pareles wrote, "Major conglomerates now own the catalogues of many labels that originally issued classic rhythm-and-blues songs. And some of them, such as Polygram and BMG, have not changed the terms of old contracts even as oldies are reissued on CDs. 'It's not about a contract; it's about doing the right thing,' said James G. Fifield, the president and chief executive officer of EMI Music, and the vice-chairman of the Rhythm and Blues Foundation. 'The right thing to do is for record labels to recognize that disparity, and to give some money to the artists who laid the foundations for our music. It's not much; I don't know why they go into freeze frame when we talk about it.' EMI, which owns recordings by Fats Domino ... and many others, has forgiven all debts for material released before 1972 and raised its royalty rate on reissues to 10 percent."

Hosted by past honorees Darlene Love and Mavis Staples, the show's "loose structure got even looser," according to the *Los Angeles Times* account, as the evening progressed. Percy Sledge introduced the Flamingos, mixing up his notes in the process, before finally bringing on the quintet. "It was the kind of evening that brought shivers through the audience several times," Steve Hochman wrote in the *Los Angeles Times*, "especially ... when the Flamingos did their first 'sh-bob-sh-bop [*sic*].'"

"We sang 'Eyes,' and when I started singing it, I'm telling you, it felt as if it wasn't my voice," Terry states. "Tommy kept saying, 'Man, it sounded like Nate came through you, and it was like Nate's voice there.' It was weird, because my wife, Theresa, said the same thing. She said it didn't sound like me, and she knows my voice. It sounded so beautiful, and when Zeke did take over and did 'I only have eyes for you,' and I did my tenor, the whole place went crazy because the original voices were there. It was like, whew." In the words of *Goldmine* magazine reporter Steve Roeser, it was "a note perfect version ... that was sheer enchantment."

Changing of the Guard

In October of 1996, New York disc jockey Don K. Reed of WCBS-FM polled his listeners over a three-week period for their all-time favorite oldies. Not surprisingly, "Eyes" ranked #4, behind "In the Still of the Night," "Earth Angel," and the Mello-Kings' "Tonite, Tonite."

Despite a lack of success in the recording studio, the Flamingos remained in demand for live performances. The Careys were now joined on stage by Ron Reace and George Spann, who had previously worked with Pookie Hudson and the Spaniels and the Dynamic Superiors. Spann had replaced Keni Michael Davis in 1995, when the guitarist decided to move to Las Vegas, finding steady work in hotels and casinos with the R&B band, Shotyme. As an instrumental soloist, a recording studio and television and motion picture soundtrack musician, the guitarist has also worked with the Radio All-Stars. "I dig it," Davis states. "Since childhood, my passion has always been playing my guitar for people. Now, I get paid for it."

Archie Satterfield, who left the group in 1992, reunited with former 1980s Flamingos member Bennie Cherry in a trio known as Touch of Silk. Along with Bobby Gant, the two former Flamingos vocalists performed everything from James Brown and the Temptations to the Eagles and Boyz 2 Men in places like the Virgin River Hotel and Casino, and the Oasis Cabaret Lounge in Mesquite, Nevada. Today, Cherry, a native of San Antonio, Texas, continues the Nevada-based group with all new members.

On December 1, 1996, the Flamingos appeared at the Nassau Coliseum on Long Island, along with R&B pioneers the Moonglows, the Clovers, Rudy West and the Keys, the Spaniels, and others, in a special tribute to ailing star LaVern Baker. Baker died just over three months later, on March 10, 1997.

On June 29, 1997, they appeared before 14,000 fans at the Continental Airlines Arena in New Jersey at Richard Nader's Doo Wop Reunion Spectacular VIII. Joining the Flamingos on their first Nader show in 20 years were the Skyliners, the Marcels, the Duprees, and Harvey Fuqua and the Moonglows. Opening with "Lovers Never Say Goodbye," they sang "Love Walked In," "I'll Be Home," "I Only Have Eyes for You," and "Mio Amore," before joining the Moonglows on stage to close with "I Was Wrong" and "Jump Children." The event marked the first time in years that the Flamingos and Moonglows had appeared on a bill together in the New York Metropolitan area. It would also be the last.

On October 4, 1997, the group appeared on "A Twistin' October Fest Oldies Concert," at the Westchester County Center in White Plains, New York. With Don K. Reed hosting, the Flamingos were joined on the card by Randy and the Rainbows, the Shangri-Las, Gary U.S. Bonds, Arlene Smith of the Chantels, and Chubby Checker. Their six-song crowd-pleasing set consisted of "Lovers," "I'll Be Home," "Mio Amore," "Your Other Love," "Nobody Loves Me Like You," and the inevitable closer, "Eyes." In the audience that night was veteran Ronze mastering engineer Phil Austin. "That was the last time I saw them together on stage. At the end of the show, I was going to go backstage and say hello, but there was such a crush of people I said, 'Ah, I'll call them in a couple of weeks.' I should have gone backstage, because I never heard from them again. But we had a great relationship over the 20 years. We just stuck together."

In November, the Flamingos traveled to the Apache Reservation in Pine Top, Arizona. The group's appearances that week at the Hon-Dah Resort-Casino would be Jacob Carey's last. Divorced from his first wife, Leah, and now separated from his second wife, Beatrice, Jake had moved south to Lanham, Maryland, in 1996. On December 10, 1997, he suffered a fatal heart attack in his Lanham home. He was 74.

Carey was survived by five children. Two were from his first marriage: Jacob "J.C." of Essex, Maryland; and Velma "Susie," of Camden, New Jersey. Three were from his second: Joel, of Philadelphia; Jeffrey, of Delaware and Deborah Petaia of Philadelphia. In addition, he was survived by one sister, Clara Morrison, eight grandchildren, and four great-grandchildren. He was buried in Cheltenham Veterans Cemetery in Cheltenham, Maryland.

Fletcher Weatherspoon, Harvey Fuqua, Pookie Hudson, and cousin Zeke Carey were among the mourners who turned out for Jake's funeral, which included an all-star cast bidding the bass singer farewell by singing the group's signature tune. "I was shocked when Jake died, and I went to the funeral," Weatherspoon explained. "Everybody sang 'I Only Have Eyes for You.' I remember that Zeke invited me up. He told me that I was the only person of color that he ever knew who couldn't carry a tune in a wheelbarrow. He invited me up with them and said, 'We're going to bring up the Godfather of the Flamingos.'"

"The Flamingos will continue," Zeke promised his fans. "Jake wouldn't have it any other way."

On May 11–12, 1999, the Flamingos joined dozens of their fellow pioneers for the historic "Doo Wop 50," a PBS-TV concert special that proved to be the most successful fundraiser in public television's history. A Rhino home video and double DVD release of the T.J. Lubinsky–produced event captured host Jerry Butler, Herb Reed's Platters, the Del Vikings, the Skyliners, the Penguins, Johnny Maestro and the Brooklyn Bridge, Lee Andrews and the Hearts, the Cleftones, the Capris, the Marcels, the Jive Five, the Channels, the Cadillacs, the Chantels, the Moonglows, the Harptones, the Spaniels, and others, performing with a full orchestra before an enthusiastic sellout crowd at the Benedum Center for the Performing Arts in Pittsburgh.

The Flamingos, consisting of Zeke Carey, Jake's son J.C. Carey, Ron Reace, King Raymond Green, and Larry Jordan, who joined in 1997 after previously working with Diz Russell's Washington-based Orioles, performed "I Only Have Eyes for You" and "Lovers Never Say Goodbye" on the extended home video release. Despite the perceptible lack of a close-up, those who knew Zeke Carey could see he was not a well man. Noticeably thin, the 66-year-old struggled with his lead vocal chores. "Zeke was sick long before he let anybody know about it," Fletcher Weatherspoon stated. "My son was playing drums for them, and he used to tell me that when Zeke would finish a show, he would go and lay down. He was sick long before he told anybody about it. The cancer worked slowly on him."

In September of 1999, the Flamingos were nominated for the Rock and Roll Hall of Fame, but failed to obtain enough votes for the honor. In November, "Doo Wop 50" exploded onto television screens across America. But while fans were singing along to the sounds of the Flamingos' television appearance, Zeke Carey's health was failing rapidly. By December, he had left his Alexandria home for the Walter Reed Army Medical Center in Washington, D.C.

Terminally ill with cancer, Carey was visited two days before Christmas by his longtime friends and fellow R&B pioneers James "Pookie" Hudson of the Spaniels and Harvey Fuqua of the

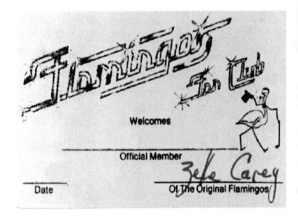

Flamingos Fan Club card, designed by Jake and signed by Zeke Carey, 1978 (author's collection).

Moonglows. "Pookie and I sang 'I Only Have Eyes for You' to Zeke in the hospital," Fuqua recounted. "Even though he was out of it, it seemed he rallied a little to join us."

On December 29, 1999, Ezekiel J. Carey died. When his death was reported in the *Washington Post* on New Year's Day 2000, the date of death was erroneously given as December 24. He was survived by three daughters, Melanie Dyer of Roxbury, Massachusetts; Tanyika Carey of New York; and Kim Turner of Clairton, Pennsylvania, along with a brother, two sisters, and five grandchildren. Zeke's older brother, Solomon, died in 2014. Zeke Carey was buried in Belleville Cemetery in Suffolk, Virginia, the final resting place for many members of the Church of God and Saints of Christ denomination including his parents, Silas and Mariah Carey. Carey's simple flat stone grave marker lists only his name and dates of birth and death.

Sadly, Fuqua later reported that next to none of Carey's friends from the music industry joined him at the Virginia service. Zeke had been the group's longtime leader and spokesman, so alerting friends and acquaintances of a significant event involving the Flamingos, such as a death, was always Zeke's job. "I didn't find out about it until it was too late to go," Fletcher Weatherspoon lamented.

"It seemed that everything stopped, and I never heard from Zeke," Phil Austin adds. "I tried to get a hold of him at his phone number in Virginia, but the number was changed. Jake had passed away. Then, one of my friends called me up and said that Zeke had died in the hospital. I tried to get a hold of somebody, but I couldn't. So, unfortunately, I missed the funeral. I wanted to go to it, but I didn't make it. To this day, I haven't been in contact with anybody connected with him. It's kind of sad. I loved the guy a lot."

Rebirth and the Rock & Roll Hall of Fame

The Flamingos were honored with induction into the Vocal Group Hall of Fame in Sharon, Pennsylvania, in 2000. "When [Mary Wilson of the Supremes] called me to represent the Flamingos, I walked onto the stage to a rapturous applause, and standing in front of the audience I broke down in tears," Hunt later wrote. "All I could think of were the other Flamingos. Nate had gone, followed by Paul, then recently Jake and Zeke. God bless them. 'I'm sorry, I can't handle this,' was all I could say."

The ultimate honor, however, came on March 19, 2001, when the group was inducted into the Rock & Roll Hall of Fame. Present for the 16th annual awards ceremony, held at the Waldorf-Astoria Hotel in New York City, were Johnny Carter, Terry Johnson, Tommy Hunt, and family members of the deceased pioneers. The class of '01 also included Aerosmith, Solomon Burke, Michael Jackson, Queen, Paul Simon, Steely Dan, and Ritchie Valens.

"The Flamingos were all seated at the same table," Hunt wrote. "Zeke's daughter sat close by. When Nate's family showed up, his son looked so much like him it almost made me cry. I was real pleased to meet [Ron Wilson, Paul's son], and he hugged me to him just as if he was hugging his dad. Finally, Jake's son J.C. came over to speak to me."

"It's an honor and a privilege," Johnson told the media. "The drag is that the dream of Jake and Zeke is finally being realized, and they're not here to see it." Terry harbors no bitterness about the length of time that passed before the group was chosen for the honor. "Not at all," he affirms. "I was shocked and surprised, happily surprised, that we were even thought of to go into the Rock & Roll Hall of Fame. To me, I didn't realize how big the Flamingos name was. I didn't realize that all these groups, the Temptations, and Frankie Lymon and the Teenagers, and Anthony and the Imperials looked up to us like we were the ones, and they were imitating our style. I had no idea that the Flamingos had that kind of reputation."

"I think it's a long overdue thing that these people are doing for us because we deserve it," Hunt told interviewer Mike Boone the night before the ceremony. "We deserve it. We put our hearts and souls into it. I always said, if people knew how much sweat that we put on the stage, us and other artists that grew up with us, they would have done this a long time ago. But at least I lived long enough to feel this excitement. It is the most exciting experience of my life. I didn't ever think Hall of Fame. Not me. When it first came up, I wanted to cry, and then I thought to myself, 'No, I deserve it.' We don't get the respect from the new set of entertainers. That's what hurts me now. It's just a look of admiration or a look of appreciation saying, we knew you were there. We followed you."

"In the past, we never received the money we should have gotten," Johnson told reporter Geoffrey Hines. "The top money we ever got was $10,000, and today, you hear about acts getting millions of dollars for signing a contract. So, getting these honors means we're finally getting our propers. To be on the same platform as Michael Jackson,

"The Ambassador of Romance..."

Terry Johnson of The Flamingos

Promotional photo, 2005 (courtesy Terry Johnson).

Queen, and all these superstars who really made the money means we're on the same level."

About this time, things started to go awry between Terry Johnson and J.C. Carey. "J.C. and I were supposed to get together," explains Terry, who had continued performing through the years with his own Flamingos group. "He called me on New Year's, 2001. He said, 'Hey Buzz, are you still active?' I said, 'What do you mean?' He said, 'Are you still singing?' I said, 'Of course, I'm still singing.' He said, 'I've got the name, Flamingos.' I said, 'What do you mean the name?' When Zeke died, his daughters went through his belongings, because he didn't leave a will. In 1979, he knew that I was working, and he trademarked the name. In the 1950s, nobody owned the name. It was just a partnership formed with a handshake. There were no legal papers or anything." Indeed, Carey was aware of Johnson's activity. A blurb in the November 17, 1979, issue of *Cash Box* claimed that "Zeke and Jake Carey, the original Flamingos, want to take action against touring groups who are using the Flamingos name."

J.C. Carey reorganized the group, replacing King Raymond Green (1950–2017), who joined the Clovers, and Ron Reace with Earnest "Mike" Gilbert, George Spann, and James Faison. Reace subsequently attempted to create his own Flamingos group, using the misleading "Rock and Roll Hall of Fame Inductees" tag.

"So, now his daughter found the trademark papers and J.C., who had worked with Jake and Zeke, decided he wanted to put a group together. He said he had a few guys, and he would like for me to be a part of the group, because I had a lot to bring to the table. I said it sounded interesting, and we kept talking, and then I said, 'Great, well, count me in.' Then, we were ready to do the Rock & Roll Hall of Fame. He called me and said, 'All right, Buzzy, I have the lineup. We're going to do 'I Only Have Eyes for You.' I said, 'Yeah, I planned on doing that anyway.' He said, 'You do the tenor part, and I'm going to let Larry [Jordan] do the lead.' I said, 'No. Hold it, J.C. You can't be telling me who's going to sing that. That's my song. God gave me that arrangement. That is me. Plus, I was the musical arranger of the Flamingos.' He said, 'Well, that was then, and this is now. I'm the musical arranger now, and I'm calling the shots.' I said, 'Wait a minute. Hold it. You're what?' He said, 'I'm calling the shots.' I said, 'Over me? I'm an original Flamingo.' He said, 'Well, that was then. I've got it now. So, you're going to go and do...' I said, 'You know what, J.C., count me out of your little thing. I'll get my own group and do my own thing.'"

Although Johnson wanted Carey to join him, Carter, and Hunt on stage to sing, the two were unfortunately unable to come to an agreement. "Since I was an original, and Tommy was an original, and Johnny Carter was an original, we three were there, and then I had them hire some other background singers. I showed them how to do what I wanted them to do. They had it where it was sounding really perfect. But I respected Paul Shaffer, and I let him rearrange it. 'He said, wait a minute, this guy, his voice sounds better in this part and...' And because I respected him so much, I let him destroy it. When we did it, it was flat. Somebody was flat, and Johnny was singing [deep bass] 'boom-bo-bo-bo-bo-boom,' instead of singing the beautiful part he should have been singing. I don't know. He had an attitude. He said, 'I want to sing Jake's part.' I said, 'Jake's part? Come on, Johnny, you're the tenor!'

He said, 'I can sing all parts.' He was snappy at me. I don't know why he did it. I was embarrassed because it was a little flat. Then I found out that Paul Shaffer could not read any music at all. He did everything by ear. I said, 'Damn. I let them destroy it.'"

After Johnson led the trio through "I Only Have Eyes for You," members of the Carey and Nelson families took to the stage. "'I Only Have Eyes for You' sounded better than I ever thought it would," Hunt conceded. "The backing singers were fantastic. We had a standing ovation, and that felt amazing. Terry did a great job singing the lead vocal."

"I had everybody come up on stage," Johnson explains. "I had Melanie and her sister, Tanyika. J.C. came up, and then I had Nate's son, Lloyd, come up, and his sister, Bunny. I thought it was only right to pay tribute to the kids of everybody that had passed. J.C. hated me for that, because he couldn't go in and do the song."

Rock Hall member Dion DiMucci inducted the Flamingos. Noted music critic Dave Marsh wrote, "The defining statement of the night came from Tanyika Carey, daughter of the late Zeke Carey, founder of the Flamingos. 'My father taught us that vocal harmony could be the highest form of democracy. It represented abstract truth and beauty.'"

Several months later, Johnson and Carey crossed paths at another awards show. "J.C. went out and sang 'I'll Be Home' a cappella with his group and they sounded really good," Johnson states. "I won't take anything from them. If it was good, it was good. They wouldn't speak to me, but I said, 'J.C., I don't know if Melanie told you, but I told her I wanted you to come up on stage with me at the Rock and Roll Hall of Fame. I wanted just him, though. Not his whole group. He didn't believe me and we've been kind of at odds with each other ever since."

Later, Carey and Johnson butted heads over the use of the Flamingos name. Carey claimed ownership of the group's name by virtue of Zeke's trademark, and performed for a spell as the Flamingos, while Johnson referred to his aggregation as Terry Johnson's Flamingos or, simply, Terry Johnson, original lead singer of the Flamingos. "I'm not trying to say that I am the Flamingos," Johnson explained at the time, "because I'm the only one of the originals in my group. But here you have a group with no original members calling themselves the Flamingos, and J.C.'s trying to stop me from earning a living. I wrote these songs. I sang on these songs. I arranged and produced them. That's just wrong."

By 2004, J.C. Carey's group consisted of George Spann, James Faison, Mike Gilbert, and Larry Jordan. Within a year, financial disputes caused the lineup to dissolve. Spann, Jordan, Gilbert, and Faison re-formed Spann's old group, the Dynamic Superiors. Carey continued on, adding old friends Doug McClure and Sidney Hall to the lineup in 2006, and they were occasionally joined on stage by Tommy Hunt, who flew in from England to perform with them at selected shows. "I hadn't performed in years," McClure recalled of his return to the stage in July of 2006. "The group had asked me would I do it, and I consented because it was local. I live in New Haven and the show was in Connecticut. I said 'why not?' I was still singing in the choir and doing solos in the church, gospel music. It's like swimming. You don't forget." In 2008, Carey, McClure, and Hall shared the stage with tenor Victor Brown and baritone-tenor Philip "Flip" Thomas.

In late 2008, McClure recorded and released his own soulful jazz CD, *Love Letters*, collaborating with John Clayton. The album included a new recording of "I Only Have Eyes for You" and versions of numerous soul and R&B classics. "It took over a year to finish," McClure explained. "My son had heard me sing at a funeral in California and he said, 'People have to hear this voice. We're doing a CD!' The songs that were chosen are about love, beautiful songs. 'I Only Have Eyes for You' is a little different from when the Flamingos did it. It has just a little more twang to it, a smooth jazz-type flavor. But it's recognizable. I had fun with it. Red Rideout, who worked with Luther Vandross, was the producer."

In the summer of 2008, the Commissioner for Trademarks canceled the Flamingos trademark registration #116194 that Carey's group was using, stating that Johnson "has Federal trademark protection over a trademark including the term Flamingos for onstage musical performances ... and the petition to cancel the trademark The Flamingos is granted." The decision stated, in part, that "Jacob A. Carey and Ezekiel J. Carey made false statements under oath that the general partnership, composed of the applicants, believed itself to be the owner of the mark sought to be registered, and 'that no other person, firm, corporation or association, to the best of his knowledge and belief, has the right to use such mark in commerce,' when they filed for the registration of the mark on December 29, 1976."

"It has been my goal to prevent anyone from tarnishing the respected name of the Flamingos with sub-par performances and claims of original members," Johnson stated when the decree was issued. "I am now the only trademarked Flamingos' group. I want to personally thank Jon Bauman, of the Truth in Music Act, for his and his staff's support and hard work in securing the integrity of this great music and its original artists."

Later, McClure and Hall broke away from Carey and performed the group's signature hits billed as "Doug McClure and Sid Hall—former lead singers of the Flamingos," and also under the name Just Two. In 2012, the pair joined forces with Jimmie Wilson, formerly of Bill Baker's Satins, and latter-day Limelites lead Al Handfield as V.O.P.—Voices of the Past. "When I'm singing, I actually live what I'm singing," McClure summed to interviewer Phillips. "I'm feeling what I'm singing. It's like telling the story, getting the point across. I don't feel like I'm a great singer, but I tell a story pretty good. It was my delivery. God's been good to me down through the years. I've been blessed." Doug McClure died on July 6, 2018, at the age of 78.

In addressing the terminology used by fans and promoters about personnel, Johnson succinctly explains, "There is a difference in the terms 'founding member' and 'original member.' The 'founding members' of the Flamingos were Paul Wilson, Johnny Carter, Jake and Zeke Carey. There were four founding members, not two. The 'original members' of the Flamingos are persons who were on the original recordings that brought the group to the height of their success. They were recognized by the Rock and Roll Hall of Fame as being Paul Wilson, Jake Carey, Johnny Carter, Tommy Hunt, Nate Nelson, Zeke Carey, Sollie McElroy and me. I believe Sollie was recognized as he should be, because he was their first recorded lead singer, and 'Golden Teardrops' is considered to be their first groundbreaking release. Any other singers that have been hired through the years for performances by Zeke and Jake Carey or me, are not members of the original Flamingos. Some consider themselves to be by association, but they are hired performers. My hope is to bring clarity to this situation, and to continue to do my best to bring a high quality of performance to the paying, supportive public."

Tommy Hunt

Following the success of "Human," Tommy Hunt toured the country constantly and continued to record for Scepter/Wand. The singer's next three releases failed to draw much national attention despite being quality productions. The Burt Bacharach and Hal David–penned "I Just Don't Know What to Do with Myself," produced by Jerry Leiber and Mike Stoller, was issued as a single in August of 1962 and served as the title track from his lone Scepter album. Although it failed to chart, the recording undoubtedly made an impression on Dusty Springfield, who cut her own successful version for Philips in 1965.

Following Dixon's departure from Scepter/Wand in 1963, Hunt teamed with the company's new musical director, Ed "For Your Love" Townsend, who produced "I Am a Witness," with backing vocals from the Shirelles, Sweet Inspirations, and Dee Dee Warwick. The soulful track, which prominently featured session great Mickey Baker's ringing guitar and the drumbeat of veteran Bernard Purdie, peaked at #71 on *Billboard*'s R&B list late that year.

After one additional Scepter release, Hunt recorded single discs for Atlantic and Capitol in 1965–66 before signing on with the Musicor subsidiary, Dynamo Records. "That was a New York–based label," Hunt explained to interviewers Boone and McGarvey. "In 1967, Luther Dixon [who had] left Scepter/Wand, came to me and said, 'Tommy, I want to record you again because I don't think you got a fair chance over at Scepter/Wand.' I said, 'Look, Luther, those kinds of things work out that way. I'm not angry because I know that as long as I'm still here, I'm not done until I'm done. Lead me to the stage and I'll sing.' So he took me to Musicor and I met Jerry Williams, who was then a hustling little trying-to-be record producer. This is the Swamp Dogg. He said to me, 'Mr. Hunt, I'd appreciate your letting me record you.'"

The first of Tommy's five Dynamo singles, "The Biggest Man," became his biggest hit in nearly six years, topping out at #29 on *Billboard*'s R&B chart, #124 on the magazine's Bubbling Under the Hot 100 list. Having performed for United States Army troops stationed in Germany in the late 1960s, Hunt settled in Wales in the United Kingdom in 1970. "I think I came to the UK because, at that time, music was changing," Hunt told McGarvey. "The Beatles had come over and created a whole new thing, and I didn't fit in. Well, a whole lot of people like me didn't fit in because we were from the rock 'n' roll days. I wanted to get on the boat and learn what I could learn. But I ended up getting married, and that was it. I had to stay then."

In 1972 and '74, respectively, he recorded single releases for Polydor and Pye, all the while working steadily in theaters and Northern Soul clubs throughout Britain. After being approached by Russ Winstanley, the British disc jockey who founded the Wigan Casino, Hunt began recording with Barry Kingston for Spark Records in 1975. His first LP for the firm, *Tommy Hunt Live at the Wigan Casino*, a collection of 1960s soul songs including "Get Ready," "My Girl," "Knock On Wood," and "Crackin' Up," was issued that year. "Barry Kingston was a house producer at Spark," the label's promotion manager Mike Walker recalled in an Internet letter. "I was familiar with Barry's work with the Sutherland Brothers, who were popular in Northern Soul circles, and worked closely with Barry on subsequent hit recordings. Tommy scored heavily with three releases … all of which were produced by Barry Kingston with, hopefully, a little help from both Russ and I."

The first of Hunt's British hits was a version of "Crackin' Up," originally recorded by the singer's early influence, Roy Hamilton. "Loving on the Losing Side" and "One Fine Morning" gained a host of airplay in 1975–76 and cemented the singer's reputation. "When I first started over there, as a brand-new artist, nobody over there knew Tommy Hunt," he confessed to Boone in 2001. "The guy that was representing me said 'I'll put you into the best cabaret clubs.' So, he put me into a place called Caesar's Palace in a small town called Luten. I said, 'Well, which part of the show do I do?'—because I thought being a small no-namer, that I would go on first. He said, 'No, it doesn't work that way over here. You're going on as top of the bill.' I said, 'I can't top the bill when people don't know me.' He said, 'Tommy, you're going on as the top of the bill.' I said, 'OK,' because I didn't know the system. What happened was, they put me there, and the show went down fabulous. I had the right songs, and the band was pretty decent—because I never really enjoyed the English players at that time. When I first got there, I never thought to myself that the English players would ever be like our soul brothers [back home]. They didn't live it. They didn't feel what we felt. I kept telling the guys, 'Look, you guys are really good, but can you play from the heart? Don't play from the music, play from the heart, because that's what we're about. We see the notes, but we play our hearts.' These English guys couldn't understand what I meant, so I said, 'Well, just play it the way you see it,' and the guys did a good job. You have to balance the singer with the band. I had to learn their way. After 35 years, I became an English-sounding singer."

A Sign of the Times, Hunt's second and final Spark LP, was issued in 1976. In 1982 and '83, he was honored with the Club Mirror Award as Male Vocalist of the Year in the United Kingdom. After cutting a couple of discs for the Trill label, "Only the Strong Survive" and "Game Player," Hunt, feeling that the activity on the Northern Soul scene was dwindling, moved to the Netherlands, settling in Amsterdam in 1986. From his new home base, Hunt traveled worldwide with his own cabaret show.

Teaming up with Jerry "Swamp Dogg" Williams again, Hunt recorded a new CD, *Until My Arms Fall Off*, for Williams's SDEG label in 1996. In 1997, one year after traveling to America to accept the Rhythm and Blues Foundation's pioneer award with the other surviving Flamingos, Hunt moved back to England, where he has found steady work on the popular Northern Soul scene once again and still performs a couple of times a month, mostly in Great Britain.

Now in his mid–80s, Hunt still enjoys working and writing music, and penned his autobiography in 2009. "There's another chance for me out there," Hunt wrote. "I feel it right now. A lot of people say to me, like, you're over the hill. I say, 'What hill? I never got to the hill yet. I ain't seen the hill. My legs ain't tired enough yet.' Since I've been in Europe, I lived in Amsterdam for 12 years, and from Amsterdam, I went to places like Iceland, Bali, Singapore, Turkey, Australia, South Africa. You name it, and I did it. After that, within the past [few] years, I stopped traveling as much as I did because, naturally, you're getting older, and you don't want to be pushing your body to a point where you won't last but a month. Now, I can choose jobs. I don't jump. Now, it's special people that I want to work for. There's no sense in jumping every time a job comes up, because you might jump up and

Tommy Hunt on stage in Europe, 2018 (tommyhuntofficial.com).

fall down and never get up. The stuff I'm writing now is basically the old stuff. All I'm doing is using the computerized crap that they have put here for us to use and see if I can get something that's going to [please] somebody's taste buds."

He's also understandably pleased with the legacy of recorded work he's already compiled. "Now that I live in England, I watch television quite a bit. We get a lot of American programs over there, and one is called *Days of Our Lives*. It is a soap opera. I was sitting there at home with my feet up, and all of a sudden, I heard this 'doo-bop-shoo-bop' come across. I said, 'What?' They were using it as a theme song in the soap opera. For me, that was a sur-

Tommy Hunt at age 85 with his Rock and Roll Hall of Fame award, 2018 (Lawrence Burrow photo).

prise, because it was maybe 30 years later. The song is still being played and recognized as one of the all-time greats."

Despite the multitude of names that have been given to popular music through the generations, Hunt is adamant when he states that it's all one and the same, and that it all sprang from what pioneers like the Flamingos created over a half-century ago. "This is what I try to tell a lot of young people, not only in England, but in Amsterdam and Germany and France," he explained to Boone and McGarvey. "When I was in Israel, there were kids coming up to me talking about the music scene and asking me why don't you do hip-hop, and why don't you do garage, and why don't you do some heavy metal. I said, 'Look, you're naming one music. There's no such thing as hip-hop, heavy metal, or garage. All it is, is somebody that created something on top of what we laid out, and they've got a new noise. There's nothing that's changed."

Hunt observes, "The British music alone in the 1970s was one of the weirdest. When I started seeing men wear lipstick, I said they're trying to go to the future before their time. They're bringing it in too fast. Kids on the streets are being manipulated by these record companies to buy this music, because I ask the kids if they can explain what message they get from this music. They can't explain, because there is no message. I'll tell you about a music that has gone by. Music that made you laugh, and it made you cry. You all don't know if you have soul. If you did, then you'd love good old rock 'n' roll. If you wanted a good ballad, if you wanted dancing, whatever, the Flamingos were the group. And, wherever they are, the Flamingos, I'm still one of you."

In the Pink

R&B vocal group collectors often pondered the history of the Whispers, who remained an enigma for well over 50 years. The only clue as to who the members were was contained on the group's original contract with Gotham Records, now in the possession of reissue giant Collectables. "The Flamingos came into Baltimore in 1956, and I went to see them, and I forgot all about the Whispers once I got into the Flamingos," Johnson admits. "I hadn't thought about the Whispers until I was in New York in the 2000s, and one of the Rob-Roys said, 'You're Terry Johnson, right?' I said, 'Yeah.' He said, 'Did you sing a song called 'Fool Heart'?' I said, 'Yeah, why?' He said, 'The Whispers? Did you sing 'Are You Sorry,' too?' I said, 'Yeah. How did you know?' A guy named Bobby Robinson from Baltimore had told him who I was, and that's how the whole thing got started about the Whispers. I love talking about this because it makes me remember, because I never think of these things. It makes me go back and remember a lot. That's so weird. They were looking for me, trying to find out who it was. I was right there all the time, and I had no idea."

Fans and collectors shared the group's original recordings with Johnson, who hadn't heard them in decades. Collectables' Gotham compilation CDs also contained an outtake of "Fool Heart." "I laughed when I heard it," he states, singing the lead lyric line in falsetto. "It was cute. It was so funny."

"We got the picture of the Whispers through a lead that [noted record collector and seller] Val Shively gave me," Theresa Trigg, Johnson's wife and business manager explains. "He sent us a copy of the 45, and told me about a printing company located in Baltimore called Global Printing who used to print all the local posters for shows around the area. I called them and said, 'I'm looking for a poster of a group named the Whispers, not the '60s Whispers but the '50s Whispers.' They said they would try to find it in their files. The next thing I knew, I got a phone call and then a fax. As the fax came through, I started smiling. Terry was asleep at the time. I took the photo into the bedroom and started singing 'Are You Sorry.' He woke up to see himself at 16 years old in a photo he hadn't seen in over 50 years. We had such a laugh!"

Renewed interest in the group resulted in Johnson's seeking out the original members of his first group. "I don't know what happened to Lump, Eugene Lewis. I went back, and I saw Billy Thompson, and I asked him about the whole group. He told me that Bill Mills had died. He told me he had seen Eddie Rogers just a few months ago. He didn't know where James was." Later, it was learned that bass singer James O. Johnson was living in a skilled nursing facility in the end stages of Alzheimer's disease. He died in Baltimore on January 1, 2009, at age 73.

Although none of the members of the Whispers expressed a desire to sing again, Johnson relearned the group's ballads for inclusion into his stage act. "Are You Sorry?" was performed live for the first time in 50 years at a November 2006 show in New Bedford, Massachusetts. He later performed "Fool Heart" and "Are You Sorry?" along with his Flamingos favorites, when Terry Johnson's Flamingos headlined a filmed concert in Burlington County, New Jersey, on October 4, 2008. "I sang them on the record, and I get a kick out of 'Fool Heart,' singing so high. I sang it in the same key, too."

Johnson's group has undergone several personnel changes in recent years, but continues to include his devoted wife and manager, Theresa Trigg Johnson, who began performing, writing and producing with Terry in 1976.

"The first group we put together after the Hall of Fame induction had Paul Wilson's son, Ron Wilson," Terry explains. "Ron got a singer from Chicago, Stefan Patterson, and then I got a guy named Ben Bagby from Miami. Theresa wasn't singing with us then. We hired guys who could sing and dance like the original Flamingos and had a lot of experience doing production revue shows with choreography. All of them had strong lead voices, and we sounded like we had been singing together for 20 years. Theresa took care of the booking, running the tracks and the sound. We wanted more than what a four-piece band could give us. We were just getting started with this front-line thing again, so we wanted more options to work with a budget that did not include a band, so we could get tight. Unfortunately, the oldies agents didn't like the look. These guys could sing, but they were young. Of course we hired guys that were young so that they could re-create the 'Jump Children' choreography that Tommy and Paul did. They tried to mimic the steps the best they could. They did a great job. They did the splits through the legs and people loved seeing it. The agents didn't care. They wanted to see older guys with a little grey in their hair so people would think there were more originals in the group. So we reformed the group in the hope of securing more work from the oldies promoters."

On May 13–14, 2003, Terry Johnson's Flamingos joined Jerry Lee Lewis, Bo Diddley, Jack Scott, Paul and Paula, Darlene Love, Johnny Tillotson, Brian

Hyland, Gary U.S. Bonds, Lesley Gore, the Avalons, the Jaguars, the Heart-beats, the Fiestas, and Danny and the Juniors featuring Joe Terry for the film-ing of *Rock and Roll at 50*, a PBS-TV concert special produced by T.J. Lubinsky and Henry DeLuca. On the Shout! Factory DVD release of the event, recorded live at Pittsburgh's Benedum Center for the Performing Arts, the group performed "I Only Have Eyes for You," "Lovers Never Say Good-bye," and "Mio Amore."

In 2003, the National Academy of Recording Arts and Sciences presented the coveted Grammy® Hall of Fame Award to the group's recording of "I Only Have Eyes for You." Established in 1973 by NARAS' National Trustees to honor recordings of lasting qualitative or historical significance that are at least 25 years old, the award is selected annually by a special member committee comprising representatives from all branches of the recording arts.

Johnson's Flamingos were invited back for *Doo Wop Vocal Group Greats Live*, which was filmed at the Sands Casino and Hotel in Atlantic City, New Jersey, on March 15–16, 2005. Broadcast on public television late that year, the doo-wop cavalcade anthology continued Lubinsky's string of successful PBS fundraising programs and spawned a four-hour, three-DVD home video package. The Cadillacs, the Skyliners, Herb Reed's Platters, Frankie Lymon's Teenagers, the Jive Five, the Cleftones, the Willows, the Harptones, the Regents, the Moonglows, the Bobbettes, the Spaniels, the Channels, Jerry Butler, Johnny Maestro and the Brooklyn Bridge, and others were represented on the program. Johnson's Flamingos, which included Theresa Trigg, Jeff Calloway (who joined in 2002), J.J. Hankerson, and William Bell, reprised the three songs that had been performed on the previous program, as well as "Love Walked In" and "I'll Be Home."

In 2005, Johnson rewrote and recorded "Let's Be Lovers" with his group as Terry Johnson, formerly of the Flamingos, with Jeff Calloway and Tee. A promotional disc jockey CD single was issued by the singer's own Hot Fun Records later that year. In a cross between ethereal soul and contemporary R&B, the veteran performer effectively linked past with present. "I was reach-ing for a new audience, but it's hard," he admits. "I have some of the old style there, and it's kind of dated. I've also said it sounds like a cross between Harold Melvin and the Blue Notes, like Teddy Pendergrass. I thought that would help it, but it dated it, because I rewrote the song. I only used four lines of what Nate and I did. I changed it around, added a bridge, and really dressed it up."

The CD single was sold through online retailers. "I had gotten a few sales here and in Japan," he states. "We did get to go to Japan a few years ago. People are playing 'My Springtime' in England, and that blows my mind.

They call it Northern Soul. It's like [people knowing about] the Whispers. It's like *huh?*"

Johnson has completed additional recordings for a full-length CD project titled *Terry Johnson is Still in the Pink*. "I have just a few of them done, but not enough," he explains. "I've gotten side-tracked, because one of the producers had gotten me into doing more of the Flamingos songs for a CD, and that stopped me from doing *Still in the Pink* stuff. I'm sorry I did slow down because I was on fire with it. It was more up to date, but it has the Flamingos sound."

In November of 2009, Johnson again took the Flamingos into a new dimension, recording and releasing a unique jazz modern harmony arrangement of "The Christmas Song" on CD via the group's Hot Fun Records imprint. At the time, the group consisted of Terry and Theresa, Jeff Calloway, and Joe Mirrione, who had joined in 2005.

On September 22, 2013, Johnson was on hand to represent the Flamingos as they received the Heroes and Legends Pioneer Award at the organization's 24th annual event in Beverly Hills, California. The ceremony was established to honor entertainers, sports figures and business executives who have not only achieved success in their areas of expertise, but have utilized their celebrity status to benefit the community, via charitable activities and community service.

That fall, Johnson was filmed by the Rock and Roll Hall of Fame for the Hall's Library & Archives department project, dedicated to preserving the first-hand accounts of the genre as told through the inductees who created it. Johnson's 1966 Gibson ES-335 electric guitar was subsequently placed on display at the Rock Hall's Cleveland, Ohio, museum.

Terry celebrated the Flamingos' 60th anniversary with a new 14-track CD, *Ambassadors for Romance*. The disc included re-recordings of several Flamingos favorites including "I Only Have Eyes for You," "I'll Be Home" and "When I Fall in Love," along with renditions of classics popularized by Lou Rawls, Nat "King" Cole, and Queen. "The kids today are not into romance," Johnson told writer Mark Voger upon its 2013 release. "It's just: Wham, bam, thank you, ma'am. So, we're trying to bring romance to the attention of the kids—how to hold their ladies' hands and things like that. Romance was so very important back then." For the 2013 release, and in their personal appearances today, the Flamingos consist of Terry Johnson, musical director, lead and background vocalist Theresa Trigg, Starling Newsome, and Stan Prinston.

In 2015, the group performed on ABC's national television program, *The View*, and Johnson and Trigg also produced ardent Flamingos fans Boyz

The Flamingos today. Left to right: Stan Prinston, Terry Johnson, and Starling New-some (Marlyn Kauffman photo).

Terry Johnson on stage, 2018 (Sonny Maxon photo).

II Men in the famed EastWest Recording Studio in Hollywood, California. EastWest, one of the world's premier recording facilities, was originally constructed by Bill Putnam, who built Chicago's Universal Studios and engineered all the Flamingos' earliest sides. Among the masters cut at EastWest through the years are the iconic Frank Sinatra classics, "My Way" and "Theme from New York, New York," Barbra Streisand's "The Way We Were," Michael Jackson's "Thriller" and the Beach Boys' iconic *Pet Sounds*.

Terry Johnson continues to pursue solo projects with global success, topping the Euro Indie Music charts twice in 2017. "Knock Knock (Let Me In)" "featuring T," spent five weeks at #1 on the list. A follow up, "Ooo Ya Wit," "featuring Starling Newsome" also reached the top of the Spotify Euro Indie Music list. Sixty-five years after the group's first record was released, the Flamingos continue to record and tour worldwide, thrilling audiences with the magical harmonies that first captured listeners so long ago.

Righting Misdeeds

Johnson reports that the Flamingos have remained woefully underpaid for the re-release of their recorded works and the utilization of their material in various multimedia productions for years. "We're still getting ripped off," he bitterly states. "I have been searching places, and Theresa is really excellent at it. I've received certain royalties that had been hidden from us. We called Rhino Records in 1990 to inquire about royalties. They informed us that they had been paying Zeke Carey with a guarantee from him that he was distributing them. He signed papers saying he would distribute these royalties evenly 'to the members of the group.'"

Rhino subsequently provided Johnson with copies of their financial statements and correspondence related to the Flamingos. "There were advances and royalties that we knew nothing about. I guess Zeke thought none of us, except him, should get the royalties. We found out that he had received thousands of dollars." Johnson retained an attorney and the matter was ultimately resolved to his satisfaction. "Tommy and I joined forces and paid an attorney and Rhino did the right thing. They decided to advance all the members who had not been paid the royalties they deserved. They also put Zeke's account in the red until all the money was paid back to them from his future royalties. As a result, Rhino pays all the members individually now. I got Johnny Carter's royalties sent to him [and his family] and I believe Sollie McElroy's wife is getting his share. Nate's wife was able to receive thousands of dollars, and Paul's wife, too. It seems like God left me here to rectify things."

Not surprisingly, Johnson's lasting memories of the Careys are less than sentimental. "I liked Jake much more than Zeke," he confesses. "Jake lost his power. You see, Zeke learned how to bully Jake. Jake was older, and was starting to lose his memory, and he would stammer a lot, and they would make fun of him, which was a drag. And so, Zeke was able to bully Jake and say, 'Sit down, Jake. You're lucky you're here.' Jake was to himself, the mumbler. And Zeke was humble when he needed me. When I was teaching him how to play the bass and teaching him his harmony notes, to get the fifth note in there, he was nice. But once he got into the business thing, and I helped him to get into that, he was too busy. He stayed away. He tried to cover me up. He tried to cover up Nate's contribution to the group. I mean, he tried to act like it was just him and Jake that did everything. In most interviews after the group broke up, Zeke never really mentioned the other members. He tried to take most of the credit for my songs and arrangements, Paul and Tommy's choreography, and even songs that were picked for the live stage show, which Nate was very instrumental in selecting."

"I didn't do any negotiating for the group," Doug McClure summed of his years with the Flamingos, which spanned 1964 to 1976. "Zeke Carey was the owner and leader of the group, and he was the one that did all the negotiations and the contracting. Zeke and Jake were the pioneers."

When Johnson sings the Flamingos songs today, he's often reminded of his friendships with, and the contributions made by, Nate Nelson and Paul Wilson. "Paul was my dearest friend. I think about Nate and Paul. They were my friends. I don't think about anybody else. I was always for the group, and whatever made us shine. I'm still that way. But I praise God. He has always taken care of me, even when the royalties could have been more for me and my family. He read my heart and I guess that is all that matters today."

The group made headlines again in late January of 2006 when a federal judge in Chicago upheld an arbitrator's decision ordering soft drink giant PepsiCo Inc. and its advertising company to pay the group $250,000 for using "I Only Have Eyes for You" in a television commercial that ran for six months in 1997 without their permission.

The lawsuit was brought by Johnson, Hunt, and the estates of Nelson, Wilson, and the Careys in 2003, citing a collective bargaining agreement with the American Federation of Television and Radio Artists that requires an advertiser to get permission and pay fees to the music publishers, the record labels, and the artists themselves. "In our case, they didn't even ask," San Francisco entertainment lawyer Steven Ames Brown, who represented the group, told reporters. "Pepsi routinely pays the Caucasian performers who appear on camera, but refuses to pay the African American singers whose voices are used in the soundtrack unless they sue," explained Brown, who had previously sued the company on behalf of the estate of Doris Troy, whose 1963 hit "Just One Look" was similarly used without permission. A Pepsi spokesman disputed Brown's claims, stating the failure to pay the Flamingos directly was an oversight and that the firm didn't realize the song was subject to the collective bargaining agreement. Newspapers and television stations worldwide reported the decision, but erroneously declared Hunt the lead singer of the classic song.

Ignorance of the group's history has also bled into some of the multitude of CD reissues featuring the group's work. One import CD on Instant Records, titled *I'll Be Home*, featured a photo of Billy Ward's Dominoes with Gene Mumford on the cover. Worst of all, MCA, in their 1997 Chess 50th Anniversary Collection package, *The Flamingos—The Complete Chess Masters Plus*, included a photo of Bill Baker's 1957 Five Satins lineup as the only group photo in the CD booklet.

Epilogue

Despite the internal conflicts that occasionally plagued the Flamingos, their legacy as one of, if not *the*, premier vocal harmony unit of the 1950s and early 1960s is assured. Interest in their recordings remains high, and radio airplay of their classic hits will undoubtedly continue long after the passing of the pioneers who created the original sounds. Reflecting on his five-decade-long association and friendship with the Flamingos, original manager Fletcher Weatherspoon was quick to praise the singers, particularly the Careys. "As people, I'd want everyone to know how regular, and pretty nice they all were. Zeke and Jake were more religious than the rest of them. They were just nice fellows to know. They were serious about their trade." Fletcher Weatherspoon passed away on October 10, 2014, in Crestwood, Illinois, at age 82.

"We always chose to be different," Zeke Carey summed. "We didn't want to sound like anybody else. So we concentrated a great deal on harmony. This happened simply because we always sang a cappella. Everything was always a cappella, and the harmony had to be fluid. The rhythm patterns had to be good. You know, whatever rhythm patterns we came up with vocally, they had to happen. As I say, we always concentrated on harmony. We established a close, very cohesive sound. We believe in good songs. Good songs. Never did believe in just shamming through a tune. Just going in [thinking] because the guy up front has the lead, he sings it very well; well, the harmony can sound like anything. The music is good, well, we don't have to worry so much with coming up with unique harmonies. We never thought that. We just believed that the whole thing was supposed to happen, and happen right."

"If I was explaining the Flamingos to some kids who had never heard us, I would tell them the structure of the way we did it," Terry states. "We were hungry, but we stuck together. We rehearsed all the time, and we were prepared when the opportunity came. I would probably play my songs, like 'Lovers Never Say Goodbye.' I know I'd play 'I Only Have Eyes for You' because of the difference in the chord structure. I just added what I had been listening to through my youth, and added to what rhythm and blues was. I just added my own flavor to it. It is really self-satisfying. It's a good thing when you hear your own music. To our fans, I'd like them to know how we appreciate them. We thank you for keeping us in the limelight. I can feel you, and I appreciate your support."

"Our music is vintage music," Jake summed six years before his death. "It's just like the wine when you're going out with your best lady. You get some wine, you get a good steak.... And the music itself, the music of yesteryear, has such relevance. They tell stories, stories that have something to do with people's lives."

The Flamingos
Discography

(Record label, label release number, contents,
and date of original release)

CHANCE
1133 Someday, Someway/If I Can't Have You—3/53
1140 That's My Desire/Hurry Home Baby—6/53
1145 Golden Teardrops/Carried Away—9/53
1149 Plan For Love/You Ain't Ready—10/53
1154 Cross Over the Bridge/Listen to My Plea—3/54

PARROT
808 Dream of a Lifetime/On My Merry Way—8/54

CHANCE
1162 Blues in a Letter/Jump Children—10/54

PARROT
811 I Really Don't Want to Know/Get With It—12/54
812 I'm Yours/Ko Ko Mo—1/55

CHECKER
815 When/(Chick-A-Boom) That's My Baby—4/55
821 Please Come Back Home/I Want to Love You—7/55
830 I'll Be Home/Need Your Love—1/56
837 A Kiss from Your Lips/Get With It [Parrot master]—4/56
846 The Vow/Shilly Dilly—8/56
853 Would I Be Crying/Just for a Kick—11/56

DECCA
30335 The Ladder of Love/Let's Make Up—6/57
30454 Helpless/My Faith in You—10/57
30687 Where Mary Go/The Rock and Roll March—7/58

END
1035 Lovers Never Say Goodbye/That Love is You—10/58

CHECKER
915 Dream of a Lifetime/Whispering Stars—2/59

CHECKER
LP-1433 *The Flamingos*—3/59
  Dream of a Lifetime
  A Kiss from Your Lips
  Ko Ko Mo [Parrot master]
  Shilly Dilly
  Whispering Stars
  Stolen Love
  On My Merry Way [Parrot master]
  Chickie Um bah
  The Vow
  Nobody's Love
  Would I Be Crying
  Chicka Boom (That's My Baby)

END
1040 But Not for Me/I Shed a Tear at Your Wedding—2/59
1044 Love Walked In/At the Prom—3/59
1046 I Only Have Eyes for You/Goodnight Sweetheart—4/59
1046 I Only Have Eyes for You/At the Prom—1959
LP-304 *Flamingo Serenade*—4/59
  Love Walked In
  I Only Have Eyes for You
  Music Maestro Please
  I'm in the Mood for Love
  Begin the Beguine
  As Time Goes By
  The Breeze and I
  Where or When
  Time Was
  Yours
  Goodnight Sweetheart
  But Not for Me

DECCA
30880 Ever Since I Met Lucy/Kiss-A-Me—5/59

END
1055 Love Walked In/Yours—7/59

DECCA
30948 Jerri-Lee /Hey Now!—7/59

END
1062 I Was Such a Fool/Heavenly Angel—11/59
1065 Mio Amore/You, Me and the Sea—12/59
1068 Nobody Loves Me/Besame Mucho—2/60
1068 Nobody Loves Me Like You/You, Me and the Sea—2/60
LP-307 *Flamingo Favorites*—6/60
    Besame Mucho
    Maria Elena
    Dream Girl
    Sweet and Lovely
    Crazy, Crazy, Crazy
    Tell Me How Long
    That's Why I Love You
    My Foolish Heart
    Heavenly Angel
    You Belong to My Heart
    Mio Amore (My Love)
    Bridge of Tears
1070 Besame Mucho/You, Me and the Sea—5/60
1073 Mio Amore/At Night—6/60
1079 When I Fall in Love /Beside You—9/60
LP-308 *Requestfully Yours*—10/60
    In The Still of the Night
    Nobody Loves Me Like You
    Beside You
    Tenderly
    Never in This World
    I Was Such a Fool
    When I Fall in Love
    Every Time I Think of You
    You, Me and the Sea
    At Night
    Everybody's Got a Home But Me
    You'll Never Walk Alone
1081 Your Other Love/Lovers Gotta Cry—11/60
1085 That's Why I Love You/Kokomo—1/61
1092 Time Was/Dream Girl—4/61

VEE-JAY (Chance Masters)
384 Golden Teardrops/Carried Away—4/61

END
1099 My Memories of You/I Want to Love You—10/61
1111 It Must Be Love/I'm No Fool Anymore—4/62
1116 For All We Know/Near You—8/62
1121 I Know Better /Flame of Love—4/63
1124 (Talk About) True Love /Come On to My Party—11/63
SLP-316 *The Sound of the Flamingos*—1963
    Too Soon to Know
    You're Mine
    Flame of Love
    My Lovely One
    The Sinner (El Pecador)
    I Know Better
    I'm Coming Home
    Moonlight in Vermont
    (When You're Young and) Only Seventeen
    Without His Love
    Ole Man River
    Danny Boy

ROULETTE (End masters)
4524 Ol' Man River—Part 1/Part 2—9/63

BELLVILLE
100 Lover Come Back to Me/Your Little Guy—5/64

CHECKER
1084 Lover Come Back to Me/Your Little Guy [Bellville masters]—6/64
1091 Goodnight Sweetheart/Does It Really Matter—9/64

TIMES SQUARE (white a cappella groups-not the Flamingos)
102 A Lovely Way to Spend an Evening/Walking My Baby Back Home—12/64

PHILIPS
40308 Temptation/Call Her on the Phone—7/65
40347 The Boogaloo Party/The Nearness of You—12/65

PHILIPS
LP-206 *Their Hits Then and Now*—4/66
    The Boogaloo Party
    I Only Have Eyes for You
    Since My Baby Put Me Down
    A Kiss from Your Lips
    Brooklyn Boogaloo
    The Nearness of You

The Yellow Rose of Texas
Your Other Love
Lovers Never Say Goodbye
Nobody Loves Me Like You Do
I'll Be Home
I'm Not Tired Yet
40378 Brooklyn Boogaloo/Since My Baby Put Me Down—6/66
40413 Itty Bitty Baby/She Shook My World—1/66
40452 Koo Koo/It Keeps the Doctor Away—4/67
40496 Do It, To It/Oh Mary Don't You Worry—10/67

JULMAR
506 Dealin'/Dealin' All the Way—6/69

POLYDOR
14019 Buffalo Soldier (short version)/Buffalo Soldier (long version)—1/70
   (reissued as Part 1 and Part 2 with same release number, 2/74)
2066–007 Buffalo Soldier/Fontaineous Combustion (UK pressing)—6/70
14044 Lover Come Back to Me/Straighten It Up (Get It Together)—9/70

RONZE
111 Welcome Home/Gotta Have All Your Lovin'—1971
LP-1001 *Color Them Beautiful*—1971
   She's Gone
   Gotta Have All Your Lovin'
   Does It Really Matter
   Dealin' (Groovin' With the Feelin')
   Welcome Home
   I Need You So
   Goodnight Sweetheart
   Suddenly We're Strangers
   You You You
   Too Young
   Dealin' All the Way

RONZE
LP-1002 Flamingos Today—5/72
   Golden Teardrops
   As Time Goes By
   Virgo, Virgin Lady
   Time Was
   Let It Be Me
   At Night
   Why Can't Susie Go to School With Lucy

LP-1003 In Touch with You—1974
  Since My Baby Put Me Down
  Making Love (Ain't Nothin' Better Than)
  Spring of My Life
  Heavy Hips
  Think About Me
  Someone to Watch Over Me
  Bump Your Buns Off
  Golden Teardrops

WORLDS
103 Think About Me /Think About Me—12/74

RONZE
115 Heavy Hips/Someone to Watch Over Me—1975
116 Love Keeps the Doctor Away/Love Keeps the Doctor Away—1976

SKYLARK (unissued Parrot Masters)
541 If I Could Love You/I Found a New Baby—1978

RONZE
CD-1000 *Welcome Home (My Love)*—1993
  Welcome Home (My Love)
  Think About Me
  Where Did Our Love Go
  I'll Be Home [a cappella]
  Making Love (Ain't Nothing Better)
  Spring of My Life
  If the Bed Breaks Down Baby
  At Night [almost a cappella]
  Time Was
  Since My Baby Put Me Down

HOT FUN
CD-24153 The Christmas Song (CD single: The Flamingos featuring Terry Johnson)—2009
CD *Ambassadors for Romance*—1/13
  You, Me and the Sea
  Smile
  You'll Never Find
  When I Fall in Love
  Begin the Beguine
  I Only Have Eyes for You
  It Had to Be You
  Till

Ebb Tide
Who Can I Turn To
I'll Be Home
I (Who Have Nothing)
Crazy Little Thing Called Love

Unreleased (recording dates listed when known)

CHANCE
September Song—12/24/53

PARROT
If I Could Love You—7/54
I Found A New Baby—11/54

CHECKER
Cry—3/56

DECCA
That Love Is You—4/19/57

END
Without a Song—10/31/58
We Were Made for Each Other—2/18/59
River of Tears—2/26/59
Happy Birthday Elise—2/60
A Kiss from Your Lips—10/20/60
I'll Be Home—10/20/60
Jump Children—10/29/60
Lover Come Back—11/17/61
Shout It Out—6/17/63

PHILIPS
I Done Fell in Love (copyright filed 11/9/65)

Bibliography

Interviews and artists' recollections were stimulated by and supplemented with facts documented from the following sources.

"Allstar Swingbill On Regal Stage This Week," *Chicago Defender*, October 7, 1961.

Armitage, Steve, "Rappin' with Tommy Hunt," published interview, source unknown.

Boone, Mike, "Interview with Tommy Hunt," March 2001, published at www.soul-patrol. com, 2006

Brooks, Tim, and Earle Marsh, *The Complete Directory to Prime Time Network TV Shows*, Ballantine Books, New York, NY, 1979.

"Burial Services for Flamingos' Wilson," *Chicago Defender*, May 11, 1988.

Büttner, Armin, Robert Pruter, and Robert Campbell, "The Parrot and Blue Lake Labels," published online at http://hubcap.clemson. edu/~campber/parrot.html, 2005.

Cash Box, various issues 1953–1996, accessed online at http://cashboxmagazine.com/archives/.

Cogan, Jim, and Bill Putnam, *Mix*, November 1, 2003, accessed online at https://www.mixon line.com/recording/bill-putnam-365354

Cotten, Lee, *Reelin' & Rockin'*, Popular Culture, Ink., Ann Arbor, MI, 1995.

_____, *Shake Rattle & Roll*, Popular Culture, Ink., Ann Arbor, MI, 1989.

"Decca Signs Flamingos," in *Cash Box*, June 29, 1957.

Ferlingere, Robert D., *A Discography of Rhythm and Blues Vocal Groups 1945 to 1965*, California Trade School, Hayward, CA, 1976.

Fileti, Donn, liner notes in "The Best of The Flamingos," Rhino Records, Inc., Santa Monica, CA, 1990.

_____, liner notes in "The Golden Era of Doo-Wops: Celeste Records," Relic Record Productions, Inc., Hackensack, NJ, 1994.

"Flamingos Correct Evil That Haunted Them," *Chicago Defender*, August 8, 1956.

"Flamingos in Personnel Change," *Chicago Defender*, June 24, 1961.

"Flamingos on TV Tonight," *Chicago Defender*, March 25, 1959.

"Flamingos Play It Cool on Religion," *Chicago Defender*, February 11, 1961.

"Flamingos Prep for Long Tour of East," *Chicago Defender*, November 29, 1952.

"Flamingos to D.C. Howard on New Year's," *Chicago Defender*, December 31, 1960.

Gart, Galen, *The American Record Label Directory and Dating Guide, 1940–1959*, Big Nickel Publications, Milford, NH, 1989.

_____, *First Pressings: The History of Rhythm and Blues*, Big Nickel Publications, Milford, NH, 1991–93.

Gonzalez, Fernando L., *Disco-File*, 4th edition, Fernando Louis Gonzalez, 2014.

Grendysa, Peter, "The Red Caps," in *Yesterday's Memories* 2, No. 1, Freezibak, Inc., New York, NY, 1976.

_____, liner notes in "The Flamingos—The Complete Chess Masters–Plus," MCA Records Inc., Universal City, CA, 1997.

Groia, Philip, *They All Sang on the Corner*, Phillie Dee Enterprises, Inc., Port Jefferson, NY, 1983.

Himes, Geoffrey, "Flamingos, Doo-Wop Royalty, to Roost in Hall of Fame," *Chicago Tribune*, March 14, 2001.

Hochman, Steve, "R&B Foundation Honorees Let Music Do the Boasting," *Los Angeles Times*, March 2, 1996.

Hoekstra, Dave, "Flamingos Return to the Home Nest," *Chicago Sun-Times*, April 3, 1987.

Interview with Tommy Hunt, Surrey, UK, March 13, 1982.

Jackson, John A., *Big Beat Heat*, Schirmer Books, New York, NY, 1995.

Jenkins, David, "The Harry Warren Website," published online at www.harrywarren.org, 2006.

Jet, various issues 1958–1967, accessed online at https://books.google.com/books/about/Jet. html.

Jones, Wayne, "Goldmine Interview: Nate Nelson of the Flamingos," in *Goldmine* 24, March 1978, Arena Magazine Company, St. Clair Shores, MI.

Kreiter, Jeff, *Group Collector's Record Guide*, 7th edition, Boyd Press, Wheeling, WV, 1999.

McGarvey, Seamus, "I Only Have Eyes for You—The Flamingos' Story, Zeke Carey interviewed by Seamus McGarvey," in *Now Dig This* 97, April 1991, Tyne & Wear, UK.

_____, "Jump Children! An Interview with Tommy Hunt," in *Now Dig This* 42, September 1986, Tyne & Wear, UK.

McGrath, Robert J., *The R&B Indies*, second edition, Eyeball Productions Inc, West Vancouver, BC, Canada, 2005.

Neely, Tim, *Goldmine Price Guide to 45 RPM Records*, 2nd edition, Krause Publications, Iola, WI, 1999.

Nite, Norm N., *Rock On*, Harper and Row, New York, NY, 1982.

_____, *Rock On Almanac*, 2nd edition, Harper-Collins, New York, NY, 1992.

"Obituary—Jacob A. Carey, Singer," *Washington Post*, December 24, 1997.

Osborne, Jerry, *Rockin' Records*, Osborn Enterprises, Port Washington, WA, 1999.

Pareles, Jon, "Thanks, Reminisces and Tunes, Lots of Tunes," *New York Times*, March 2, 1996.

"Paris Club's Show Is Star Studded Hit," *Chicago Defender*, July 2, 1953.

Propes, Steve, *Those Oldies but Goodies*, Collier Books, New York, NY, 1973.

Pruter, Robert, *Doowop: The Chicago Scene*, University of Illinois Press, Chicago, IL, 1996.

Pruter, Robert, "The Flamingos: Earl Lewis discussed their 'roots' with Robert Pruter," in *Goldmine* 36, Arena Magazine Company, St. Clair Shores, MI, May, 1979.

_____, "The Flamingos—The Chicago Years," in *Goldmine* 16, No. 7, Krause Publications, Iola, WI, April 6, 1990.

_____, liner notes in "The Golden Era of Doowops: Parrot Records," Relic Record Productions, Inc., Hackensack, NJ, 1993.

_____, liner notes in "The Golden Era of Doowops: Parrot and Blue Lake Records-Part 2," Relic Record Productions, Inc., Hackensack, NJ, 1994.

Pruter, Robert, Armin Büttner and Robert L. Campbell, "The Chance Label," published online at http://hubcap.clemson.edu/~campber/chance.html, 2006–2018.

Rallo, Lou, interview with Sollie McElroy, in *Discoveries*, Arena Publishing, Fraser, MI, November, 1997.

Rosalsky, Mitch, *Encyclopedia of Rhythm & Blues and Doo-Wop Vocal Groups*, Scarecrow Press, Lanham, MD, 2000.

Salem, James M., *The Late Great Johnny Ace and the Transition From R&B to Rock 'n' Roll*, University of Illinois Press, Chicago, IL, 1999.

Sbarbori, Jack, "The Dells: Then & Now," in *Record Exchanger* 4 No. 6, Vintage Records, Anaheim, CA, 1976.

_____, "Sollie McElroy," in *Record Exchanger* 3 No. 3, Vintage Records, Anaheim, CA, 1975.

Silvani, Lou, *Collecting Rare Records*, Times Square Records, NY, 1992.

Smith, Wes, *The Pied Pipers of Rock 'n' Roll*, Longstreet Press, Marietta, GA, 1989.

Tamarkin, Jeff, "The Flamingos" in *Goldmine* 64, Arena Magazine Company, St. Clair Shores, MI, 1981.

Tancredi, Carl. "The Flamingos—The Early Years" in *Bim Bam Boom* 1, Issue 4, Bronx, NY, 1972.

_____, interview with Zeke and Jake Carey of the Flamingos, 1964, © Nikki Gustafson and Jim Dunn, www.harmonytrain.com, 1998–2004.

"Teenagers, Flamingos Spotlight Rock 'n' Roll," *Chicago Defender*, August 21, 1956.

Tyler, Lee, "Billy Paul: Soul Searching," bluesandsoul.com, 2009.

Warner, Jay, *The Billboard Book of American Singing Groups: A History 1940–1990*, Billboard Books, New York, NY, 1992.

_____, "Harmony in History: The Flamingos," in *Discoveries* 61, Arena Publishing, Fraser, MI, June, 1993.

"Weatherspoon Presents The Flamingos," *Chicago Defender*, March 21, 1987.

Whitburn, Joel, *The Billboard Book of Top 40 Hits*, 4th edition, Billboard Books, New York, NY, 1989.

_____, *Top Pop Singles 1955–1993*, Record Research, Inc., Menomonee Falls, WI, 1994.

_____, *Top R&B Singles 1942–1988*, Record Research, Inc., Menomonee Falls, WI, 1988.

White, George R., Robert L. Campbell, and Tom Kelly, "The Chess Label," published online at http://hubcap.clemson.edu/~campber/chess2.html, 2006.

Williams, Otis, with Patricia Romanowski, *Temptations*, Fireside-Simon & Schuster Inc., New York, NY, 1989.

Index

239